"This is the practical approach I wish I had
my career. Calvert provides a strong guidi
consultancy projects from beginning to end.
easily accessible for anyone who wishes to deliver their particular expertise
into a client organisation."

Cynthia Pexton-Shaw, Elevation Learning

"A book that gets to multiple editions is clearly a classic of its sector.
Calvert's is in its seventh, and will probably go on to many more. It achieves
a threefold feat: of being useful to the expert and to the recently qualified and
to the student. Even those of us who have spent decades in this profession
need a consultancy bible to refer to. Calvert shows how to be rigorous and
systematic, but the book is packed with practical advice from one who is
both an academic expert and a senior practising consultant. This is both
The Art and The Science of Consultancy."

Ian Watson – Chair, The Institute of Consulting

"This book explains in plain English the role and daily challenges of life
as a management consultant, and has been an excellent source of reference
in building our business. Calvert presents a practitioner's view covering
the requisite soft skills as well as the mechanics of solving the client's
business problems."

Martyn Evans, Consulting Director, Altus

"In a world of disruption and the supremacy of technological advancement,
Calvert reiterates the leading role of the human component, where
professionalism and ethical behaviour rule. The communication, presentation
and influencing skills backed by strong knowledge will remain key attributes
in a profession which must reinvent itself more often than others."

*Sorin Caian, Immediate Past Chairman of ICMCI / International
Council of Management Consulting Institutes*

CALVERT MARKHAM

The Art of
CONSULTANCY

Legend Business Ltd,
107-111 Fleet Street, London, EC4A 2AB
info@legend-paperbooks.co.uk I www.legendpress.co.uk

Contents © Calvert Markham 2019
The right of the above author to be identified as the author of this work has
been asserted in accordance with the Copyright, Designs and Patents Act 1988.
British Library Cataloguing in Publication Data available.

Print ISBN 9781789550818
Ebook ISBN 9781789550825
Set in Times. Printing managed by Jellyfish Solutions Ltd
Cover design by Simon Levy I www.simonlevyassociates.co.uk

CONTENTS

Foreword   9

Preface   11

Introduction   12

Chapter 1 — Overview of the delivery process   15
Entry   17
Contracting   18
Diagnosis   20
Intervention   24
Closure   24

Chapter 2 — Entry   23
So, who am I?   23
Consultant roles   25
The consultant as an outsider   28

Chapter 3 — Contracting   30
Revisiting terms of reference   31
Planning a consultancy project   32
Preparing the project plan   33
Practical operating   41
Questions of standards and ethics   44

Chapter 4 — Diagnosis 47
Problem solving 47
Data collection 50
Constraints on data collection 54
Forming conclusions 63

Chapter 5 — Intervention 66
Recommendations are conclusions adjusted for the process of change 67
Organisational readiness for change 70
The process of change 72
Techniques for assisting change 79
Words of consolation 85

Chapter 6 — Closure 86
Completing a project 86
Deriving ongoing commercial value 87
Deriving value for the practice 89

Chapter 7 — Analytical tools and techniques 90
Generic data collection techniques 91
Structured data collection tools 98
Data analysis techniques 114
Some useful models 123

Chapter 8 — Reporting to clients 126
Reports to clients 127
Preparation 129
Writing reports 143
Making presentations 146
Informal presentations 165
Review 166

Chapter 9 — Influencing clients 167
The power of the consultant 168
The response to consultants' influence 171
Preparing and presenting a persuasive case 172
Processes of social influence 185
Improving your influencing skills 190

Chapter 10 — Designing and presenting training sessions and workshops 191

Creating a training specification 192
Designing training sessions 194
Improving training presentations 201
Running workshops 202

Chapter 11 — Marketing and selling consultancy projects 203

The marketing and sales process 205
Promotion 208
Prospection 211
Proposition design 216
Pitching 219

Chapter 12 — The business of consultancy 225

The consultancy business process 226
Rule 1: Maintain utilisation 228
Rule 2: Invest non-fee-earning time carefully 234
Rule 3: Control the cash 238
What do the three rules mean in practice? 240

Chapter 13 — The practice environment 242

Becoming a consultant 243
A model of the consulting business 247
Working in a consulting practice 252
And finally… 254

References 255

Publishing history 256

FOREWORD

There is perhaps, a paradox in an industry that thrives on and promotes change, and yet has enduring features such as the skills of change management and relationship building. In fact, this is unsurprising because change is always a question of perspective. Or rather, continuity is always close by, even if it is often less celebrated, visible or feared.

Such a tension is especially evident today when the consulting industry seems to be transforming, both in terms of its structure and its fields of activity. We are now constantly told how the industry, and the big firms especially, face disruption from many sources, notably the 'gig economy', regulation and globalisation. My own research too points to the fact that consulting has become so successful in many contexts that it is now part of the management mainstream, making it less distinctive. Likewise, in a recent survey seeking to identify the consulting skills of 2030, emerging areas of expertise are highlighted such as cyber security, artificial intelligence, big data and robotics. But there will always be new knowledge and without this, consultancy would indeed die out. Also, even if the large firms have had their heyday, consulting skills will be needed by those inside and outside the industry, whatever label is given to them.

This book epitomises that which is enduring and widespread in consultancy whilst simultaneously being 'of the moment'. It is in its seventh edition now and is fundamentally practical. For an academic, like me, it has far too few references in it! But this is because it is both tried and tested in practice – of both consulting and training consultants. It is aimed at those who wish to do consultancy not explain it, although it is also informed by various models. Finally, its lineage also means that it is distilled down to the essences of consulting – comprehensive, succinct and efficient (and so ideal for those with little time) – whether as a sole practitioner, part of a network or an 'old fashioned' employee!

Of course, in highlighting the continuities of consulting – its art – there is a risk of leaving the new and difficult in the shadows, but actually, they work together in the consulting cycle of relationships, projects and, hopefully collaboration.

Andrew Sturdy
Professor of Management and Organisation, University of Bristol, UK and management consultancy researcher and writer.

PREFACE

Consultancy is delivering specialist skills in a client environment. The critical word in this definition is 'client', implying a relationship in which an outsider makes their knowledge and experience available to an organisation. But clients (however defined) have a choice about whether to engage a specialist, and whether to take that specialist's advice. Incompetent consultants will quickly lose their clients.

There are skills involved in being a competent consultant – more than simply being a subject matter expert – and it's these that this book seeks to cover.

Consultancy is a buoyant and expanding sector. More and more people are entering the profession and all need consulting skills. Much of my career has been spent in training consultancy skills and in this book I hope I have been able to capture the key areas that are going to be of value to someone taking up the profession of management consultant.

However, as many routine tasks have been automated away, managers are also expected to seek performance improvements through change. They too must engage in projects and influence rather than command — the same skills as a consultant — so the study of consultancy and the skills needed are now a common feature of postgraduate business courses. And an understanding of consulting is of value to executives who need to hire and work with consultants.

Consultancy services are now offered by a much wider range of organisations and in recent years there has been the growth of emergent consultancies — organisations whose main business is not consultancy, but who now offer their know-how to outsiders, either simply to generate revenue or to make their primary product lines more competitive.

The world of work has increasingly been about accelerating performance through change, with which all these communities are involved. Consultants have been called agents of change and I hope that this book will be of interest and value to all of them.

Calvert Markham   **March 2019**

INTRODUCTION

This book addresses the two main processes involved in consultancy, which are delivering consultancy projects (consultancy is usually delivered as a project), and selling the project in the first place. An empirical description of the two processes is shown in Exhibit I.1. (These are empirical as they are based on observation and experience rather than detailed research).

Exhibit I.1 The consultancy sales and delivery processes

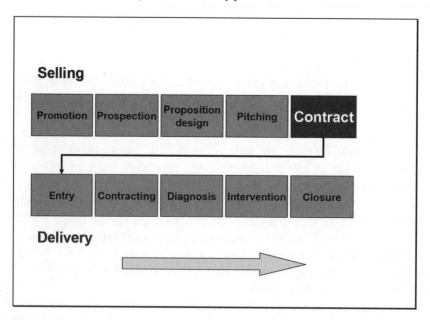

The four stages of the sales process are:
- *promotion* — in which you are seeking and establishing relationships with potential clients;
- *prospection* — in which you are identifying suitable opportunities to work together;
- *proposition design* — where you are fashioning the details of how you would address this opportunity,
- *pitching* — in which you sell the proposition to the client.

The five steps of the delivery process are:
- *entry* — in which you establish a relationship with a client;
- *contracting* — agreeing what you are going to do and how you do it;
- *diagnosis* — in which you gather information and work out how the client's situation is to be addressed;
- *intervention* — where you work with the client to put your solutions in place, and
- *closure* — completion of the project and withdrawal.

Clearly, there are similarities in the two processes between:
- promotion and entry;
- prospection, proposition design and contracting;
- pitching and intervention.

This is not surprising, as in both cases you are seeking to influence a client: when selling, to buy the project; when delivering, to 'buy' your recommendations. (Indeed, in many ways selling is simply unpaid consultancy!)

These processes provide the framework of this book and as most consultants are primarily involved in delivery, this is where we start. There are also some underpinning skills that are needed in some measure at all stages, and the following chapters deal with these.

As their experience grows and their careers progress, consultants will need to take on responsibility for selling and so we then look at marketing and selling consulting projects.

Finally, consultancy has to be done in a commercial context, and this affects the disciplines that apply to all these skills. For those who enter consultancy having previously worked in different environments, the transition can be difficult. Understanding the commercial imperatives can illuminate some of the peculiarities of the sector — why, for example, you need to record your time. So the book finishes with two relevant chapters, the first being about the business of consultancy, with the imperatives needed for commercial success. The second – the final chapter – comments on working in the practice environment, which (as anyone who has worked in a consulting practice will know) has its own peculiarities!

CHAPTER 1

OVERVIEW OF THE DELIVERY PROCESS

They said that the job could never be done,
But I with a will set to it;
And I tackled that job that couldn't be done —
And found that I couldn't do it!

Anon

The purpose of the consultancy delivery process is to enable the consultant to add value to the client.

At a basic level, a consultant can simply provide a piece of advice. For example, a lawyer might be asked a question on a basic point of law and be able to provide the answer in a short telephone conversation. Such an instant response is not appropriate in addressing most of the predicaments which motivate organisations to involve consultants; usually a programme of work is involved and this is embodied in a *project*. So, the project is the vehicle by which value is added to the client.

Clearly, the detailed programme of work needed will vary from project to project, but a practice may have developed its own methodologies based on previous operating experience or research. These can be categorised as follows.

1. *The standard service*: this is a highly product-orientated approach. The client is buying a standard service that will vary very little in

the amount of time required (or, if it is likely to vary, the swings and roundabouts cancel each other out). Examples might be:

- a house conveyance by a solicitor;
- personality profiling using psychometrics.

In each case, the service will be much the same on each occasion and its design requires little or no new planning. Very little management consultancy falls into this category.

2. *Royal roads* are again standard approaches, but adapted to the circumstances of a client. Examples might be:

- introducing a job evaluation scheme;
- computerising a stock control system.

The work content of 'royal road' type projects can be predicted with some certainty — not only because it is fairly well known, but also because of previous experience. The amount of time required to conduct a 'royal road' approach will depend on the nature of the application. The details of the work involved may also vary.

In both these cases the consultant is mediating a standard process; a lot of the value that the client is buying lies in the process rather than in the capabilities of the individual consultant.

Much of management consultancy however consists of a journey of exploration rather than a walk along a well-worn track. These projects must also be planned, which presents more of a challenge than the 'standard service' or 'royal road' approaches. What is needed is a delivery process that sets out the generic phases that comprise a consultancy project which can be applied generally.

These are shown in Exhibit 1.1, and this short chapter provides an overview of the process. Each phase is described in more detail in the following chapters.

Exhibit 1.1 The delivery process

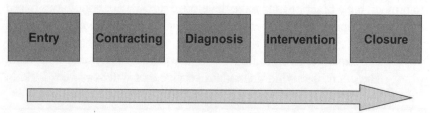

Before embarking on a description of the process — a health warning. The process is empirical, based on observation, rather than a statement of absolute and exclusive truth! It should, therefore, be regarded as a tool — a servant rather than a master. So, use it but if the circumstances of your situation cannot fit the process, then adapt it, or indeed abandon it.

Let's now take a look at each stage of the delivery process.

ENTRY

A consultant's first contact with a client may be either in the course of selling an assignment[1] or starting a project that has already been sold. In either case, careful preparation is required and you should aim to make a favourable impact.

Preparation should ensure that you know:

- background client information — nature of their business, key people;
- key aspects of their business, for example, how they make money, recent performance, current issues in the public domain;
- the history of any previous relationship between your consultancy and the client, and particularly any previous discussions that might have a bearing on the project;
- what the objectives of the introductory meeting are;
- what expectations the client has of the first meeting (often you can set these yourself by a preliminary email or telephone call).

The client will be seeking to form an impression of you throughout your early contacts, whether written or telephone, but the first meeting is when the client will be particularly able to do so. There is no second chance to form a first impression and so you should aim to make as favourable an impact as you can.

Early in a project, it is important to allow time for familiarisation. This will be necessary not only for practical matters (such as who's who, office

---

1   Each consulting firm has its own language. For example, the first practice I worked for referred to consulting *assignments* rather than consulting *projects*. I have used both words in this text with I hope, a little more precision, in that consultants are *assigned* to work on consulting *projects*.

layout, etc.) but also for understanding the informal rules and climate of the organisation. The latter includes such items as:

- specialised language used in the business;
- ways in which people work together (e.g. can you walk into people's offices, or do you have to schedule a meeting first?);
- current affairs or hot topics for the organisation.

CONTRACTING

EXPECTATIONS AND OBLIGATIONS

As soon as contact is made there will be expectations and obligations created on both sides besides the formal agreement set out in the terms of reference.

A major cause of client dissatisfaction is when a consultant fails to meet the client's expectations. These expectations relate not only to meeting commitments in the terms of reference, but also in how the consultant carries out the project, for example:

- the consultant's conduct;
- what the consultant wears;
- when the consultant arrives and leaves client premises;
- the apparent priority the consultant attaches to the work done for the client.

Likewise, the consultant will also have expectations of the client; these will be reflected, largely, in the commitment the client shows towards the project.

The sponsor (the member of the client's staff commissioning the project) will, presumably, be committed to it, but you will have to consider the commitment of others. Will the project require the co-operation of more senior or more junior staff and, if so, are they committed to its success? Beware of sponsors who do not appear to be committed to the project or who are carrying it out as a personal crusade.

Also consider the impact of a consulting project on a client's workload and systems. Any project will create a demand on client time, but you also need to consider whether the client's usual management systems will support the project adequately. The way I put this is: 'ordinary business can be run within the ordinary arrangements in an organisation; extra-ordinary activity may need extra-ordinary support.' So, for example, during a change programme the frequency of communication with staff may need to be increased.

ESTABLISHING TERMS OF REFERENCE
Consultancy is an intangible product and terms of reference are a way of expressing the product definition. It may seem surprising that this is a topic relevant to delivery; after all, doesn't the contract that is the product of the sales process express this?

The answer is 'yes', but there are several reasons why an understanding of terms of reference is relevant to an operating consultant:

- Operating consultants need to understand terms of reference if they are to fulfil the terms of the contract;
- The consultant may be involved in formulating a contract as a member of the sales team;
- Operating consultants will get to know the client organisation much better than the sales team, because they will be exposed to it for longer. Better knowledge may show that terms of reference need to change.

The key elements in terms of reference are:
- *scope*: the areas of concern that the consultants are to address;
- *deliverables*: what the client is going to get.

Larger projects can be broken into work packages, each a small project in itself, with its own scope and deliverables.

WORK PACKAGE MANAGEMENT
The work package is the means by which the deliverables are to be achieved. The key elements of managing a work package are:
1. The *methodology* or approach to be used, usually described as a series of tasks;
2. The *plan*, which describes when these tasks are to be carried out;
3. The plan will also indicate the *resources* required, which may include client as well as consultant effort;
4. How the work is to be *managed* and integrated into the client's usual management process.

DIAGNOSIS

THE PROBLEM-SOLVING PROCESS

Diagnosis is based on some sort of problem-solving framework. Problem solving is the route between problem and solution and the process provides guidance on what needs to be done at each stage.

In particular, consultancy is often a journey from the unknown into the known (or making tacit knowledge explicit), and hence necessarily involves data collection. A robust problem-solving approach helps in defining what data needs to be collected.

DATA COLLECTION AND ANALYSIS

Paradoxically, you need to consider analysis before deciding what data you need to gather: you have to know what you are going to do with it when you have got it, and this is the purpose of an embracing, problem-solving approach. Data gathering is time-consuming and you need to make sure you confine yourself to gathering only that which is necessary and sufficient for your purposes.

In simple terms, the consultant will start the project with a view (perhaps expressed as a series of hypotheses) of what the detailed nature of the problem is and how it might be solved. Data gathering will be used at the start to verify these hypotheses and subsequent data gathering will be used to form new hypotheses or add more detail to the original ones. Data analysis will lead to possible solutions.

There is a variety of data collection techniques. The choice of which is most appropriate will depend on the nature of the data to be collected. Moreover, you will almost certainly need to compromise on what data you collect; some may be unobtainable or it could be too costly or time-consuming to collect all that you might.

FORMING CONCLUSIONS

Data collection and analysis should lead to a better understanding of the areas of concern and how they might be addressed. This will usually be embodied in some conclusions, which are an 'ideal' view of what needs to be done. But these need to be tempered by reality in formulating what in practice can be done — intervention takes this into account.

INTERVENTION

By 'intervention' we mean the culmination of the project when the consultant engages with the client to address the issues identified. Most often the intervention will consist of developing recommendations and, perhaps, their implementation.

DEVELOPING RECOMMENDATIONS
In making your recommendations they have not only to be technically 'right' but also acceptable to those responsible for authorising their implementation. During the project you should develop an idea of what is or is not acceptable and devote effort to 'pre-selling' your preferred solution.

Your recommendations should also be feasible; that is, the client must be able to implement them. No points for making technically excellent recommendations, which the client embraces enthusiastically and then finds cannot be implemented because the resources or skills to do so are not available.

Recommendations should, therefore, also include proposals for how they might be implemented in practice.

CREATING CHANGE
In many instances, clients want consultancy support not only in formulating a solution but also in implementing it. This may be because their organisation doesn't have the resources (e.g. skills, manpower) to do the work; or they want to reduce risk; or they want to acquire know-how; or a mixture of these or other reasons.

Consultants are also seen as agents of change and they may, therefore, be better positioned to undertake this work.

The challenge of change, however, is not simply that of task management — ensuring that things get done — but also in dealing with the people dimensions. Poorly handled change generates resistance where there should be commitment.

CLOSURE

If anything, consultants are change junkies, and so the finish of one project is often overtaken by the excitement of the approach of the next. Closure is therefore frequently overlooked.

The value of closure can be considered from the points of view of both client and consultant.

Firstly, as a consultant you hope that this is not the end of the relationship that you have with this client. We have noted already that most business arises from previous clients, and so you want to complete the project so that the client will come back to you again, should the need for your services arise. (This will be the job of the account manager, should you be working for a larger practice.)

Secondly, consultancy is a knowledge-based business. One of the reasons for a consultant to be part of a practice is to profit from and contribute to the experience of others in that practice. Review is the means by which this is done, but it is often not done or not done well. Getting the knowledge out of the heads of individual consultants and making it corporately available needs specific effort. Although the simplest aspect of the process, it is the real means by which consultancy practices can grow their value to both individual consultants and to clients — see the comments in Chapter 13 on the practice environment.

CHAPTER 2

ENTRY

*I eyed the man fixedly. His head stuck out at the back and his
eyes sparkled with pure intelligence.*

Bertie Wooster on Jeeves in *The love that Purifies*
(P G Wodehouse)

New consultants can suffer a form of identity crisis. They are put in front
of clients and immediately a number of doubts can take hold:

- Am I meant to be able to answer any question they ask? What if I
  don't know the answer?
- How can I be worth a daily fee rate that is a multiple of my salary?
- What if they ask me how long I've been a consultant?
- How can I cope with clients who don't like consultants?

These anxieties diminish with experience and confidence. Even so, there
are challenges for all consultants engaging with a client for the first time
and this is what the entry phase is all about.

SO, WHO AM I?

We know from everyday life that we are inclined to take people at their own
valuation. We shall see in Chapter 9, when we review Cialdini's research
on influencing, that people are influenced not only by authority but also by
the appearance of authority.

LOOK LIKE A CONSULTANT

Knowing that you are well dressed and presentable adds to your self-confidence — and you have to look like you are worth whatever exorbitant fee rate you are charging. You should also behave like a consultant. Remember that you never get a second chance to make a first impression, and so good initial impact is essential. Research shows that initial impact depends largely on how you *look* and, secondarily, on how you *sound*. *What you say* is of minor importance compared with these. Check this out next time you meet someone for the first time: reflect on what you make of this person, and what evidence has led you to this conclusion; it will be primarily and inevitably on these superficial matters. As we get to know this person better, we may revise our views but, plainly, consultants should aim to make a favourable first impression.

There are two factors influencing visual impression:
• how you are dressed and groomed;
• your body language.

This is deemed to be so important that some consultancies provide training by image experts. And while inappropriate attire doesn't mean that you are necessarily a bad consultant, why make life difficult for yourself?

There are some simple guidelines to follow. Grooming rules are fairly obvious but are worth summarising:

1. Hair should be clean, tidy and cut regularly. Nails should be clean and neat.
2. Similarly, clothes should be clean. One item often overlooked is footwear; I once heard a client say that dirty or scuffed shoes counted against a consultant in the sales process!
3. Maintain personal hygiene; watch out for body and breath odour and don't drink alcohol before meeting a client — it can stay on the breath and give a bad impression.

(These points may seem obvious and not worth stating but I have met consultants who have broken each one of these rules!)

Dress is a more difficult area, with casual dress expected, indeed the norm, for many businesses in recent years. The simple rule here is to dress how your clients expect their consultants to dress. This may be different from how the clients dress themselves. If in doubt, err on the side of formality; it is better to be overdressed than underdressed.

The second area of visual impact is body language. You need to remember that body language is learned before spoken language — it is the way that we communicate as babies. When we distrust people, it is often because their body language is at variance with what they are saying.

Body language is a manifestation of what we are feeling but, equally, how we feel can be influenced by our body language. So if we feel confident, we look confident; but equally if we behave confidently, we will feel more confident.

So, identify those behaviours that you adopt when you are feeling confident; they might be for example:

- standing or sitting in a relaxed way;
- moving and speaking in an unhurried way;
- using expansive gestures;
- keeping your head erect rather than bowed.

These behaviours typically demonstrate confidence and, if you adopt them, will help you to feel more confident.

Finally, there is the matter of the voice. In the UK, we tend to class people by their accent, but a regional accent is nowadays rarely an impediment. As a consultant however, you are frequently involved in presentations and meetings, so you need to make sure that your voice is clear and strong. (If it isn't, there are vocal exercises you can do that will help — consult your local drama school!)

Image is important, but never try to pretend to be something that you are not. Attempt gradual changes and improvements and make sure you are comfortable with them; for example, choose clothing that suits you and in which you feel comfortable.

PROFESSIONAL BEHAVIOUR

From the point of view of the client this means:

- you should be seen to act in their interest;
- while charging them fees, you should be working for them (i.e. not be always on the phone to your office or other clients);
- you should be seen to be operating at a high work rate (one firm advised its consultants always to walk quickly on clients' premises, and always to carry a piece of paper or a file to give an impression of great industry);

- if you are working at the client's offices, you should keep their office hours and preferably those of the client's executives, which will be longer;
- you should bring a standard of excellence to other activities you undertake, for example, in chairing or contributing to meetings, in responding to queries promptly and so on.

Remember that, if you work for a firm of consultants, you are the embodiment of that firm to your client. A record of first-class operating is enormously valuable to individual consultants and a tremendous sales aid to their firms.

CONSULTANT ROLES

One way of looking at the client–consultant relationship is as doctor and patient; the patient has an ailment of some kind and goes to the doctor to diagnose and cure it. But there are other ways in which a consultant can provide help.

In certain circumstances, a consultant might be appointed to hold an executive position temporarily as an interim manager. For example, a company may appoint a consultant as general manager for a short while to mastermind a turn-around. Once complete, the consultant can leave and an individual with different qualities can be appointed to rebuild the company.

In a less dramatic way, an organisation may find it needs an IT manager to bridge the loss of one and the arrival of a replacement, and will call on a consultant to help.

Interim management positions are highly interventionist roles — ones in which consultants are making decisions as if they were executive employees of the organisation. At the other extreme is the role of consultant as facilitator, working totally through the client's staff; in this situation the work of the consultant enables the client organisation to initiate and manage change for itself. For example, the management team of a UK company, which had been acquired by a US conglomerate, had to reorganise its structure and systems to meet the requirements of its new parent. This was a new task for the management team, and one that required them to work together in a way they had never done before. The job of the consultant who worked with the team was not to plan the reorganisation required but to help the group to do it for themselves.

The roles of executive and facilitator are widely divergent. Schmidt and Johnston (1969) analysed consultant roles in more detail and suggested a continuum of behaviours, which is shown in Exhibit 2.1. The continuum is from client-centred to consultant-centred. Client-centred behaviours use the client's experience and knowledge: the role of the consultant is to help the client use this experience and knowledge effectively. At the other end of the spectrum are consultant-centred behaviours that focus more on the consultant's direct knowledge and experience.

Exhibit 2.1 The continuum of consultancy behaviours

Client centred

Consultant role	Consultant behaviour	
	Refuses to become involved	Use of client's experience and knowledge
	Listens	
Facilitator	Reflects	
	Classifies	
	Interprets	
	Probes	
Consultant	Gathers data	
	Diagnoses	
	Adds new data	
	Identifies options	Use of consultant's specialised experience and knowledge
	Proposes criteria	
	Recommends	
	Prescribes	
Executive	Plans implementation	

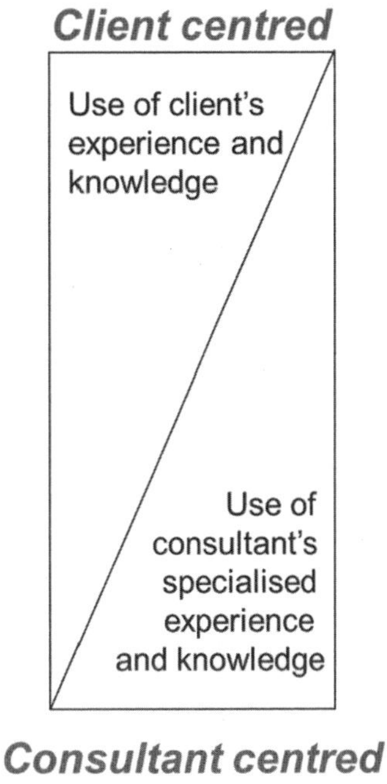

Consultant centred

Schmidt and Johnston also considered the circumstances favouring behaviours towards either end of the spectrum and classified them according to:

• factors unique to the client;
• factors unique to the consultant;
• factors in the client–consultant relationship;
• factors in the situation.

These have been simplified and presented in Exhibit 2.2.

This analysis brings home the point that consultancy projects are joint efforts between consultant and client, and consultants should vary their role according to the circumstances to get the best results. So, whether you are an experienced consultant or a novice, it is worth reviewing projects.

- Where on the continuum am I functioning and is this appropriate?
- Do I tend to operate at one position on the continuum and not take the other roles when they might be more suitable?

Exhibit 2.2 Factors influencing the consultant role

	Favouring client-centred	*Favouring consultant-centred*
Factors unique to the client	Client wants: Independence To understand and learn about the problem To make decisions	Client has: Little experience High need for help No great ownership of status quo No vested interest
Factors unique to the consultant	Consultant wants: Client to grow and develop To prevent dependency	Consultant has: Considerable relevant experience and expertise Established reputation High understanding of client
Factors in the client–consultant relationship	Little empathy Consultant not totally acceptable	High mutual trust Previous experience of working together Congruent goals Open communication
Factors in the situation	Penalty for wrong solution is high Affects complex systems Problem is dynamic or has a long time perspective	Problem is: Clearly defined Urgent Of low complexity Of little consequence on culture

THE CONSULTANT AS AN OUTSIDER

By definition, a consultant is not part of the client's hierarchical structure. (So, an internal consultant should ideally be in a management structure separate from that of their client department.) This provides an advantage of perspective — by coming fresh to a situation, a consultant is less burdened by legacy thinking and past decisions. Inevitably, this perspective diminishes with time; after a period working with a client, a consultant starts to take on the assumptions and mind-set of the client — a process known as 'going native'.

At the same time, the consultant needs to adopt a measure of 'protective coloration'. Organisations are like the human body they may have the equivalent of an immune reaction to outsiders. Consultants have to get to know clients pretty quickly. This is not just about them as people but also the jargon, style, and in summary, the culture, that prevails.

One client said to me, 'You know us so well, I keep forgetting you're not a member of my organisation'.

I'm still not sure whether to take this as a compliment or a criticism!

UNDERSTANDING THE CLIENT

Because they are outsiders, consultants need to understand the political environment of their clients. This is essential if they are to be effective.

Stakeholder analysis (see Chapter 7) is a useful way of assessing individual motivations, while power mapping (also described in Chapter 7) provides an insight into interpersonal relationships. These topics provide a way of recording information and can point towards gaps in knowledge where further information is needed. This information needs to be collected during the entry phase (whether or not collected by the organised methods described, consultants tend to do this intuitively).

The political environment then needs to be appraised. Who are likely supporters or opponents on this project? Who are the key influencers whom you need to get on side?

Be cautious early on in aligning yourself with any political factor within a client's organisation; it is wise to try to position yourself as everybody's friend at the outset of any project.

CHAPTER 3

CONTRACTING

A verbal agreement isn't worth the paper it's written on.
Louis B Meyer (attrib.)

Consultancy is amongst the least tangible products. If you were told that you are to receive a can of baked beans tomorrow, you will have a pretty good idea of what you are going to get. By contrast, if you are told you are getting some consultancy on Monday, what might you expect?

One of my colleagues says that consultancy is all about the sale and delivery of promises. Contracting is about the definition of these promises, which are usually embodied in a project.

A consultancy project is only one part of an ongoing relationship between a client and consultant. It represents a particularly intense period of the relationship and can influence it significantly, either positively or negatively. After the project has finished, the relationship will continue to need managing if the consultant is to obtain follow-on work or new projects; this is an aspect of ongoing account management.

Having good client relations is vital in maintaining a network for a professional practice and the foundation of this is how the relationship starts — the contracting phase. When consultant and client come together, there will be expectations and obligations on both sides. The basis of a successful consultancy project (and hence a good ongoing relationship) is, therefore, a clear understanding between consultant and client about:

- the scope of the project — what areas of concern need to be addressed;

- what deliverables the client will receive;
- how it is to be conducted;
- how much it will cost.

These need to be embodied in clear terms of reference setting out expectations from the start. Many difficulties on a consulting project arise simply because of a mismatch of expectations rather than any failure in execution. Expectations will usually be embodied in a proposal, which is the basis of the contract that exists at the conclusion of the selling phase.

As well as achieving the proposal promises, a consultant responsible for operating a project has other priorities, notably:
- to keep the client happy (delighted would be better), so that repeat business is placed with the practice,
- to complete the project within the time and cost limits established at the outset.

These objectives can be met by careful planning, monitoring progress against plans and conducting the project competently.

REVISITING TERMS OF REFERENCE

Those involved with selling consultancy projects will be responsible for drafting and agreeing terms of reference for a project with a client (see Chapter 11). This section is called 'revisiting terms of reference', as the operating team needs to be familiar with these for the project in which they are currently engaged.

There are some particular features of terms of reference that are relevant to operating consultants.

BEWARE OF SCOPE DRIFT
A common pitfall is to take on work that is outside the terms of reference. In practice, this is free consultancy. Consultants accept tasks (perhaps doing work as a favour to the client) for which there is no budget.

There could be a good reason for doing this, for example, to help a client who is faced with a temporary difficulty. The principle involved here is that the relationship will be strengthened and perhaps the favour returned (Cialdini calls this 'reciprocation', see Chapter 9). But taking on extra work needs to be done with open eyes, not blind agreement!

CHECK THAT THE TERMS OF REFERENCE REMAIN RELEVANT

The sales team will have taken a view on what needs to be done and how best to do it, based on the information they have to hand. The operating team usually has a more extensive exposure to the client and the reality they encounter may be different from that anticipated by the sales team.

Under these circumstances, the terms of reference may need revision.

HAVE A CHANGE PROCEDURE

Terms of reference may need to be changed to accommodate additional requests from the client, or changed circumstances or understanding. Consequently, there needs to be a process by which changes can be defined and agreed with a client and accommodated within revised terms of reference and plans.

Change is a norm: organisations and their business environment change, as do the roles of people within them. You would not expect any business to be identical 12 months hence to what it is now and so the requirements of any project may well change over time.

PLANNING A CONSULTANCY PROJECT

Not all professionals plan their projects; for example, a solicitor working on a particular matter may simply respond to outside initiatives and charge for the consequent time spent. Such an approach can be risky for consultants who are engaged with projects which are all different and which have to meet the project objectives against a fixed-fee budget. In 99 per cent of cases, therefore, consultants need to plan their projects.

A plan for a consultancy project should show:
- what is going to happen;
- when it is going to happen;
- the resources required.

These elements lead to the benefits of planning:
- It enables you to monitor progress;
- It helps to provide a standard of performance to pace your work, otherwise, it is easy to let one project fall behind because of pressures of other commitments;
- It enables you to schedule consultant resources — you know whether you have space in your diary for more work;

- It provides a basis for estimating fees;
- It can be used to communicate expectations to the client.

Good planning is required for the simple commercial reason that consultants are selling time. It is consultancy stock control.

Planning is important in managing the client's expectations, because the client will need to schedule their resources and, at a more prosaic level, need to know if you are going to be around two days a week or full time.

PREPARING THE PROJECT PLAN

Although an outline plan may have been set out in the proposal, the consultant will need to prepare a detailed operating plan for any project other than the most simple. The principles of planning a consultancy project are the same as those for planning any other project, but a brief recap is worthwhile.

As an example, imagine there is a consultancy run by Tom, Dick and Harriet – TDH; we will be hearing more about them throughout the book. They have won an engagement with a client, ABC Ltd, which is to set up a new stock control system, which Dick is handling.

1. Dick's first task is to break the job into discrete tasks, and break these tasks themselves, if they are large, into separate elements. Exhibit 3.1 shows the breakdown for the first phase of a project to specify a new stock control system.

Exhibit 3.1 Outline programme

Phase 1 Specification of new system
1.1 Familiarisation
1.2 Appraisal of present production and stock control procedures
1.3 Formation of steering group
1.4 Identification of priorities and requirements for new system
1.5 Specification for new system drafted for discussion and approval

Again, each one of these steps consists of smaller steps, as shown in Exhibit 3.2.

Exhibit 3.2 Detailed programme

Phase 1.3 Formation of steering group
1.3.1   Determine who are the most influential people in sales and production
1.3.2   Draft shortlist of possible steering group members and consider solicitation method
1.3.3   Discuss shortlist and method at progress meeting on 7 April. Get confirmation/alterations
1.3.4   Carry out solicitation programme
1.3.5   Convene first meeting of steering group on 21 April

Where there is a distinct order to the tasks (as in Exhibits 3.1 and 3.2) then it may be helpful to show the tasks on a logic diagram reflecting these relationships.

2. Assess the time required for each step, in terms of both consultant input and calendar time. Calendar time is usually more than consultant time — it allows for delays whilst client staff are carrying out part of the project, or are unavailable. Remember to allow time for yourself for thinking about the project, or discussing it with professional colleagues.

3. For complex projects, more sophisticated tools such as network analysis might be useful. For short or simple projects, however, I have found the Gantt chart quite adequate for my needs, and an example of this, for a quite different project this time, is shown in Exhibit 3.3. The practical test of any plan is: does this plan tell me — or can I infer from it — what I am meant to be doing on this project today? If it does not, it is probably inadequate.

4. If there are several consultants on a project, they will need to be allocated specific tasks. The job of project management is made more simple if these tasks are 'mini-projects' within a work package breakdown — the consultant has to achieve defined goals or deliverables within a certain fee budget and calendar time.

Allow some time for familiarisation with new clients at the start of a project. Familiarisation can include:
*   visiting the various sites of factories and offices;
*   knowing 'who's who';

Exhibit 3.3 Example of a project plan for a new performance appraisal system

ACTIVITY	Oct				Nov				Dec		
	6	13	20	27	3	10	17	24	1	8	15
1. Completion of systems design											
1.1 Preparation of draft documentation	X										
1.2 Review of draft documentation		X									
1.3 Final documentation and procedures agreed			X								
2. Pilot trial											
2.1 Announce the pilot trial to staff				X							
2.2 Train assessors				X							
2.3 Prepare performance appraisals					▬▬▬▬▬▬▬						
2.4 Performance appraisal 'clinic'						X					
2.5 Review performance assessments							X				
2.6 Hold appraisal meetings								▬▬▬▬▬			
2.7 Review system with assessors and those assessed								X			
2.8 Evaluate pilot trial										X	

- understanding the key processes in the organisation (for example, in a profit-making organisation, the principal methods of adding value);
- understanding the jargon used in the business — every organisation has words or phrases that it uses in a specialised way.

After this initial immersion into the client culture, the consultant should have sufficient knowledge to speak the language of the client.

Accept that planning cannot be comprehensive at the start of a project and allow for this. It may not be possible to define what later phases of a project may contain in detail until the initial diagnosis is carried out. It is after this that detailed planning can then be done. All you can do in making your estimate at the outset is to use your best guess. This simply requires you to make your planning assumptions explicit. These can then be checked with the passage of time to see if they remain valid. For example, a planning assumption might be, 'The new marketing manager will be in post by September 1'; if this becomes no longer true, the plan will need re-examination.

QUALITY CONTROL
In this context, I mean the quality of output of the consultancy project.

Management consultancy projects often break new ground by the novel application of existing techniques and thus the consultant is undertaking work that, in some respects, is unique. This creates difficulties in controlling quality because there are no basic standards to compare with. If, by contrast, you are manufacturing a standard product, you can decide what the key quality characteristics should be, establish measurable criteria of acceptability and check whether each item falls within the criteria. It is less easy to do this in a service industry, and particularly difficult to do it within a consultancy project. It is important, however, to define what standard is adequate. Given more resources, any job can be improved (and consultants are by nature relentless improvers), so where do you stop? The starting point is to establish the standards by which a project is to be judged and these should be embodied in the terms of reference. (Indeed, it is a good test of terms of reference to see whether they indeed do provide a basis for this judgement.)

There are other, fairly obvious, criteria to be met, such as having a satisfied client and carrying out the job in an appropriate manner. However, there is something more required, which is professional integrity. A major trap for the new consultant is to assume that a satisfied client means that they have done a good job; this may not necessarily be the case.

For example, given a choice of alternative courses of action, the client may be relying on the consultant to recommend the best. Initially, the client will not be able to judge the choice but will be satisfied because a choice has been recommended.

Equally, the client may not want to hear or do what is best, but to speak the unspeakable could be the most helpful thing a consultant does — this is the advantage of being an outsider.

Most projects should result in satisfied clients but professional judgement is the responsibility of the consultant.

Two heads are better than one

This is, certainly, the case for quality control in consultancy and it is well worthwhile involving a colleague in a project for other reasons too:

- Often the discussion of a project is a helpful way of identifying the key issues, solving problems and creating new ideas;
- You can be blind to flaws in your thinking that may be obvious to someone else — better that the 'someone else' is not the client;
- You may have rationalised away the need to deal with certain important issues. Working with a colleague should spur you to confront them;
- It is as well to review key items of documentation, particularly reports, with a colleague who can check them for clarity, as well as proofread them;
- It may also be useful to refer to a colleague's expertise, not just in technical matters but also to tap into their expertise on consultancy matters.

Larger firms often embody this role into a supervisory system; a more experienced consultant is appointed to supervise less experienced ones on projects perhaps with written procedures to be followed. The supervisor might have other responsibilities too, such as training the consultant. If you are a sole practitioner, however, this approach becomes more difficult. Nonetheless, sole practitioners can and do seek the help of fellow professionals to ensure high-quality work.

Individuals new to consulting firms can be daunted by their quality control procedures. In their previous jobs they may not have been subjected to such high standards; some find it difficult to adjust to having their professional judgement questioned.

CONTROLLING RESOURCES

Whereas quality control is about controlling the output of a project, controlling a project also involves controlling the input — the consultant's time.

Once the plan is made, it is necessary as with any project to monitor progress. As there are plenty of excellent texts about project management, here we will consider only those features that are peculiar to control in a consultancy project.

The consultancy time spent must be carefully controlled. It is useless waiting until the end of a project of any size to see what time was spent on it. It needs to be monitored at suitable milestones, and feature on the agenda at each progress review.

Client staff also have to contribute to the project; this means being available for meetings, and carrying out other work entailed by the project. (A consultancy project usually entails an increase in the client's workload.) The availability of client resources to work on a project is a constraint on its pace; there are others too, for example:

- If a project requires new equipment, there may be a lead time associated with acquiring it;
- The pace at which change can be absorbed within the client organisation.

Managing time

These factors should have been considered at the time the consultant and client agreed to carry out the project. The agreement probably will have estimated:

- the number of consultant days required;
- the calendar time for its completion.

The control of time on a project interfaces with the internal accounting system for the consulting company (see Exhibit 3.4).

Exhibit 3.4 Controlling time

Internal accounts		Project data
Time spent on various projects	←→	Time spent on this project
Forward loading	←→	Time required to complete this project

It is essential that consultants ensure they are spending their time gainfully employed. This means careful diary control. There are, therefore, two essential controls required for internal accounting for time spent, namely:

- how time was spent during the last period;
- how time is to be spent in the future.

The same breakdown can be used for both and Exhibit 3.5 shows the type of form that might be used.

Professionals often charge by the hour — or, indeed, a fraction of it if their work does not usually occur in large enough units to merit a whole hour's effort. On the other hand, an audit clerk may be assigned to a client for days or weeks. So, the nature of the work does help to determine what is the most appropriate method of monitoring a consultant's time. I believe that accounting for a consultant's time on fees by the day or half-day is most appropriate for fee-earning work. Other aspects, however, such as selling, marketing or administration, do not necessarily occur in such convenient periods, so you may wish to account for these in smaller units.

Exhibit 3.5 Loading chart

Name													
Week commencing		April				May					June		
Chargeable	Project no.	3	10	17	24	1	8	15	22	29	5	12	19
Alpha plc		2	1	1		½		1	3				
Delta Ltd			2		2	2							
Gamma Bros.		½	1	2	1								
Allocated													
Zeta plc						1	1	1	1	2	2		
Total chargeable		2½	4	3	3	1½	3	2	4	2	2		
Selling													
Bloggs		¼	1	¼									
Cloggs						¼	¼						
Floggs						1		¼	¼				
Total selling		¼	1	¼	1¼	¼	¼	¼					
Other													
Projects		1											
CPD						1							
Office admin.													
Holiday		1				1		1			4		
Total other		2				2		1			4		
Total allocation		4¾	5	4¼	4¼	3¾	3¼	2¼	4	3	2	4	-
Free days		¼	-	¾	¾	1¼	1¾	2¾	1	2	3	1	5

Data on time spent can be collected weekly or less frequently, depending on the nature of projects and the invoicing cycle. For example, if invoicing is done weekly (to keep accounts receivable to a minimum), then time needs to be booked weekly. If the projects are long term — say a full-time engagement, typically for a month at a time, then monthly reporting may be more appropriate. Even so, individual consultants need to keep a record of how they are spending their time on a weekly basis – it can be difficult to remember what happened a month ago!

Forward loading is usually difficult to do in any detail more than a few weeks ahead, but even so, it is worthwhile looking beyond that. There needs to be some distinction on the plan between confirmed commitments to fee-earning jobs and those that are only tentative. A method of showing this is also given in Exhibit 3.5, within the category 'allocated'.

Data from the internal system then can be used to monitor how much time has been spent on the project. Exhibit 3.6 shows a simple control sheet that Dick might use on the ABC project if Tom and Harriet are also making an input.

Exhibit 3.6 Project control sheet

ABC Ltd Project										
Week ending	Tom		Dick		Harriet		Totals			
							Week		Cum	
	Bud	Act	Bud	Act	Bud	Act	Bud	Act	Bud	Act

All records are time in days on the project

Bud = budget; Act = actual; Cum = cumulative

One of the great dangers for consultants is over-commitment. They need to control future commitments so that they have sufficient flexibility to respond to any additional operating requirements on existing jobs.

PRACTICAL OPERATING

PLANNING FOR A GOOD CLIENT RELATIONSHIP

As well as achieving the results promised in a proposal, Dick will have the aims of keeping the client happy throughout the work and establishing a good relationship so that TDH will be considered when the next requirement for outside help arises.

To this end, your planning should enable you to do the following:

1. Keep the client informed about progress: the plan should schedule regular progress meetings with the client to report on problems and successes, and future plans. Make sure you do not leave long gaps between reports, particularly at the start of the project and above all avoid unpleasant surprises for your client.

2. Whatever the rank of your client, not only do they have to be assured of the continuing success of your project but they also have to be able to assure their boss, colleagues and subordinates, some of whom may not be as enthusiastic. A well-informed client is able to refute rumour and, of course, will be more convinced that the project is being professionally run.

3. Allow yourself a safety margin in both consultant and calendar time for completing a project. It is embarrassing (and makes for poor client relations) if you have to increase the fees, or fail to meet deadlines.

4. Remember, too, that operating several assignments part-time is less efficient than a single full-time assignment (as encapsulated in the equation $2\frac{1}{2} + 2\frac{1}{2} = 5\frac{1}{2}$ days/week).

5. Part-time operating has to be more carefully planned and organised than full-time; it wastes time, and it can be frustrating to visit a client and find the people you need to see are away.

6. Within a short time of the project starting, you should demonstrate some 'quick successes'. A quick success consists of delivering a benefit to the client sooner than expected. In Dick's case, he might find a way of reducing inventories of finished goods in a few areas. If this can be done very soon after starting, he will have shown his worth.

7. Aim to do a little more than was promised. This can vary from doing more on the project to providing help in other areas of the business. This has to be kept in check however — there are no points for providing so much extra in other areas that the original project falls behind.
8. Schedule your invoicing so that the client has a bill to pay when they have a sense of having received value from you, e.g. after delivering a report rather than before it.

DURING THE PROJECT
Here are a few practical tips on operating management consulting projects.

Keep the initiative
The consultant should provide a sense of direction and set the pace on a project — the client should strive to keep up with you, rather than the other way around. Initiative applies not only to project management, however, but also to thinking. The consultant should be initiating the ideas and recommendations on a project rather than the client.

Keep client staff informed
This is not simply those in contact with the project, but also other senior staff, whose impression of the project may be formed solely from casual conversations with you. You should be careful what you say on these occasions as an unguarded remark can have unfortunate repercussions. Years ago, a colleague advised me how to cope with this. 'Always have a "news item" up your sleeve,' he said. 'A "news item" is some simple, quotable recent piece of information about your project which puts it in a good light. It will be passed along by word of mouth and generally result in the project getting a good name.' Examples are:
- 'Savings should be more than we originally expected';
- 'We have completed this phase of the work faster than we expected';
- 'Old Harry (who had been against the project) is now putting a lot of support into the project'.

(If you are a junior consultant working in a large firm of consultants, this technique might also be used to impress senior colleagues!)

Keeping a project diary
Some consultants habitually maintain a diary — a log of events, meetings, agreements and other significant items and events — on all projects. Others rely on progress reports. A project diary is more appropriate, however, if the project is long or complex, or is likely to be contentious — e.g. if there is challenging employee relations content, or there are individuals who actively oppose the project.

Keep documentation secure
Many projects involve sensitive information that should not be freely available to the client's staff, so when committed to paper, it needs to be kept secure. This means keeping it under lock and key if it is left at the client's premises, or better still not leaving sensitive documents there at all.

Documentation, of course, is often computer-based, so you should ensure that your computer files are appropriately secure. Nowadays, a laptop computer is a standard tool in the consultant's kit; obviously, this too should be kept secure when used on client premises, as indeed should any memory media which contain confidential information. So, for example, it is good practice to log off when your computer is unattended.

First-name terms
It is common practice in most areas of business in the UK, and more widely in the US, to default to using people's first names but this is not a universal habit. There are a few sectors in the UK, and certainly many other countries, where use of someone's first name at first meeting would be considered over-familiar and damage the relationship.

If in doubt, err on the side of formality — or do what I do, which is to see if the client uses my first name and then follow suit.

Do not undervalue the project
It can be undervalued in two ways — by you or by the client. Because it is competing with other pressures for your time, it should nonetheless receive the necessary attention from you. If the client feels you are not giving sufficient priority or attention to the project, they will rapidly become discontented.

Similarly, the happiest outcome for some client staff might be that the project stops and you go away. They may, therefore, belittle the project and hope that you will do the same. Don't.

On being thrown out

Sooner or later, it happens that a consultant gets thrown off a job. This can happen to inexperienced and experienced consultants alike; it may be obvious and dramatic or become clear only in retrospect and can be no fault of the consultant. The fastest I have come across this was years ago when a consultant who went to start a project in the morning was back in his office just after lunch because 'his face didn't fit'. Another example was the consultant who worked with a client on a project for 18 months, who was then asked to withdraw because of a change in political balance — he was identified with the old regime.

Happily, this does not happen very often, but when it does it can devastate a consultant's self-confidence. The only consolation is that it has happened to a lot of good consultants, who are still highly regarded by their other clients.

When things go wrong, in your role as account manager, consider what you can do to rebuild the relationship. The test of a service organisation is how well it handles breakdowns in service. And bear in mind this is a problem for the client as well as you; joint problem solving can be a powerful way of building a relationship and dealing expeditiously with an operating problem is a way of doing so.

QUESTIONS OF STANDARDS AND ETHICS

Questions of standards and ethics arise for the consultant in two areas:

1. What are the standards of professional behaviour and personal conduct that I should adopt in my work?
2. How should I resolve dilemmas arising from the applications of these standards?

Most professions have standard codes of conduct and the various institutes of management consultants around the world are no exception. An example of a code of conduct (drawn from the UK Institute of Consulting) has principles as follows:

1. *Meeting the client's requirements*: a member [of the Institute] shall regard the client's requirements and interests as paramount at all times.
2. *Integrity, independence, objectivity*: a member shall avoid any action or situation inconsistent with the member's professional obligations

or which in any way might be seen to impair the member's integrity. In formulating advice and recommendations the member will be guided solely by the member's objective view of the client's best interests.

3. *Responsibility to the profession and to the Institute*: a member's conduct shall at all times endeavour to enhance the standing and public recognition of the profession and the Institute.

These are sound principles; I have a simple test that I also apply to any question of standards:

If this action were reported fully and fairly in the press, or to my clients, would this enhance or detract from my professional reputation?

This embodies two criteria:
1. *Transparency:* is this an action that would be defensible in the full glare of publicity?
2. *Vulnerability:* what would be the impact on me and my business were this to become widely known?

It is not, however, questions of professional standards themselves that give most difficulty; it is their interpretation in different situations that can be tricky, when there can be a conflict in doing what is right for more than one party. Examples of dilemmas that may arise are as follows.

1. Engaging in work for a client whose culture and ethics are different from ours. For example, the attitude towards bribes or the treatment of women is quite different in some countries outside the UK. How should consultants respond? Do they refuse to change from the standards in use in the UK or should they adapt to the local practice?

2. Situations arising where serving a client's wishes and interests may be in conflict with our own standards. For example, the marketing director of the client confides to you that he is about to change jobs but does not plan to announce it until the annual bonus (which will be substantial in his case) is paid. The CEO — your client — at a subsequent meeting asks you if there are any foreseeable defections. Do you tell him about the marketing director?

3. Conflicts between the demands of our own practice and that of a client. For example, a consultant was assigned to a project where

— unbeknown to him — his qualifications had been exaggerated to the client by the colleague who made the sale. It would be embarrassing (and commercially difficult) to withdraw — besides which, the colleague comments, 'The job is 90 per cent common sense — if you need some specialist help outside your expertise, just ask for it.' What should the consultant do?

As you can see, each of these dilemmas ends with a question. In many cases, any given answer to the question is going to upset somebody — there is not necessarily a perfect answer that will satisfy all.

It is often difficult to take an objective view of an ethical dilemma that involves you. For this reason, ethical guidance does not consist of prescribing the answers to sets of dilemmas; it involves communicating principles (such as those to do with transparency and vulnerability mentioned above) and acting in accordance with them within an organisation so as to encourage good practice.

If you are in a large consultancy practice, therefore, this is what should be done. Smaller firms and sole practitioners may not have the resources to set up an internal system; a qualified outsider in all cases, though, may be helpful to resolve ethical dilemmas.

CHAPTER 4

DIAGNOSIS

Things should be made as simple as possible but not any simpler.
Albert Einstein

*A hot-air balloonist had lost his bearings when he landed in
a field and saw a man approaching on foot. The balloonist
asked the man where he was. 'You are in the basket of a hot-
air balloon, in the middle of a field,' came the reply. Factually
correct but totally unhelpful.*

Diagnosis is the process that results in a consultant being able to form valid
conclusions about how a client's areas of concern might be addressed. At
its most trivial, this might simply be providing advice in response to questions. So a tax adviser might be asked, 'When should I have completed
my personal tax return this year?' In most cases, a consultant would need
additional information, and so diagnosis requires some data collection. The
issue then is, what data do I need, and how do I acquire it? This is predicated
on the problem-solving method that you are using.

PROBLEM SOLVING

A simple illustration of problem solving is that used by your family doctor.
You visit the doctor and describe the symptoms that have prompted your visit.
On the basis of what you say, immediate observations and perhaps referral

to your medical notes, the doctor forms some hypotheses — preliminary conclusions — about your condition. Next, the doctor may ask questions or conduct an examination to test these hypotheses. These may be validated or prompt the formation of further hypotheses. At the conclusion of the consultation, the doctor may prescribe a treatment plan and/or decide how the diagnostic process might be pursued — e.g. by referral to a specialist.

This example illustrates the key elements of diagnostic problem solving. This can be interpreted as follows for consultancy, as shown in Exhibit 4.1 below.

This can be an interactive process, which can be applied to answering a series of questions. Taking the medical analogy again, these might be:

1. What is wrong with this person?
2. How should we best treat it?

Exhibit 4.1 Diagnostic problem solving

Doctor	Consultant
Listens to what the patient says	Agrees terms of reference with the client
Forms some preliminary conclusions about what could be wrong	Forms some preliminary hypotheses about how the client's areas of concern might be addressed
Takes a history and conducts an examination	Identifies data needed and collects it
Decides on treatment plan	Forms conclusions

In consultancy, we might refer again to the project that Dick of TDH Ltd is doing with ABC Ltd (see Chapter 3). Here, the presenting symptom is the desire for a new stock control system. Dick's questions might be:

1. Where is the existing system deficient?
2. How can it best be improved?

So the first phase of his consultancy project might be to determine the key problem areas; the second phase would be to recommend how each of these should be addressed.

This approach might be labelled *exploratory* problem solving, which is particularly helpful if you are approaching a new situation. At the other extreme is the standard approach or methodology (see Chapter 1), which prescribes the work to be done in addressing the client's problems. A half-way house between these is using a model of performance to help.

CHOOSING A MODEL OF PERFORMANCE

Data is needed:

- to determine the nature of the problem and the model to be used to understand it;
- to build a more detailed picture according to the model chosen.

Applying this to the story of the balloonist at the start of this chapter, the former is about deciding which of many maps to refer to and the latter, having chosen the map, to find out where you are on it.

The process of familiarisation helps the consultant to select and build a mental model of the issue to sort out. Often this model will not be articulated; it may be intuitive, but it will be there. Consultants with different specialisations look at situations from their own specialist point of view. The marketer will see problems from the marketing standpoint; the information systems specialist will see the data-processing problems and so on. Because consultants bring their own specialist biases to a project, it is important that they make their assumptions explicit. Questioning the client's assumptions is a major value of a consultant's intervention. Likewise, consultants need to articulate and question their own assumptions!

Referring back to the stock control problem in ABC Ltd cited in Chapter 3, the problem initially cited by the client might be that of wishing to introduce a new computerised stock control system. Although recognising that the problem is not necessarily about logistics, Dick's experience might indicate that the process of familiarisation could be best accomplished by drawing up a material flow diagram. His first step will be to collect data at level 1 above to understand what the material flows are. The results are depicted in Exhibit 4.2.

Dick would build up this picture by discussions with a few key people in the company, at the same time illuminating the problem he has to address. He might, therefore, investigate the following:

1. What measures are used to determine the performance of the stock control system, wholly and in part? These might be:
    - to deliver goods within a given time of receiving the order;
    - to keep inventories of stocks low;
    - to keep rejects below a given percentage.

Exhibit 4.2 Material flows at ABC Ltd

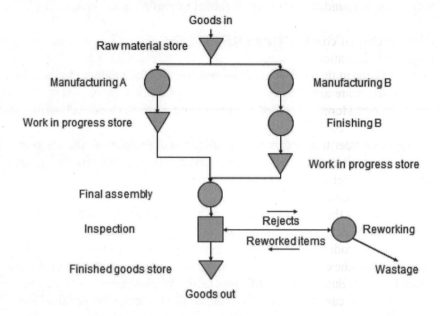

These objectives might be in conflict and the stock control system will have to lead to the right trade-offs.

2. Who takes decisions that affect the performance of each part of the system? If different managers are responsible for pursuing each of the objectives above, then the system could itself cause conflicts between the managers.

DATA COLLECTION

You will see that already in the example, Dick is embarking on data collection.

In management consultancy, as with all problem solving, you need to identify the data you require very carefully. From childhood, our life is taken up with collecting and sorting data and trying to make sense of the world. Similarly, management consultants collect and sort data to make sense of the organisation and issues they are working with.

A difficulty facing the consultant, however, is not the shortage of information but its abundance, and it can be difficult choosing which information is relevant.

Perversely, of course, despite the availability of data, it is rare to have all of the information you ideally would like. This applies, particularly, to predictions about the future, especially people's behaviour. Cost is also an element: the more accurate or extensive the data required, the more costly it is to collect. Moreover, I suspect it obeys the law of diminishing returns: the effort involved in getting data to one per cent accuracy is an order of magnitude greater than getting it to ten per cent accuracy.

Management consultancy has its roots in work study, which itself is based on the careful observation, measurement and analysis of work and involves large amounts of data collection and analysis.

Similarly, in the other areas into which management consultancy has developed, projects almost always involve some initial research; it is rare for data to be readily available in the form required to address a particular issue. The data the consultant collects will be facts and statistics — i.e. hard data — but soft data, such as opinions, signals, assumptions, speculations and other clues can be just as relevant to the successful implementation of a project.

It is difficult to distinguish between data collection and data analysis because there is little point in collecting data unless you have some idea of what you are to do with it. Data collection can be very time-consuming (indeed, it can be the single most time-consuming element in a consultancy project) and a lot of time — and thus money — can be wasted if it is not done properly. The specific and detailed techniques associated with any discipline can be seductive: it can be easy to embark on a highly structured programme of data collection without reflecting what the data is to be used for. Once started, the danger is that the means become the end — the process of collecting, analysing and presenting data overshadows the original purpose of the project. There are masses of consultants' reports languishing on managers' shelves around the world which, although masterpieces of data collection, have failed to address the important issues. Alternatively, the important issues have been recognised, but too late; the data collected does not match that required to address the issues and the conclusions are inadequately supported.

Starting a new consultancy project is a bit like being the balloonist referred to at the start of the chapter: you are put down in the middle of a field and have to find your way around. There is some comfort in taking action — any action — and rushing around collecting data may give you and your client the impression of progress. The purpose of this chapter is to avoid doing unnecessary work. At the start of a project, therefore, don't just do something — sit there and think!

DECIDING WHAT DATA TO COLLECT

One of the popular methods of teaching business analysis has been the use of case studies. I have a book of them in front of me and they vary in length from 2 to more than 20 pages of closely typeset information. Even so, 'real life' is vastly more complex; a case study, however long, offers a small volume of data compared with the real world in which the significance of data may not be appreciated, or it is unavailable, or there are other priorities competing for attention. Deciding what data to collect is trying to sort the signal from the noise. It is an important task and can be a hard one.

As indicated above under 'problem solving', the consultant is able at an early point in the project to have a pretty good guess at what the likely conclusions might be and thus organise data collection to test whether these are right.

For example, Dick's initial hypothesis concerning the stock control problems at ABC Ltd, following the familiarisation stage, could be that managers are working towards conflicting performance goals. The data he will choose to collect initially will therefore be about performance measures and managerial responsibilities.

Consultants are great post hoc rationalisers (they are not alone in this!) and when reporting retrospectively on a project, will show that the process of data collection is in the following sequence:
1. Define the objectives of the project.
2. Determine the data required.
3. Develop and implement a plan for collecting the data.
4. Analyse the data.
5. Draw conclusions and make recommendations.

In practice, unless the project follows a standard methodology, the process is messier and, for example, Dick's project would probably follow a series of iterations:
1. Definition of the project objectives beforehand.
2. Get to know the client.
3. New slants to the issues identified. Possibly project objectives are slightly shifted and initial hypotheses formed.

4. Crude data collection.
5. Items worth exploring identified in more detail.
6. Revise/substantiate hypotheses.
… and so on.

Despite this process of reaching hypothetical conclusions early on in the project, the consultant must keep an open mind.

> On one project, the consultant quickly identified what he considered should be the outcome of the investigation. A number of data collection meetings with senior executives in the company had been set up but the consultant made the mistake of pre-selling the proposed solution at the meetings. In the event, most of the executives agreed with his conclusion, except the chairman of the company, who was the last to be seen. He totally disagreed with the consultant's solution. The consultant lost face with the chairman for having reached what appeared to be a firm conclusion without sounding the chairman out, and also lost face with the executives because he could not deliver the proposals to which he had got their agreement.

A development of this method of choosing what data to collect comes from giving some thought to the content and structure of the final report early on in the project. If Dick, for instance, reckons that ABC Ltd ought to have a new stock control system, he might decide that his case will be best made by presenting data on:
- benchmarking of stock levels in ABC Ltd with those expected in high-performance organisations elsewhere;
- quality of delivery;
- timeliness and accuracy of information produced by the system.

Having decided what evidence he wants to present in his final report, Dick could then go one step further and lay out how it might be presented. This would consist of drawing up the tables, diagrams, graphs and charts, etc. to assess what data would be needed to complete them.

A further refinement is to fill in the charts and tables with dummy data (before starting data collection) to make sure that there are no gaps, nor is data to be collected which is unlikely to be of much use. You need an active imagination to do this effectively and it is more difficult with qualitative than with quantitative data.

CONSTRAINTS ON DATA COLLECTION

Dick will have to make sure that he does his project within the consultant time allocated, and this might restrict the information he can collect. For example, it could be very useful to have information on how satisfied ABC Ltd's customers are with delivery times, but visits to customers could be difficult to arrange and time consuming. Moreover, there is the danger that asking questions about the adequacy of delivery dates may create questions in the customers' minds which were not there before.

Summarised below are the major constraints on data collection, which will limit both the range of data collected and the methods of its collection.

TIMESCALE
The first constraint is the calendar time available for the project. (The amount of effort and the consequent limitations in terms of cost are discussed in the next section.)

The effect of a limited timescale may itself constrain the amount of effort that can be put in by a project team. For example, if a new product is to be launched to catch the retail Christmas market, there may be severely limited time for test marketing if it is started too late.

> *On the other hand, do not let a limited timescale deter you from collecting vital information. This happened to a consultant pressed for time on a number of projects, who had to take on another which had to be completed within a short timescale. Most of the factual information required was collected but, because of the time constraints, the deeply political environment in the organisation the consultant was required to advise had not been recognised. The consequence was that a major presentation to the board of directors went very badly and jeopardised the project that the consultant was engaged with.*

The moral is, if there is insufficient time to collect vital data, either extend the timescale or limit the terms of reference of the project — at least initially — to that which can be accomplished within the available timescale. If clients expect work to be completed within an unreasonably short timescale, a firm stand by the consultant is necessary to persuade them otherwise. If this is not possible, you have to question whether you should be involved with the project at all.

COST
The expense of data collection arises mainly from:
- the consultant's time and the expenses incurred;
- the method of data collection and analysis;
- the time and effort of client staff.

For example, if attitudes are to be assessed throughout an organisation using a questionnaire, costs will arise from design and printing or creating web pages for online completion, the time spent completing it and the collation and analysis of completed questionnaires.

Expenses can also arise from using specialist survey techniques involving proprietary questionnaires and the computer software required to analyse them.

Travel expenses can also add considerably to the costs of the project, as they did in a project run from the UK in an African country, part of which was to advise on the suitability of particular computer software. The software was available and in use only in the USA and so the consultants had to make several intercontinental trips, which added significantly to the project cost.

Sometimes a consultancy may subcontract research work and this can be another form of expense. Even published editions of market or economic research reports focusing on highly specialised topics can cost thousands of pounds.

If the associated expenses of data collection are likely to be significant, they should be included in the preliminary cost estimate.

Finally, remember that data collection often involves time commitment from client staff. Clients may be concerned about the opportunity cost of the time of their own people becoming involved in meetings. The consultant needs to be prepared for, and sensitive to, this point.

WHO SHOULD BE INCLUDED?
In the story of Sleeping Beauty, a curse was placed on the princess by a fairy who was not invited to her christening. Beware the same process happening on your projects! If you are to carry out a survey, it is important

to cover not only those who have data but also those powerful individuals who will feel that they should have been consulted. It is better to see too many people than run the risk of needlessly creating a powerful antagonist.

Data collection also provides an opportunity to meet a wider cross-section of the top people in the organisation than the consultant otherwise would. It gives a chance to assess what they are like whilst at the same time being able to establish a good relationship with them. There is a military maxim that 'time spent in reconnaissance is rarely wasted'. The same is true of data collection; you may well have a complete compendium of hard data to collect, but equally you need to have information about the key people in the organisation and their views relevant to your project (see stakeholder analysis in Chapter 7). And, as is obviously the case, you can learn a lot from meeting them.

For example, sometimes consultants will receive a certain amount of disinformation — information that purports to be accurate, but which, at best, is only partially so. This is often provided by those wishing to score political points or follow their own agenda, particularly at senior levels.

Happily, consultants can often spot this happening, and so will have acquired a useful piece of data in itself — the peculiar objectives being followed by the provider of disinformation.

CONFIDENTIALITY AND SECURITY

Consultants are sometimes used to carry out external research where the client wishes their identity, or the fact that they are engaged in a particular project, to be kept confidential. Executive search (headhunting) is an example of this: the client may not want it to be generally known that they are seeking to fill a particular position (perhaps because of personnel or commercial repercussions), or may wish to sound out a prospective candidate's interest through an intermediary.

It is more difficult, however, to collect data if the identity of the client is to be kept secret from those providing the data — for instance, if you require competitors to pool data. The way around this is to offer respondents a suitably edited version of the research carried out in exchange for their taking part. Product managers will be more ready to give their views on the changing market for widgets if they know that they are going to receive a distillation of the views of similar managers amongst competitors, than if they are to receive nothing in return.

Sources of information, sometimes, have to be kept confidential from your clients. Thus, a consultant commissioned to carry out a salary survey may have gathered data on the basis that specific providers would not be identified; to do otherwise would therefore be a breach of confidentiality.

Perhaps the most difficult problem of confidentiality is that of keeping the nature of an enquiry from staff. For example, a consultant advising on the feasibility of a company moving its head office from one location to another may need to know how many staff would consequently resign, preferring not to move. One way of finding out is to ask them — and indeed, that may well be done later on in the project — but at the stage of a feasibility study, the resultant speculation would not be in the client's best interest. So, an alternative method of data collection needs to be used, so as to keep the reason for it confidential.

One consultant faced with exactly this problem asked heads of departments — who knew about the prospective move — to guess for each employee whether they would resign. A further alternative might be to collect the data under the guise of a survey oriented to a different end, for example one on job satisfaction. (Although, this needs care too; make sure you do not jump out of the frying pan into the fire.)

In any case, a consultant is a new face in an organisation and, inevitably, questions will be asked about who they are and what they are doing there. If you are not going to tell the whole truth, you must ensure you have a good cover story beforehand!

METHODS OF DATA COLLECTION
There are essentially only three ways you can collect data:
- From observation;
- From dialogue with people;
- By examining documents or other material.

In consultancy, data is generated using investigative techniques, the most common of which are:
- the interview — a meeting with a single interviewee;
- the discussion group — a meeting with several people;
- the questionnaire — a way of creating documentary information.

Information on each of these, and the pros and cons of each, is given in Chapter 7.

There are also structured data collection tools available. The following analytical techniques are outlined in Chapter 7, together with their advantages and disadvantages and some practical hints for using them:

- Critical incident technique;
- Delphi technique;
- Stakeholder analysis;
- Power mapping;
- Repertory grid technique.

CHOOSING THE METHOD OF DATA COLLECTION

General considerations of cost, timescale, etc. will influence the choice of data collection method but the nature of the data you seek will also affect how you go about collecting it.

It might exist already in a form you can use. Hard data abounds in an organisation on matters to do with its business and so there is much to be gleaned by examining documents such as:

- management accounts;
- business results and forecasts;
- business plans;
- organisation charts;
- personnel statistics;
- advertising material.

There are sources outside the company too, for example:

- published market research;
- investment reports (for large companies or sectors);
- newspapers and periodicals;
- vast quantities of information available on the web.

Most projects, however, involve the consultant having to research data. In selecting the method you have to consider the structure, nature and detail of the data required.

Structure

Structure means the degree of variety in the answers that can be given to the question asked. A highly structured question is, 'How many people work in this factory?' The answer will be a number. An unstructured question is, 'How effective is the stock control system in this company?'

Unstructured questions invite further qualification; in the case above, it might be, 'Effective in what terms?' It invites comparison with a number of yardsticks; does the stock control system:

- keep working capital requirements low?

- minimise waiting time on key pieces of manufacturing machinery?
- enable customers' orders to be delivered within the required time?
- help production operations to be planned efficiently?

There will need to be some research into which of these, or any other yardsticks should be used to assess the stock control system.

The nature of a consulting project is to move from relatively unstructured to more structured data collection. At the start, the consultant will try to approach an issue with an open mind; this phase is largely exploratory. The data collected initially helps to focus later enquiries. The danger of starting with too much structure is that you are asking questions of the kind, 'When did you stop being late for work?' which contains at least four assumptions which could be wrong! Later on you can use structured data collection, which can be used to verify or validate conclusions that have been reached.

It is much easier to analyse structured data than unstructured. Examples of structured and unstructured questions are shown in Exhibit 4.3.

Exhibit 4.3 Structured and unstructured questions

Unstructured	What do you think of this Company's employment policies?
Structured	Show your degree of agreement with the following statements using the boxes below.

	Agree strongly				Disagree strongly
The Company pays well					
The Company provides secure employment					
The Company provides equal opportunities to all					

There will be a wide variety of responses to the unstructured question, which will then have to be classified. In the structured case, the classification has already been done; it assumes, for example, that pay, security of employment and equal opportunities are the appropriate measures of the attractiveness of the company's employment policies. If, however, the major concern of those surveyed is that they feel they work in unpleasant surroundings or they do not like the hours of work, these points will not emerge in the structured questionnaire.

In summary, then, structured data needs a lot of preparative work before collection to make sure it is defined correctly but is relatively easy to analyse afterwards. Unstructured data does not require as much preliminary work, but needs a lot of analysis subsequently.

Facts v *opinions*
Facts should be verifiable, but opinions can also provide valid data. Answers to questions that follow are matters of opinion:
- what do you think of the company's employment policies?
- is company publicity being adequately dealt with?
- could we do our training better?

Opinions are subjective and with all subjective data there is the danger of distortion — that respondents will slant their response to some particular end — perhaps to please the questioner. A question such as, 'What do you think of the company's employment policies?' could be distorted — for example, if respondents believed a critical answer would be held against them.

If distortion is likely, better-quality data can be obtained by face-to-face data collection than by questionnaire, and by trying to eliminate value-laden language as far as possible.

The advantage of face-to-face collection is twofold: firstly, most people lie less well face-to-face and, indeed, are more reluctant to do so. Secondly — and probably more significantly — people will speak their minds face-to-face with the consultant (who, hopefully, establishes some sort of rapport with them) far more openly than if they are required to document their comments in writing, which may be seen by anyone.

It is sensible to avoid value-laden language in all data collection. By 'value-laden' is meant the implication that some answers would be more welcome than others. Thus, 'Is your company a good employer?' is a value-laden question because of the use of the word 'good'. It is probably better in this context to ask a question such as: 'Which employment policies in this company do you consider wholly satisfactory and which would you like to see changed?'

People are, sometimes, uncomfortable being critical so if you are seeking data that requires them to disclose honest criticism, there are two further things you can do:

- Allow them to make positive as well as negative comments (as in the example above);
- Convey the sense that it is safe to make negative comments (and this is far easier to do face-to-face than via a questionnaire).

Level of detail

The detail required might also affect the data-collection method used and there is a major distinction between qualitative and quantitative data. Much of consultancy (particularly at strategic levels) is about qualitative data, such as:

- how do we compare with our major competitors?
- what are the most probable technological threats to us?
- which markets offer the best growth opportunities to us?

Detailed, statistically accurate information is not necessarily required but it is important to distinguish those cases which do. For example, some years ago, a logistics firm was planning to spend £1 million to upgrade their scheduling system. They had specified a response time of three seconds. After some research it was found that this response time was required for only a fraction of the users while the needs of most could be achieved by a modification to the software costing only a few thousand pounds. Arriving at this conclusion involved collecting fairly precise numerical data; and the benefits of this cheaper solution had to be balanced with the difficulties faced by those who needed the fastest response times.

Generally, the need for detailed numerical data is greater in technical consultancy such as:

- introducing a new software system;
- moving the office to another location;
- deciding on a new salary system.

Strategic consultancy is concerned with policy and requires the definition of policy options and how choices are to be made among them. This may be a matter of opinion but it is possible, nonetheless, to apply statistical analysis to opinions through such methods as the Delphi technique (see Chapter 7).

The touchstone for determining the level of detail required is: what is the data to be used for and how much accuracy is required to define and distinguish between options?

An example

To illustrate how a data-collection method might be chosen, we will continue with the example of Dick's stock control project at ABC Ltd. He has used the notion of 'individual performance analysis' (described in Chapter 7) to arrive at his hypothesis that the conflict between departments arises because their goals are in conflict. If he is right, he will need to clarify and possibly rearrange managerial responsibilities.

Exhibit 4.4 Dick's performance model for ABC Ltd

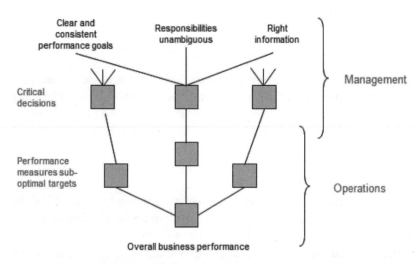

The performance model Dick uses for the next stage of data collection is shown in Exhibit 4.4. Business performance, overall, depends on the performance of its component parts; there will be measures for each of these, but performance targets have to be set sub-optimally (i.e. what is best for part of the business is not necessarily best for it overall; for example, responding to an urgent customer order may result in inefficient production, but be necessary to provide competitive customer service).

Dick's model shows that the quality of performance depends on how well key decisions are made, and these in turn depend on each manager having:
- unambiguous responsibilities;

- clear performance goals, which are consistent with those of other managers;
- the right information for the decisions he or she needs to take.

Dick's hypothesis implies that these criteria are not met and he needs to define and collect the data necessary to verify it.

Suppose, then, that Dick wants to check whether managers' responsibilities are ambiguous; he needs first to define which responsibilities are relevant to the stock control system. This is highly unstructured data and his initial data collection will attempt to give it more structure. One of the features of ambiguity is that it not only arises out of fact, but also because individuals' perceptions are unclear or mistaken. Dick will, therefore, need to use a data-collection method which gathers opinion and, given that the number of respondents would be small, he should use interviewing.

FORMING CONCLUSIONS

Consultancy is not science. The human and organisational systems it deals with make it difficult to gather and analyse data with the same comprehensiveness as would be required for a specific experiment. Data will be partial and judgement is called for.

Nonetheless, it is important that the conclusions you reach are supported by data. Some of the skill of a consultant involves making tacit knowledge explicit. Communicating back to a client what you have learned from them may enable them to come to a new understanding of their circumstances.

The three comments that follow, I believe, are of great significance in problem solving, data collection and analysis, which merit the attention of all consultants.

DATA COLLECTION IS AN INTERVENTION INTO AN ORGANISATION: TREAT IT AS SUCH

Since the Hawthorne experiments in the 1920s, it has been known that an observer will have an effect on people working. Consultancy involves interacting with an organisation, and collecting data is part of that interaction. The knowledge that a consultant is involved can make people curious or feel threatened, so imagine the repercussions within an organisation resulting from the following data-collection activities of a consultant:

- They ask publicly for information on staff numbers;
- They ask at an interview, 'Do you think you are paid enough?'
- They ask for comments on the consequences of shutting down plant X;
- They ask what is needed to double production.

Consultants are agents of change and any request for data, however innocent, may imply that there is to be change in the matters to which the data relates. So, in collecting data, remember there are no limits to the conclusions to which imaginative and paranoiac minds can jump.

Data collection is also the point at which the consultant is going to become more widely known in the organisation. How well it is done will influence the organisation's view of the consultant.

In a project involving a team of consultants, one of them circulated a questionnaire amongst client staff, which was poorly designed and very difficult to understand. The only replies the consultant got were protests about the questionnaire; none was returned completed, and the episode severely dented the consultant's credibility with the client.

MAINTAIN A HEALTHY SCEPTICISM

One of the reasons consultants are employed is because of their objectivity. One of the ways in which this is most useful is in challenging conventional wisdom, which straitjackets thinking and stifles innovation. Comments such as, 'We tried that five years ago and it didn't work,' although true, carry the unspoken corollary — 'and it won't work now.' The consultant must ask 'Why?'

Conventional wisdom — 'well-known facts' and conventional thinking — needs to be verified. Consultants must satisfy themselves that the data they are working with is sufficiently reliable and not be surprised or afraid of radical conclusions.

USE YOUR STOMACH AS WELL AS YOUR BRAIN

Not a suggestion to increase the number of business lunches attended, but encouragement to make use of gut feelings.

This means trusting your instincts — those impressions or conclusions which cannot be explained wholly rationally. The brain is a powerful organ, which no one fully understands and is immensely capable. In the course of work you absorb many impressions, many of them unconsciously. Similarly, there are unconscious mental processes, the output of which is gut feelings.

On those occasions when I have let reason overrule gut feeling, I have almost always been mistaken. So, notwithstanding the apparent reliance of consultancy on data and logic, trust your instincts. You can always rationalise your conclusions afterwards!

CHAPTER 5

INTERVENTION

We trained hard, but it seemed every time we were beginning to form a team we would be reorganised . . . we tend to meet every situation by reorganising, and a wonderful method it can be for creating the illusion of progress while producing confusion, inefficiency and demoralisation.

Attributed to Petronius Arbiter

The client was a manufacturing company in the Midlands; the project was to improve business performance, which had been falling drastically. On the first day of their assignment the two consultants drove up to the head office and parked their car in the spot directly outside the front door, marked 'Reserved for the Chairman'. They marched in to announce their arrival. 'Tell the managing director,' said one to the receptionist, 'that the consultants have arrived!'

I have always liked this story, which a former colleague swears to be the truth. It portrays the consultant as Superman, and it is delightful to be regarded as such. Sadly, however, in reality a consultant is more like Donald Duck; sailing forward serenely on the surface but paddling furiously under the water.

Much of the paddling is to do with creating change. Change is at the core of consulting projects and the management consultant has a key role in helping it happen. Organisations of people are amongst the most complex entities on this planet and there has been — and, undoubtedly, will continue to be — a considerable volume of research into their behaviour. This research has thrown up a host of theories and models, all of which give insights into the behaviour of organisations in different circumstances. To date, however, there is no universally applicable theory that the consultant can use to determine what has to be done to create particular changes. The best approach, in my experience, is to select those theories and models that you find personally helpful.

I do not believe that you need a tremendous body of theoretical knowledge to create change. Change is normal and we encounter it throughout every aspect of our lives. Everybody has their own theories, based on experience, of how and why organisations and people change, and will apply them to consultancy projects. Furthermore, a consultant is rarely concerned with change *per se*, but changing *something* as a means to an end.

This is how *intervention* is connected with the *diagnosis* phase of the consultancy delivery process. By the end of the diagnostic phase, you should have reached some conclusions. These will, perhaps, be technically excellent and aesthetically pleasing to the specialist but will almost certainly need modification to work in the client environment.

RECOMMENDATIONS ARE CONCLUSIONS ADJUSTED FOR THE PROCESS OF CHANGE

So recommendations are the result of adjusting conclusions. The question is on what basis they should be adjusted? An understanding of the process of change helps the consultant to recognise what is feasible and what needs adaptation.

If you want to achieve something different, you have to do something different. Interestingly, the manifestations of change may, within the major scheme of things be small, for example entailing changes for individuals to:

- their place of work;
- the teams they work with;
- the tasks they carry out.

For those involved, however, these apparently superficial changes could be profound: a change of status, a loss of authority, the need to learn new skills. The human dimension is all important.

THE PROBLEM WITH CHANGE IS GETTING PEOPLE TO ACCEPT IT

Perhaps people can be ordered to comply with a change but the result will always be less satisfactory than if their commitment had been won.

Resistance impedes commitment and it would be tempting to see winning commitment as simply overcoming resistance. This is an inadequate view. It is better to mobilise the energies of those involved so that they carry through the change successfully. That is commitment. Where energies are directed to opposing the change, that is resistance.

One writer has suggested that resistance should be honoured. This view emphasises that there is usually (in the mind of the other person) a sound foundation for that resistance. Recognising, understanding and accommodating resistance may lead to better ideas, improved methods of implementation and greater acceptance of change.

Many people enter consultancy from a technical background that emphasises finding solutions that are 'right'. The people dimension can easily be overlooked. Much of the remainder of this chapter is therefore about people and change.

CHANGE IS MORE DIFFICULT THE DEEPER IT GOES

Exhibit 5.1 suggests an empirical hierarchy of change. (I am indebted to Alan Elliott who conducted research into the validity of this model at the City University Business School. As a result of this he suggested the interpolation of 'strategies' into the hierarchy.)

Exhibit 5.1 A hierarchy of change

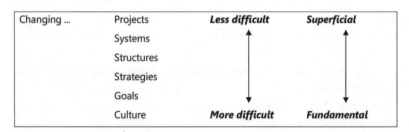

Projects for the purposes of this definition are accomplished within the existing systems, structures and procedures of the organisation. Examples may be the test marketing of a new product, the repainting of a factory, or the installation of new equipment. Projects may be part of a more fundamental change — for instance new computer equipment will probably entail changes in systems and, possibly, some changes in organisation structure.

Systems are the processes regulating activities within the organisation. As well as the management information system for reporting and control, there will be many other systems manifest as procedures, for example, for regulating when people arrive at and leave their work, for determining the allocation and use of resources, the flow of work and so on.

By *structures* I mean the organisation of tasks in relation to one another within the enterprise. One way of looking at an enterprise is to see it as having to accomplish a host of tasks relating to internal and external transactions. These tasks are collected into convenient groups called jobs. Structure is all about these task groupings and how the jobs relate to one another.

Changing *strategies* involves redirecting the business of the organisation, which occurs when entering a new market or business. Strategies are the routes by which the goals of the organisation are achieved.

Goals are about the purpose of the organisation — goals in this context do not mean transient targets or budgets (e.g. £1m profit this year). What is meant are the mission(s) of the organisation, for example:

- 'To provide health care to all residents in the UK';
- 'To sell road transport facilities';
- 'To make a living repairing TV sets'.

A redefinition of goals can have dramatic repercussions for a business. Thus, a bank might change its mission from 'to provide credit, banking and money transmission facilities' to 'to provide financial services to the general public', which might involve entering new lines of business such as insurance and pensions and withdrawing from corporate finance.

All this is grist to the mill of the corporate strategist. More fundamental though, is organisation *culture* — the underlying values and norms of the organisation. This will be manifest in an enormous variety of aspects: what dress is *de rigueur*, the manner of addressing one another and all the traditions and habits of the organisation. It is the corporate personality.

Only in a few situations will it be necessary for a consultant to intervene at the corporate culture level. Indeed, many of the superficial interventions will, themselves, effect a change, albeit slight, in corporate culture. Thus, a change in organisation structure or in the systems in use will have an effect on the organisation's culture in the same way that experience can affect the personality of an individual.

Modifications of a corporate culture ought to be approached with some moral caution. The consultant has to be able to justify the changes to be made and this cannot simply be the superimposition of their own value system on that of the client. There must be sound business reasons for cultural change. Occasions when a change in culture might be required are the following:

1. The retirement of an autocratic and long-standing chief executive (possibly the founder of the company) who has no obvious successor. In this case, the organisation would need to change from being centred on a particular individual to, perhaps, one where the organisation structure is more significant. (Roger Harrison has developed an organisation typology in which this change is typified as from 'power-centred' to 'role-centred' — see Harrison, 1972.)

2. A decline in traditional markets requiring a firm to become innovative and entrepreneurial. In a mature market, the usual practice would be to maintain the status quo — standard production processes, routine selling and distribution patterns and so on. Innovation and entrepreneurialism run counter to the status quo. (Large organisations may form separate business divisions or subsidiaries to accommodate those different styles to avoid conflict between the two cultures.)

ORGANISATIONAL READINESS FOR CHANGE

The ease with which change can be accomplished also depends on how ready the organisation is for it. Research shows that change in organisations occurs discontinuously — periods of upheaval are separated by interludes of relative stability. Change often coincides with the arrival of a new leader or in response to circumstances which threaten the organisation.

Gleicher, quoted in Beckhard and Harris (1977), has developed a formula that gives an insight to this shown in Exhibit 5.2.

The formula shows that if change is to take place, the elements A, B and D must be present. Moreover, they should together weigh more than the 'cost' of undertaking the change —not just financial but also for example the upheaval, the time, the discomfort, the frustration of personal ambitions. Organisational readiness for change will be insufficient if A, B or D are too small.

Exhibit 5.2 Gleicher's formula

$$C = (ABD) > X$$

Where

C=change

A=level of dissatisfaction with the status quo

B=a clear desired state

D=practical clear steps towards the desired state

X=cost of the change

Deficiencies in each of these can be characterised as follows:

A: 'We're happy with the way things are.'

B: 'Although we're not very happy with the way things are, we've no clear idea about how they could be better.'

D: 'We know how we'd like things to be but we don't know how to start.'

Analysing readiness can help the consultant decide where effort might most profitably be invested to achieve the required change, for example, by:

- confronting the client with the facts to show how unsatisfactory the situation is (sometimes, the act of collecting this data can, by itself, increase the level of dissatisfaction) (A);
- helping the client to define the 'ideal state' of affairs or investigate the potential for improvement (e.g. by benchmarking) (B);
- using experience from elsewhere to show how the improved state can be achieved (D).

And do not overlook X, the 'cost' of change; even though the elements A, B and D may be significant, they may be less than the perceived cost. As an alternative to increasing A, B or D it may be possible to reduce X. Remember, it is the *perceived* cost — so reducing X can be achieved by changing people's perceptions of the cost, as well as the cost itself. For example, part of the perceived cost could arise from fear of the unknown. Good communications and explanations from the consultant can reduce this fear and, hence, the perceived cost.

THE PROCESS OF CHANGE

Consultants need an understanding of the change process as it evolves in a consultancy project. It can be unbundled into four stages, and we consider the key elements that apply to each stage. The stages are as follows.

1. *Planning*, in which the change is dealt with only in concept.
2. *Initiation*, in which the change is started.
3. *Implementation*, in which the change is carried out.
4. *Completion*, in which the change is 'cemented' into the organisation.

These are not watertight compartments; often the understanding of the nature of the change may develop during implementation. Planning has to be flexible to accommodate this.

In each stage of change, the consultant needs to be able to answer the questions:

- What is going on;
- What ought I to be doing about it?

Exhibit 5.3 illustrates the answers to these questions for each stage.

Exhibit 5.3 Stages in change

	What is going on?	*The critical items to manage to deal with this*
Planning	Vision – defining where we are heading	Mobilise influential opinion
Initiation	Reaction: • welcome • questioning • uncertainty • resistance	Energy raising Expectations Communication Processes
Implementation	Response: • acceptance • fall in performance • alienation	Participation Confidence building
Completion	Making change permanent: • internalisation • revisionism	Reward Review

PLANNING

The starting point of a change is a *vision* held by the client of how things will be after the change has been accomplished. Sometimes, it may be the task of the consultant to help the client to articulate this vision.

It is worth noting that the vision may alter or develop as the change proceeds. Initially, it may be only broadly understood; with time its detailed nature will become more apparent. Next, there has to be a *climate of opinion* amongst the client's colleagues, superiors and necessary opinion-formers that supports the vision. Obviously, the more powerful an executive, the less reliant they are on others' support; usually, however, the executive needs to drum up support as part of the planning stage. The consultant can help in forming an assessment of the degree of support; the technique of force field analysis, described in Chapter 7, is helpful in doing this.

INITIATION

Whenever a change is announced there will be a *reaction* amongst those affected. Some may *welcome* it; others may *resist*. All will *question* what it means and, for many, it will occasion disturbing *uncertainty*. That there will be a reaction is inevitable; the task of the consultant is to try to get a reaction most conducive to the change being introduced.

People will base their judgement of a change in terms of its personal impact. If they feel they are going to be adversely affected, then they will resist; if they think they will be better off, they will support it. This will depend on their perceptions of the change — not necessarily objective reality!

Before a change can take place in a group, they have to be ready. Gleicher's formula, described earlier in this chapter, is useful in analysing this. To recap, four conditions have to be satisfied.

1. There is dissatisfaction with the status quo.
2. There is a vision of how things might be after the change has been implemented.
3. There is some idea of, at least, the first few steps in getting the change started.
4. The benefits of the change need to outweigh the costs.

These criteria have to be satisfied for all those who are involved in the change. In particular, there has to be an incentive to change; if everybody is happy, there is no reason to change. Consultants can use data feedback to show the disadvantages of maintaining the status quo. Remember, however, that the announcement of an impending change may, itself, create a climate in which change is more likely to be accepted.

> *For example, one organisation was often undergoing change. The technique the general manager used was to let it be known, informally, through his immediate subordinates that a reorganisation was impending. He then waited for an interval, by which time everybody was so tired of the ambiguity that they welcomed any change that resolved the situation.*

> *This method is described to show the effects of uncertainty rather than as a prescribed method. Indeed, the effect was devastating on the morale of this organisation and it has since gone out of business.*

Having created an awareness of the need for change, the consultant must help the client to 'sell' the vision of how things might be after the change, to those who are likely to be affected by it.

These activities serve to *raise energy levels* of all concerned and direct them towards the change. This is also known as 'unfreezing', and it is aimed at making people more receptive to the idea of change. Unfreezing involves:
- clear signal(s) that things are going to be different;
- encouraging behaviours that are different.

Symbolic behaviours by the leaders in an organisation can raise the awareness of change.

> *For example, a new chief executive who wanted to transform the organisation quite deliberately always ran, rather than walked, up the stairs whenever visiting any of the outlying offices. This demonstration of energy was symbolic of the new energy he wanted released in the business.*

It is easy to underestimate the importance of symbolic behaviours in change unless you recognise the impact of past experience. All organisations have stories (myths, legends), 'case law' and so on, into which a newcomer will informally be indoctrinated. These have a powerful effect in that they illustrate what are meant to be the right ways of behaving or taking decisions. When you introduce change, you have to rapidly change the appropriate aspects of organisational folklore by promulgating examples that underscore the new behaviours or ways of taking decisions.

Again, change programmes are sometimes launched by seminars, conferences or other kick-off meetings. As well as performing their role in facilitating communication, these can act as rites of passage, which encourage people to behave differently after attending them. (An example of a 'rite of passage' in everyday life is a wedding ceremony. Although it lasts a very short time, it has a profound impact on the way in which a couple think about themselves and on how society regards them.)

Expectations are a key component in change; what people expect of the change and how it might affect them is going to condition their response. Managing expectations is vital. One result of uncertainty is that if people do not know what to expect, they will draw their own conclusions — which may be totally wrong. So good communication is essential.

Good communication at times of change may require extra effort; routine arrangements may be inadequate to deal with the communication requirements of a major change. Organisations deal with this by having special briefing sessions, newsletters, meetings, etc. Often these communication channels are one-way (such as a newsletter) but communication must be two-way; not only should managers tell their people about the change, but should also listen carefully to their response. The consultant must ensure that the right communication channels are in place, so that people know what the change is, why it is necessary and how it will affect them.

In the same way that change may require new methods of communication, it may also require new *processes* of problem solving and decision making. Different problems require different approaches; one method alone is insufficient for all managerial problems and decisions. The consultant should make the client aware of this and introduce new (often more participative) methods of problem solving and decision making as required.

IMPLEMENTATION
Implementation is the core of change and can take a considerable time — months, if not years.

Some people will *accept* the change quite happily. They represent an asset for the consultant, as they can help to persuade those who are as yet unconvinced. It is easy to become preoccupied only with those who are being resistant, but those who have accepted the change can help to build the confidence of those who have not.

Sometimes, the confidence of managers can be eroded when *performance falls* after the introduction of a change. The fact is that change usually involves people doing things differently, and doing things differently requires people to learn to do them. While they are learning, people cannot be expected to attain optimal performance immediately. Change, therefore, often entails a decline in performance in the short term. A client who is unprepared for this may be tempted to abandon the change.

Performance will suffer particularly if change takes people into completely unfamiliar areas. *Alienation* results when people:

- have no idea of what the change means, what it requires of them or where they now fit in;
- feel powerless: they have no influence over the change or how it affects them.

The result of alienation is, at the least, resistance to the change. In extreme cases, it can create considerable stress and lead to people psychologically resigning from the organisation — losing all interest in their work and caring little about their performance.

The risks of alienation can be reduced by employees' *greater participation* in:

- information: knowing what is going on and what is planned for the future;
- decisions concerning the implementation of the change.

The importance of two-way communication has already been mentioned; this leads on to the influence that the rank and file have over decisions: how much attention is going to be paid to the information that is fed back.

If people feel that whatever they say they are powerless to influence the change, they will become alienated; change will be something that is 'done' to them. If they can influence it, they will become more committed. This empowerment is a major factor in implementing change. (Conversely, negative power – the power to say 'no' – is widely distributed. So if people cannot influence change, they will resort to the use of negative power, using it to stop change).

In practice, this means delegating decision making. The decisions over which people most want influence are those which affect them personally. Delegating these decisions has the advantage, too, that they are being taken by experts — those who are actually doing the job. So a consultant should encourage managers to delegate decisions, within the necessary constraints, as far as possible.

Confidence building is another important element during implementation. Where a change is spread across different areas, the confidence of those involved may not be all the same. In such cases, you can only work within the level of commitment of whichever group you are dealing with. Some groups may be able to progress well; others more slowly. Attempting to change a group more quickly than it can cope with will be frustrating for all concerned. Confidence building can be achieved often by allowing those who are less confident to observe the success of those who are more advanced in implementing the change.

'War stories' of success elsewhere can help in building confidence in a group. Likewise, early success can also help in building the confidence of a group.

One further feature of change is saying goodbye to the past. Change is like a journey; to go elsewhere, you have to leave where you are now. Sometimes it can be very hard to leave the old ways behind, particularly if the change implies that past activities were of little value. A consultant can sometimes help by getting clients to honour the past by some form of exhibition, for example, or a souvenir edition of the company newspaper.

As a consultant, it is often difficult to understand resistance to change; from our position, it may seem rational, for the benefit of the majority and so on. But to implement change, you have to start from where people are at — not assume that they are with you.

A helpful analogy is that of giving someone a lift in your car: if you are to arrive at your destination together, you first have to rendezvous at the beginning of your journey. If you are the one with the car, you are the one responsible for getting together with your passenger to start off with. Likewise, consultants must fully appreciate the starting points of those undertaking change.

COMPLETION

The desired state after implementation of a change is that people have taken it into their usual way of working — it is no longer seen as a change, but as the norm. This process is called *internalisation*. But there may be those who want to go back to the old ways — the *revisionists*. They are like those who, when everybody else is undertaking a journey, do not want to leave home. If they cannot be persuaded to leave home, they must ultimately be left behind. If a person finds it very difficult to accept a change, sometimes the only way forward is to put them in a position where they do not need to accept it. Sometimes, it may mean a job transfer; sometimes it may mean the individual looks for a more congenial job elsewhere. It is often painful for managers to deal with this type of problem, so the consultant should help them confront the issues and deal with them.

People drive to where they see their *rewards* lying. In this context, reward does not mean only what they are paid — it is how they obtain career advancement, the approbation of their superiors, recognition from their colleagues and so on. The basis on which people are rewarded needs to underwrite the change. A change will flounder if the basis on which people are rewarded is not also changed to fit the new circumstances.

As well as money, a key motivator of people at work is: 'How do I please my boss?' If the boss is not committed to the new order of things, then it will be difficult for their subordinates to make the change. Commitment to a change has, therefore, to percolate through all the layers of an organisation if it is to be successful.

Finally, there is the process of *review* — what can the client learn from the way in which this change was carried out? The learning from one change may help the organisation to be better equipped to carry out the next. The consultant can see that a review is carried out as part of the closing stages of a change programme.

In recent years, the capacity for organisational agility – the ability of an organisation to instigate and make change – has formally been recognised as a desirable feature of organisations.

PROBLEMS OF TRANSITION

Before moving on to techniques for assisting change, it is worth mentioning one final point about the process of change. It is this: sometimes the difficulties of making a change do not lie in getting a client's agreement to the promised land that lies at the end of the change; rather, the difficulties lie in plotting out the route which will take him or her from here to there and getting agreement to it. Resistance to change goals may therefore arise because the client cannot see how they might be achieved. In these circumstances, there will need to be a number of modest transitions en route to achieving the desired changes in the longer term.

The problems of transition (as compared with those of goals) are the problems of 'how?' rather than 'why?' and this point has been made above in the discussion of Gleicher's equation.

Confronting the client with transition problems and working with him or her to address them can help the changes required take root. A small-scale instance is the following.

A client was setting up a new business and the new management team came together for a two-day meeting to discuss procedures.

There was rapid agreement about the objectives of the new operation, and the session seemed complete after the first half-day. The consultant then suggested the group should draw up action plans (who was going to do what, and when) to achieve the objectives they had set out.

What then emerged was that the general language of objectives masked a considerable divergence of views about details and confusion about how the group should work together.

By working on the problems of transition for the rest of the meeting, the group was not only able to develop plans (which were subsequently successfully implemented) but also to build up its strength as a team.

TECHNIQUES FOR ASSISTING CHANGE

This section covers a number of techniques that can be used on consultancy projects but beware the trap of making change seem more complicated than it really is. If the change required is only superficial, and all that is required is for those subject to it to agree to comply with management instructions, then special techniques are unlikely to be needed. In more demanding circumstances, however, I have found all of the following techniques useful at some time or another.

THE USE OF A LAUNCH WORKSHOP
A launch workshop (or kick-off conference), perhaps presented as a training course, can also be used to legitimise new behaviour, and, as such, is similar to an anthropological rite of passage. (See above under Initiation.)
    A training course can be used in a change programme to encourage a change of attitudes and behaviour. To be effective, the course should:

- be away from the workplace (and preferably residential);
- last at least a whole day and preferably longer;
- be intensive (and the intensity can apply to the informal sessions around the bar as well as in the classroom).

These arrangements are distinctively different from what goes on at work. They must be a punctuation mark in the working lives of participants and thus the event must have impact. The overall effect should be to unfreeze the attitudes of participants, to make them receptive to new ideas and willing and able to undertake the changes required. The content of the training given on the course should complement these processes.

> *By way of an example, a major company wanted to improve managerial performance significantly. The programme adopted had two components:*
> - *A performance improvement element with an incentive; if a workgroup could show an improvement in performance of ten per cent, staff within the group would get a ten per cent pay rise;*
> - *A training element, aimed at helping managers in the programme to carry out the process involved as well as performing the new tasks required of them.*
>
> *A very large number of managers went through the training programme, which developed a reputation conducive to its success:*
> - *Participants were expected to behave differently on their return;*
> - *They enthused about the training they had received;*
> - *People competed to attend the training programme.*
>
> *Those who had attended were able to display a certificate that showed they had been through the training programme.*

The reason for giving the example is that it illustrates how a training programme can be successfully used as a rite of passage and, in the example, it achieved its objective: the improvements in managerial performance were achieved.

DECIDING WHERE TO START

If you are introducing change into an organisation, it may be something that is all or nothing (e.g. the amalgamation of two divisions) but very frequently there may be scope for more gradual introduction. In these circumstances you need to decide where to start.

One way of doing this is to select a part of the client organisation that is going to be easiest to change, introduce the change there and use this to demonstrate its effectiveness to other departments who might be less receptive.

You thus start with a 'pilot trial' prior to general implementation. There are three advantages to this approach.

1. It reduces change to more manageable proportions — for example, there will be fewer people involved and therefore less time involved in briefing, training, meetings and so on.
2. It allows you to 'debug' the new system prior to its general implementation. Almost inevitably there will be unanticipated difficulties in any new way of working, necessitating changes in design and so on.
3. It provides demonstrable proof of the viability and usefulness of the change. Furthermore, there will be a caucus of client staff involved who can speak with authority on what is entailed and the pros and cons.

The difficulty lies in selecting the starting point. Some parts of the organisation may be ruled out for administrative or other reasons, such as a peak of workload, so the choice may be limited anyhow. The most sympathetic part of the organisation may not be the best place to start, either, if success there does not carry much weight elsewhere. Only once, however, have I come across an organisation who wanted the consultants to start a project off in a difficult area; their reason was, 'If we wanted to work in an easy area, we'd do it ourselves'.

A related question is, should you start change at the top of the organisation and work down, or at the bottom and work up?

In almost all circumstances, it is best to start at the top. Senior management has greater power to get things done — or to stop them happening. The circumstances in which you might start at the bottom of the organisation are:

- if the change affects only this level;
- if it is essential that people at this level co-operate for the project to work, i.e. the balance of power is shifted because they have considerable negative power — the power to stop things happening.

CHOICE OF CLIENT STAFF TO WORK WITH

It is rare for a change project not to involve client staff in some role or other in the project team. For example, if engaged on an IT project, they may be seconded from the client's own IT department. There may be no choice of who works with you — it may be simply by virtue of the job incumbent. On other occasions, it may be possible to set up project teams over whose membership you have some choice. Referring back to the start of this chapter, it is worth choosing a team that has the right type and amount of power and influence.

> *A good example of this was a project within a local education authority. It involved devising a work pack for use by teachers in schools within the county to encourage children to save energy. Experience had shown that the work pack would be most likely to be accepted if it was devised by a team of teachers who worked in the authority. In the past, teachers in the county had not been receptive to work packs designed by non-teachers, and were even inhibited about using those designed by teachers from another authority. So the project team was comprised mainly of teachers drawn from the county and the work pack was well received.*

Such an approach could have emerged by using a combination of force field analysis (FFA) and stakeholder analysis described in Chapter 7. FFA would have shown that a key factor was to get the support of class teachers and stakeholder analysis would have shown that they were most strongly influenced by the recommendations of their colleagues.

CHANGING ATTITUDES

Organisations and people often behave like a large rubber ball in respect of change; they change under pressure but when the pressure disappears, they revert to their old habits. With many of the changes introduced by consultants the option of changing back will not exist: for example, the old computer system has been replaced, so the new system must be used. With more fundamental changes (as defined in Exhibit 5.1), the opportunity of changing back is more likely to exist, and so a real change of attitudes is required.

There has been much research into the process of attitude change and it would be tempting, but not particularly helpful, to quote some of the theories here. But as this book is about practice, there seem to me to be three general points to be made.

1. We are not too concerned about what goes on inside a person's head. The consultant has to be concerned about what people do — the decisions they make or actions they take.
2. People are not inherently opposed to change *per se*. Resistance to change occurs more often as a failure in communication, its insensitive introduction or that the change is simply wrong. (I leave aside here those changes that adversely affect the individual. Few will welcome a change against their self-interest, for example, being put out of a job.)
3. Attitudes can frequently be changed by changing the way people look at things, and this in turn can be achieved by providing them with activities and experience that change their perspective.

Taking the last point, for example, resistance to change often comes from fear of the unknown. In this case, special effort needs to be put into explaining the change, the reasons for it and what the consequences are likely to be. Even then, there will still be those who feel threatened and with whom the consultant must use confidence-building measures. A simple confidence-building measure is allowing those subject to a change to discuss it beforehand with others who have made it already, thereby allaying their fears. For instance, the introduction of a new piece of equipment may be facilitated by seeing it operating in another location where it has already been successfully introduced. It is more difficult to demonstrate new managerial systems unless they have been successfully implemented elsewhere already — hence the value of a pilot trial to demonstrate what really happens.

Further confidence-building measures need to be taken at the implementation of a change. However careful the preparation, however good the communications and training prior to its introduction, at its early introduction a change needs a high level of support — what some consultants call 'nursing'. This means being on hand to answer queries, overcome difficulties and put right those things which inevitably go wrong.

What can you do when, despite your confidence-building efforts, participants lack the confidence to go on? First, of course, you need to reassure yourself that their lack of confidence is not well founded: is there some factor that you may have overlooked that gives substance to their doubts? You could also work with them on a cause and effect diagram, to assess all the possible causes of failure and see that they have been addressed.

These, of course, address rational concerns, but fear can be irrational. Ultimately you may have to give them a push — like an able swimmer lacking the confidence to go out their depth. Once they have made the change successfully, they should have the confidence to continue.

USE OF FEEDBACK

Finally, there is the use of feedback to encourage change. Numerous tests have shown that people seem to perform better if they know how well they are doing. Combined with target setting, this can be a powerful motivator.

In the context of change, feedback between different levels and groups can be effective, as well as amongst individuals. Examples illustrating this are as follows.

> *A colliery displayed the cumulative weight of coal mined, year to date, on a big sign at its entrance. One year, it became clear that the workforce might achieve a million tons for the first time. By unprecedented effort and teamwork they achieved this — but it would not have happened without feedback on a regular basis on how they were doing.*

> *A group of managers who had similar concerns about certain aspects of their performance had never discussed them. The consultant discovered this, and was able to raise the subject at one of their group meetings. Therefore the discussion of a subject which previously they had felt uncomfortable raising was legitimised.*

Management often sees employee communication only as a downward process. But it should also be upward. The consultant can encourage the feedback of views from junior levels to senior levels and this can frequently be instrumental in changing top management attitudes. For example, a management team which considered it did a good job of keeping employees informed would need to reconsider its views if they found out that staff felt poorly informed.

One of the key jobs therefore for a consultant concerned with change is to keep client staff informed about how things are going. Beyond this, remember that recognition is a most powerful motivator; in the UK we have the whole honours system to prove it! So make sure that top management recognise and congratulate those involved in a change for their achievement.

WORDS OF CONSOLATION

Organisations are the most complex systems with which a consultant has to deal. No surprise, then, that no one has devised a comprehensive way of ensuring that change is guaranteed. All you can do is improve the odds for change being successful and this chapter should provide a basis for doing so. Even so, if it is any comfort, like all consultants, you will have your failures.

There is a danger also that 'change' becomes overplayed and is made to appear overly hard. But change, not stasis, is a natural state of affairs. Everybody, from the moment they are born, undergoes continuous change and as a species we are fairly well adapted to it. So, notwithstanding all the advice in this chapter, the best way of achieving a change may simply be to ask people to get on with it.

A final exhortation, however. Everybody has their own theory of how individuals or groups or organisations respond to change. It will be based largely on past experience and may include precepts and rules that are empirically deduced. It is well worthwhile bringing your own particular theory out from the back of your mind to examine it carefully. Do the beliefs and assumptions you have made about change make sense in the context of the projects you are now handling?

CHAPTER 6

CLOSURE

The opera isn't over until the fat lady sings.

Anon

A speaker at a consultancy conference ran through the sequence of phases in a consultancy project and asked participants to raise their hands for the phases that enthused them. There was a large show of hands for the early phases, but hardly any were raised for the phases relating to closure.

Closure receives scant attention from consultants. At the completion of a project there should be a standard procedure to ensure that maximum value for the consultancy has been obtained from the work. A project might have value in that it provides operating credibility in a particular business sector, or provides useful experience in the development or application of particular techniques. The larger the practice, the more important it is that there is a formal system for ensuring that project experience is recorded so that it can be used with effect throughout the practice.

COMPLETING A PROJECT

Before completing a project, you need to make sure that the client is also ready for your withdrawal. This you do with the process of transfer.

Transfer means leaving the client with the ongoing capability to maintain the changes and systems you have introduced as a result of your work. Transfer therefore includes:

- training client staff;
- setting standards and procedures;
- establishing systems and records;
- providing manuals.

Remember these are a major chunk of your legacy to your client on this project and therefore should be provided to a high standard.

The client should be of the view that the project is complete – that you have delivered adequately against the promises that were made in the terms of reference at the start of the project, or as subsequently revised.

In the same way that it is useful to have a 'rite of passage' to kick off a project, a similar process might be used at the end to mark its successful completion – perhaps a party or some other celebration in keeping with the client's corporate culture.

DERIVING ONGOING COMMERCIAL VALUE

How you treat this final stage depends on how you see the relationship between you and your client. Ideally, you are one of your client's specialist advisers to whom they will turn whenever there is a problem you can help with. But whilst working with this client you have the chance to find other areas where your practice can help develop the client's business. Hopefully, you can turn these opportunities into further sales.

A consultancy project during its course offers commercial opportunities for further work with a client, for example by greater involvement in the current project through:

- taking on work which would otherwise be carried out less effectively by the client's staff;
- becoming involved in later stages of the project, e.g. its implementation or replication at other sites or divisions.

Members of the consulting team may also be able to see opportunities for additional work outside the present project with the client, either for themselves or for other members of the firm.

There are other areas of commercial value you might explore. Clients will have their own network of contacts locally and in the industry. If you have done a good job, they will probably spread the word; they may be prepared to introduce you to other organisations which could be interested in your services. Less directly, the project may provide a useful reference, both in terms of the work carried out and the experience of working in a particular business sector. (Indeed, you and your client may want to issue a press release to mark the successful completion of an interesting project). This can help in bidding for similar projects or work in the same industry.

The completion of the project need not mark the end of the consultant–client relationship. On a practical point, there may be the need for follow up servicing visits to ensure that new systems continue to work well, or to carry out further training of the client's staff. Servicing visits also provide a 'right of entry' to the client organisation, during which new opportunities might be revealed.

If you cannot extend, you disengage. This is not the end of the relationship and you and your client will now have a better knowledge of each other. Remember that past clients are the best sales prospects for the future and you should keep in touch. Even if there is no further work with that client, they should be subject to an account management process to maintain a suitable relationship with the practice. (Account management goes on whether or not there is consulting work being undertaken.)

There are all sorts of vehicles for keeping in contact with past or prospective clients, i.e. those organisations with which you are not currently working. Email offers a cheap method of contact, and this might be complemented by less frequent postal mailings. Face to face events might be social – e.g. lunches or other corporate entertainment or seminars; these are sometimes combined into breakfast meetings, which have become increasingly popular in recent years. Contact has to be managed sensitively; you do not want the client to feel you are too importunate. A good rule of thumb is that you should limit prospection meetings to about twice a year (unless the client indicates otherwise), but you can circulate documents more frequently.

You need to have a clear objective in promotional contact: the chances of your approaching a client on the day they have a need of your services is pretty remote; instead, you want to keep your own practice at 'front of mind' – i.e. that they think of you when they have a need for services such as those that you offer.

The pressure of present projects can crowd out this important work, however, and it is best to have a systematic approach to follow up. Do not neglect your former clients — they can be your best market.

DERIVING VALUE FOR THE PRACTICE

The ending of a consultancy project is as significant as its launch; quite apart from the commercial aspects of completion, the consultancy practice needs to make sure that other aspects of value are also drawn from the experience of conducting this project.

Remember that while some of the value of an assignment consists of the corporate experience gained by conducting it, it might also provide a reference for future work. It is important, therefore, even when no formal evaluation is conducted, to assess the value of an assignment and what the consultancy has learned.

You may also wish to conduct a formal evaluation of the project. This consists of comparing what actually happened with the original (or amended) terms of reference. You should keep the terms of reference to hand throughout a project and refer to them frequently to ensure that the work you are doing remains relevant. It is easy to go on interesting but time-consuming digressions. Ideally, all clients will be satisfied at the end of a project, but when they are not, it is frequently because you had different expectations at the outset rather than through any failure of operating. It is therefore essential to make sure that the terms of reference are clear throughout.

It is sensible also to conduct a commercial assessment: how profitable was this project? This can provide information useful for pricing and operating future projects.

Finally, the main question that needs to be answered at the end of any project is, 'What did we learn?' Consultants should have developed their expertise through its exercise during their assignment to this project; there will have been mistakes and lessons learned. There will also have been successes and these should be celebrated.

CHAPTER 7

ANALYTICAL TOOLS AND TECHNIQUES

Management consultants . . . are people who borrow your watch to tell you what time it is and then walk off with it.
Robert Townsend in *Up the Organisation*

There are of course a whole range of management and consultancy techniques, some of which have become well known. Indeed, the consulting practice Bain & Company has for many years published a list of the most popular management tools and trends.

This chapter, however, looks at more basic and enduring tools and techniques — ones that can be of use in a variety of disciplines and applications. It is by no means comprehensive, but includes techniques that I have repeatedly found helpful.

They are collected under four headings:
- Generic data collection techniques;
- Structured data collection techniques;
- Data analysis techniques;
- Some useful models.

GENERIC DATA COLLECTION TECHNIQUES

Although the subject of what data is needed has been covered under the diagnosis part of the process, data collection occurs at all stages of work with a client. Set out below are the advantages, disadvantages and operating hints for three generic methods: interview, discussion group and questionnaire.

THE INTERVIEW

The interview is a one-to-one meeting between the consultant and a member of the client's staff. (Incidentally, I rarely refer to them as interviews when discussing them with the client — I always call them meetings. Some people would object to being interviewed but meetings are a part of their routine work.)

Advantages
- It allows personal contact with client staff which may not otherwise be possible. This is particularly useful when interviewing the senior people in an organisation, which gives you the opportunity to make your mark with those who might be strongly influential in determining the success of the project.
- It can be used in an unstructured way. It enables you to follow the interviewee's train of thought, priorities and emotions, rather than forcing them into the predetermined structures required in most other forms of data collection.
- It enables the client's staff to feel they have contributed to the project (and thus they are more likely to accept the conclusions).
- It allows you to get a 'feel' for the organisation and people in it. If interviews are held in interviewees' offices, what is the experience like? Are they always being (and allowing themselves to be) interrupted? Have they got a clear or untidy desk? Are there any interesting charts or graphs on the wall? All this could be useful intelligence.
- Personal contact can be used to draw out more data than otherwise might be forthcoming in two ways: firstly, the interviewee may be more confident about making disclosures face-to-face. Secondly, they may have data handy which they can share with you.

Disadvantages
- It is time consuming.
- It is sometimes difficult to decide who should or should not be seen. (I usually define the criteria and let the client select. Almost always

this means having to see more people than you originally budgeted for.)
- Subsequent analysis is difficult as much of the data collected is unstructured.
- There is always the possibility of selective bias on the part of the interviewer.
- It can be difficult to integrate the interview notes of different interviewers.

Operating hints

Allow sufficient time for interviews. Those at the start will normally take longer because you are at the bottom of the learning curve. As you get to know more about the organisation you will need to ask fewer questions of clarification and also the focus of your questions will become sharper.

Ensure that you and the interviewee have a common idea of how much time is required for the interviews. It is frustrating to have only half an hour available for an hour's discussion, so if possible book the time in their diary in advance. (If possible, book a little longer than needed — it allows for interruption or overrun.)

Do not try to do too much. Interviewing is hard work — it requires 100 per cent attention all the time to hear and understand what is being said while at the same time directing the conversation. As a rule of thumb, I operate at 50 per cent capacity: assuming I work an eight-hour day, I would schedule four one-hour interviews — perhaps at 90 minute intervals. The extra half-hour can be used for extending the interviews, allowing for late arrivals and for writing up notes. I recognise that the six or seven hours thus allocated will not be totally taken up with interviews, so I usually take other work I can do to fill in the odd spaces.

Use some form of structure which will help you to develop the discussion in a logical way and, subsequently, to analyse the response. This is particularly important if more than one consultant is carrying out the interviews. Exhibit 7.1 shows an exploratory interview agenda that develops 'areas of enquiry', in this case a study of the finance function in a bank. It shows the type of question which might be used to start the discussion on the topic; the numbering system can also be applied to the responses (by noting the reference in the margin of your interview notes) so that they can be analysed more easily later. Also remember to introduce the interview — what it is about, what it is to be used for and how long it will take. At the end, thank the interviewee for their help and mention, if possible, what will happen next.

Exhibit 7.1 Areas of enquiry

1. Current organisation of function
1.1. Your job and the structure reporting to you.   1.2. The role of the group for which you are responsible.   1.3. Responsibilities of your job and specialist skills/knowledge required.   1.4. The responsibilities of those reporting to you and any specialist skills/knowledge required.
2. Operation of your function
2.1. *Imperatives and obligations* (Imperatives: are there any statutory (e.g. reporting) obligations the function has, and what are they? Internal obligations – e.g. timing for internal accounting purposes.)   2.2. *Interfaces* – information flows and/or decisions. Frequency (importance etc.). (Within finance function; with other parts of the bank; outside the bank.)   2.3. *Scope* (discretionary aspect). (Has your group a formal remit, and if so, what is it and how was it set? How would this remit be changed? In particular, how do you know if some things you do are no longer required, or if additional tasks are required?)   2.4. *Performance* (How can you tell if your function is doing a good job/things are going wrong? Priorities/vulnerability; what are the most important task/tasks which have serious repercussions if they go wrong?)
3. Future developments

3.1. What do you see to be the major influences which may change the nature of your function? (Business change/organisational; statutory/regulatory change; information technology; other.)
 3.2. What are the results of these influences likely to be in terms of the tasks and responsibilities of your group; the volume of work; the skills required; other?
 3.3. What influences are there likely to be on other parts of the finance function and what are the consequences likely to be?
 3.4. Are there other changes which would be desirable to enable your group or the finance function as a whole to increase its performance?
 3.5. In particular, comment on:
 • the interface between central and local finance function with subsidiaries/overseas offices;
 • how the function should be organised to deal with:
   • different specialisations;
   • different subsidiaries/overseas offices;
   • different businesses.

4. Personal development
4.1. What is your career history?   4.2. How do you see your future?
5. Is there anything else you would like to add to your comments?

Do not forget the technique of the experienced interrogator — people will say more when they are relaxed. At the end of an interview you can put down your pen and notebook and show by your mien that it is over. At this point an interviewee will sometimes relax and provide you with more useful data which they were uncomfortable disclosing during the formal part of the interview. Remember also the virtue of silence which can sometimes prompt an interviewee to say more than intended.

In the interests of good client relations you may wish to drop a 'thank you' note to those who have given up time to see you, either after you have seen them or at the end of the interview programme. It is not always appropriate doing this — in some circumstances it might be considered too formal — but it is worth considering.

THE DISCUSSION GROUP

The discussion group is an interview at which more than one of the client's staff are present. There is a variant called a 'focus group', which is usually more structured than an interview, and is often used in market research.

The discussion group has many similar advantages and disadvantages to those of the interview; the following points are worth noting by contrast.

Advantages
- You can meet far more people in discussion groups than in one-to-one interviews.
- A discussion group is a higher-profile event than a one-to-one meeting, and can therefore be used to publicise your project or as a building block in a change programme.
- You can observe how participants interact and the group dynamics.
- Individuals may feel more confident about giving their views if they realise that others in the group are being open. They may also spark ideas off each other.

Disadvantages
- The more people there are, the less time there is for each to talk. You will therefore get a less comprehensive view from each individual and one or two people may dominate the discussion.
- People may be inhibited about opening up in front of colleagues.
- Meetings will probably need to be held in a meeting room — so you will not get the advantage of seeing others' offices.

- It is harder work; you have to regulate a more complex discussion as well as taking a record. For this reason it is often useful to have two consultants involved — one to lead the discussion and the other to take notes — but obviously this is more costly.

Operating hints

Have some ground rules for determining the composition of groups. Should each consist of members from the same department or from a cross-section? Should there be a mix of levels? Take the decisions on these, bearing in mind the type of data you want to collect, and remember they can also be an instrument of change. For example, if you wanted to confront departments with others' views of them in respect of a problem, you might use mixed groups.

Unless there are strong reasons for doing so, avoid forming discussion groups with the top executives in an organisation. You will be the outsider in the group of powerful people who will know each other well. Whatever you are trying to achieve may be overshadowed by the agendas they are working out amongst themselves.

You have both to regulate the discussion and to keep a record, and this is more complicated in a discussion group than in an interview. As noted above, ideally there should be two of you involved, so that one can lead the discussion while the other can keep notes. If this is not possible, you can make your task easier by:

- *More structure*: you keep control of the topics covered more tightly than in an interview.
- *Greater focus*: you concentrate on finding out about a narrower range of more specific items.
- *Simplified note taking*: you will not be able to collect all the data that becomes available at a discussion group meeting and the difficulty is compounded by also having to lead the discussion. You may wish to resort to recording (more difficult because of the size of the group), but an alternative with a large group is to record the key points on a flipchart. This has the additional advantage of giving participants the opportunity to make sure you have recorded and understood the key points they are making, as well as being able to refer back to and synthesise with previous points.

THE QUESTIONNAIRE

The term 'questionnaire' is used here to include any document designed by the consultant to elicit data from respondents. Examples of their use are:

- an attitude survey, to find out the state of staff morale;
- a survey of remuneration within a specific industry sector;
- a study of the buying habits of car users.

Everyone will have at some time completed questionnaires and will have views on their design. Some specialist consultants may use standard questionnaires (for example, occupational psychologists use them to assess aptitudes). In what follows, we will assume that the questionnaire is non-standard and is self-administered (i.e. respondents complete it themselves rather than under the supervision of the consultant).

Advantages
- A very large number of people can be sampled if necessary and it is cheaper than interviewing.
- Responses can be analysed fairly easily.
- It may be less time consuming for the respondent, or more easily fitted in with their work, than an interview.
- Nowadays web-based questionnaires are a simple way of capturing views.

Disadvantages
- You will get responses only to the questions you ask. You must therefore be sure these are the ones you want answered.
- You have no chance of explaining it to the respondents — so it must be clear and unambiguous.
- Respondents may feel inhibited about committing themselves honestly in writing.
- Similarly, unless you provide for it in the questionnaire, you will have no idea of the relative strength of feeling attached to a given response.
- People may ignore the questionnaire or be dilatory in completing it so a 100 per cent response is unlikely, possibly leaving you with an unbalanced sample.

Operating hints
Whereas much of the work in interviews lies in analysing them after they have taken place, with questionnaires effort has to be put into their design before data collection takes place. In particular you must make sure that:
- you ask questions in logical order;

- the wording used is clear and unambiguous and does not bias the respondent toward a particular answer;
- the questions are answerable.

Treat the questionnaire in the same way as a report in PR terms. If it has a wide circulation, it may be the only basis respondents have to form a view of you, the project you are carrying out and the organisation you represent. So make sure it is well presented and does you justice.

You need also to consider the question of anonymity. Do you want the respondents to be identified at some future time? One way of addressing this is to provide respondents with a unique one-off code that gives them access to the questionnaire, but does not enable them to be identified.

It is always worthwhile having a pilot trial of the questionnaire with a small sample of prospective respondents before giving it full circulation. This will help you to spot any poor wording or design that needs improvement.

Use the pilot trial to test not only the questionnaire but also the subsequent processing. Are the responses easily analysed to give you the information that you require?

Even after all this testing, you may wish to include a telephone number or email address to be contacted if a respondent has difficulty in completing the questionnaire.

Do not forget about the administration of the questionnaires. You need to ensure that you have made adequate arrangements so that:
- the questionnaires get to the right people;
- they know what they have to do when they have received them;

If questionnaires are sent by email or if you are using hard copy you need to make sure that:
- respondents know how they are to be returned;
- the questionnaires actually get back to you.

Do not forget to include questions about the respondents themselves (so-called 'demographic data') covering relevant facts about them and their work. You may, for example, wish to contrast different sites, or differentiate according to age, sex or some other distinguishing feature. (I am always amused by the apocryphal personnel department that provided information on 'employees broken down by age and sex'!) Consider also whether you want to identify individual respondents or whether you will get a better response by preserving anonymity.

Use scales and tick boxes to record varying responses. Exhibit 7.2 shows an example of this.

Exhibit 7.2 Example of a questionnaire

Canteen	Very good	Good	Average	Poor	Very poor	No view
31. How do you rate the quality of the food?						
32. Is the variety of the dishes...						
33. How do you rate the service?						
34. What do you think of the décor?						
35. Overall, how do you rate the canteen?						

Beware of creating skewed scales that bias answers: for example, the scale below is biased towards favourable remarks.

Excellent
Good
Above average
Average
Below average

STRUCTURED DATA COLLECTION TOOLS

These are data collection techniques with a purpose. The data needed will be collected by one of the generic methods noted above.

Set out below are:
- Critical incident technique;
- Delphi technique;
- Stakeholder analysis;

- Power mapping;
- Repertory grid technique.

CRITICAL INCIDENT TECHNIQUE

This is a means of eliciting data from people about effective and ineffective behaviour. The data generated can be used in studies of job design, individual or group performance, selection and training and equipment design.

It is most useful in situations when there is a lot of variety, ambiguity or flexibility and it is necessary to define what behaviour or circumstances lead to the best result.

The way this is done is to gather a number of 'experts' and collect data from them about critical incidents. A critical incident is an event which they observed as having a notably successful or unsuccessful outcome. It is best to describe the technique by means of an example.

Suppose a bank wishes to improve the quality of customer service amongst counter staff, the application of critical incident technique would be as follows:

1. Gather together a group of counter staff or their supervisors. It is important that the group has been able to observe ineffective and effective customer service and hence are 'experts' on it.

2. Collect information on critical incidents from them. These are descriptions of occasions when they have observed effective or ineffective customer service, and you would ask for three pieces of information:

   - What the circumstances were;
   - What the member of counter staff did;
   - The outcome of what they did.

You can use a standard form to collect this data, and a completed example is shown in Exhibit 7.3.

Data on critical incidents does not have to encompass dramatic events — most of the events will be part of the routine of everyday work. The data will be collected in a discussion group (as in the present example) or you can ask the experts to note their observations down over a period. It is important, too, that effective and ineffective incidents are separated clearly.

Exhibit 7.3 Critical incident form

What were the circumstances?

A customer complained at the counter about the bank charges made to her account. She had become aware of them only when she had received her bank statement.

What did the member of counter staff do?

The teller explained the basis for the charges, he looked at the bank statement and gave advice about how the customer might avoid them in future. He gave her a leaflet explaining bank charges and how to avoid them.

What was the outcome?

The customer was still unhappy about the unexpected bank charges but said, 'Thank you for your help.'

---

3. The next step is to analyse the incidents. They provide a rich source of data and you could look for features under headings in addition to behaviour — for example:
    *   Systems: bank charges levied without explanation or breakdown of their basis;
    *   Skills: dealing with a complaint courteously, demonstrating knowledge of the basis of bank charges and how to avoid them.

In this case, both features might be relevant. The start of the analysis process is to write each feature of the incidents onto cards. (This helps in sorting them out later.) This is a task that can be done by the consultant either alone or in collaboration with the experts.

The cards can then be sorted into generically similar categories. This is a task that the experts should do. One method is to divide the experts into two groups which come up with different categories and then bring them together to combine their conclusions. In the example, therefore, customer service incidents might be categorised under:

*   handling routine transactions;
*   dealing with complaints;
*   coping with failures in back-up systems;
*   recognising when others need to get involved;
*   other.

4. The behaviour in each of these categories can then be scaled according to their effectiveness. The scales created are sometimes

called behaviourally-anchored rating scales, or BARS. One such, on a five-point scale, is illustrated for 'dealing with complaints' in Exhibit 7.4.

The BARS or other scales are a major output of critical incident techniques. The example in Exhibit 7.4 could provide helpful input in assessing how well individual counter staff deal with complaints or provide guidelines for training in handling complaints.

Exhibit 7.4 Example of a behaviourally-anchored rating scale

5	Demonstrates concern that customer has a complaint and energetically seeks to resolve it.
4	Listens sympathetically to complaint.
3	Listens passively to complaint.
2	Aggressive reaction to customer.
1	Gets into argument with customer.

DELPHI TECHNIQUE

The Delphi technique (named after the Oracle at Delphi renowned in classical times) was developed by the Rand Corporation in World War II. It is very useful in collecting data about complex or unclear situations from experts, who may have widely different viewpoints. It is therefore often used in planning as a means of projecting the future. It has also been used as a method of problem solving. Examples of questions which might be addressed using the Delphi technique are:

- What will be the nature of customers' needs in retail banking in the next ten years?
- How will the transport choices of passengers change with increasing traffic congestion?
- What education will be required to ensure a sufficient supply of plumbers in the next 15 years?

The approach is fairly laborious and should therefore be used only when the questions are of some moment.

In the Delphi technique the 'experts' are required to complete a series of questionnaires, each questionnaire is based on the responses to the previous one. There is thus no need for the experts to meet, and therefore it is possible to include experts from outside the client organisation or who are physically distant.

The technique consists of three stages, although each may involve more than one round of questionnaire.

1. Establish the major responses to an initial open-ended question.
2. Determine the relative weighting of these responses.
3. Establish the reasons for experts' views which are significantly different from the norm.

Establish the major responses to an initial open-ended question
A simple example illustrates how the technique works. Suppose you are planning a strategy for a food-processing company and you want to establish the impact of technology on food production over the next 10–20 years. First of all you would assemble a panel of experts — people who might reasonably be expected to have a view on this. Some of these will be in the client's firm, but there will be others, for example:

• Customers of the client;
• Manufacturers of processing and packaging equipment;
• Competitors (who may of course take part only if they can share in the results of the study);
• Food technologists;
• Shippers.

The first questionnaire will be qualitative and ask questions around the theme:

> *In your own area of business, what do you see to be the significant developments in technology which will affect food processing?*

Each member of the panel will give responses from their own viewpoint. For example:

• Customers (probably food distributors and retail outlets) will comment on consumer trends; for instance, an increasing number of single person households might result in increased demand for high-quality ready-made meals;

- Manufacturers of packaging equipment might predict that short batch runs will become more cost-effective, thus allowing 'own label' brands to be produced for small customers;
- Food technologists could point to the use of genetic engineering in improving the production of synthetic food;
- Shippers might foresee new preservation techniques that make a greater variety of exotic fruit available.

There will also be a host of other predictions.

Determine the relative weighting of these responses
The next questionnaire will seek the degree of agreement among experts in these matters. Exhibit 7.5 illustrates a portion of the questionnaire. At this stage the data collected is the degree of agreement with the statement. From this the strength of any prediction can be judged.

It is possible to have an intermediate stage that categorises the statements and asks respondents to add others that might be prompted by this list. Next, you could ask for an assessment of the importance of each statement. The statements which were thought to be most important could then be assessed using the form in Exhibit 7.5.

Exhibit 7.5 Example of extract from Delphi technique questionnaire (part 1)

Mark the following statements on a scale of 1 – 5 according to whether you agree strongly (1) or disagree strongly (5) with the statement. If you do not wish to comment, mark with a zero.

4. Consumer trends	No comment	Strongly agree	Agree	Average	Disagree	Strongly disagree
4.1 Increasing demand for microwave oven ready meals	0	1	2	3	4	5
4.2 Trend to fresh food from frozen	0	1	2	3	4	5
4.3 Trend to frozen food from fresh	0	1	2	3	4	5
4.4						

A popular marketing ploy for a consultancy is the use of a survey to create publicity for its services in a particular area. Surveys of this kind are frequently carried out using a technique based on the first two steps of the Delphi technique as described above. For example, a firm selling consultancy in telecommunications may decide to get publicity by publishing a survey of trends in corporate telecommunications over the next ten years. The firm will start off by taking a number of basic questions and (using stage one of the Delphi technique) get the major responses. The initial questions might include, 'How will telecommunications affect business activity over the next ten years?' The responses could be:

- Increased use of advertising and ordering via mobile phones;
- Voice traffic static, but the split between land line and mobile phone expected to shift to mobile;
- Data traffic on fixed-line systems continues to grow rapidly.

The consultancy could then poll a large number of telecommunications equipment users to assess the degrees of agreement with these (or rather more narrowly defined) statements. The results could be presented in a statistical format which could be very useful to those involved in business planning in the telecommunications industry.

Very often the surveys will show how responses to each question were split. For example, the responses to a different question are shown below:

In how many years' time do you foresee genetic research leading to the possibility of 'regrowing' lost limbs in humans?

5-10	3%
11-15	15%
16-20	27%
21-25	25%
More than 25	5%
Never	25%

Establish the reasons for experts' views which are significantly different from the norm
The third questionnaire feeds back data to the experts on how their opinions compared with the averages for all those that commented. This is illustrated in Exhibit 7.6.

Exhibit 7.6 Extract of example of Delphi technique questionnaire

The table below shows how your opinion compared with the average for all experts ✓ = your opinion; ■ = average				
14. Drivers of telecoms growth in 5 years				
Growth factors (%)	100 – 200	200 – 300	300 - 400	400+
14.1 Channel to market	✓	■		
14.2 Use of mobiles		✓	■	
14.3 Data traffic		■		✓

The request for explanatory comments at the end again enriches the data. In Exhibit 7.6 for example, the difference in opinions may be because the respondent believes that smart phones will supplant computers.

Bear in mind the increasing interest in what are called 'outliers' – data that is outside the common areas of observation. The idea of the 'black swan' – the set of circumstances that is rare but not impossible – has become of interest in recent years. So do not neglect observations that are far from the norm.

From the above it is obvious that the Delphi technique is hard work. It needs a lot of analysis work on the part of those administering it and time and effort from those responding. With large panels it also needs careful organisation. It is a useful technique for consultants to have in their kit bag but one to be used sparingly.

STAKEHOLDER ANALYSIS

Stakeholder analysis is a simple way of looking at who the people of influence are in a situation, and their motivations. You can also note the nature of their influence. The form for recording your observations is shown in Exhibit 7.7.

Exhibit 7.7 Stakeholder analysis

Name of individual	*Measure of influence on this topic*	*What he or she wants to happen/motivations on this*

Note that the degree of influence is situational; a person can be highly influential in one situation but not in another. For example, I may know the chief executive of a global corporation, but this may be of little help in winning a consulting project in a subsidiary with a manager who is perhaps several ranks lower, who is in charge. Stakeholder analysis can be used to:

- help you identify the likely response to a proposal or recommendation you are going to put to a client;
- help plan how to communicate with a client.

For example, if two influential people have objectives that are in conflict, they may waste all the time at a meeting together engaged in conflict rather than moving things along.

The information needed to conduct stakeholder analysis will arise quite naturally during the course of meetings with clients. The form can also help you to identify areas where you need to find out more.

POWER MAPPING

Whereas stakeholder analysis considers each individual in turn, power mapping looks at the influence they have on one another. Exhibit 7.8 shows an example. Influence can, of course, be both business and personal: two individuals who, for example, regularly enjoy playing golf together may well influence each other's opinion. Position in the business will also be significant, and there can be negative influence too – if A dislikes C, then if A supports something, C's natural inclination is to oppose it.

Power mapping is helpful in deciding, for example, who are the key people to convince in a given situation. In the figure for example, if you can win over E and C, then there is a good chance of there being a favourable response from the others.

REPERTORY GRID

The repertory grid is a method of finding out how people look at things — the factors that they use in making judgements about significant differences between them. These factors are called 'constructs' and the objects to which they are applied are called 'elements'.

The first step is to define what is being evaluated. A common example in the world of work is the value of a job for the purposes of job evaluation, which is used to create a job structure and often used to inform the basis of a salary structure. You would then take a number of different jobs (the elements) and invite those people making judgements to compare them

Exhibit 7.8 Power mapping

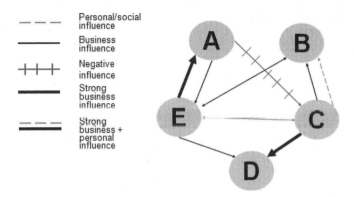

- - - - Personal/social
influence

──────── Business
influence

+++++ Negative
influence

──────── Strong
business
influence

─ ─ ─ Strong
business +
personal
influence

in respect of their value to the business. As an illustration, the consultant might ask the judge, 'In terms of their value to the business, which is more important, Job A or Job B?' The judge answers, 'Job B'. 'Why is this?' asks the consultant. The judge replies, 'Because Job B controls a bigger budget.' So the consultant has elicited that the judge reckons that the value of a job depends on the size of the budget that is controlled.

Having illustrated the principle, let's look first at an informal use of the method and then a highly structured approach.

Informal use

I use the repertory grid concept quite frequently in interviews when trying to find out about values in organisations. For example, if I want to know how managers judge their subordinates, I ask a question such as:

> *Think about the best person in your team and the worst. Imagine them standing side by side and tell me about the differences between them in terms of their performance.*

The response to this question will explain quite a lot about how performance is judged in the organisation. The same question repeated at interviews with other managers should begin to show some consensus. This data can then be used, for example, to see if it is consistent with business objectives, or with the views of subordinates on the ways they are appraised.

There are two key points in the phrasing of the question. The first is the choice of elements, which in this case are the people in the manager's own

team. The second is the context in which distinctions are being made —
their performance. Changing either of these will affect the data elicited, as
can be inferred from Exhibit 7.9.

Exhibit 7.9 The importance of phrasing the question

Element	In terms of
People	Looks
Factory	Pollution
Product	Safety
Salespeople	Sales performance
Company	Quality of employee relations

Each of these combinations will give the views of the judge on different matters. 'People in terms of looks' will yield different constructs from
'People in terms of safety'.

The analytical approach
Where you wish to combine views of different judges, a more analytical
approach is better. For the purposes of illustration, imagine that Harriet
(of TDH Ltd, introduced in Chapter 3) has been commissioned to collect
the views of a community on how they valued public service, and she is
meeting an individual – Tony – to solicit his input. First she would identify
a number of elements, in this case a number of jobs – say:

• fireman;
• nurse;
• classical pianist;
• lawyer;
• refuse collector;
• carpenter.

One way in which constructs can be elicited is to invite judges to take
three of the elements and to look for the similarities between any two, which
distinguish them from the third. Taking three of these elements — say,
fireman, nurse and refuse collector — Harriet would ask Tony what two of

these have in common which distinguishes them from the third. For these Tony might note that for him the main constructs are:

- Works indoors — works outdoors
- Job held by mostly men — job held by mostly women
- Concerned with matters of life and death — not concerned with matters of life and death
- Long training required — little training required
- 24 hours a day job — day work only

These differences, however, do not tell us much about Tony's views on public service. So Harriet might ask, 'In terms of their value to society, taking these jobs in groups of three, what distinguishes one job from the other two?'

Tony might argue with some justice that his answers for these jobs would be the same as the list above but Harriet might want to penetrate a little further; she can do this by asking, 'Is this construct important and if so, why?' This could yield further constructs. So, applying this question to point 1 above — working indoors or outdoors — Tony might comment, 'Working outdoors is less comfortable than working indoors,' so another construct, the comfort of the working environment, has been generated.

Similarly, Tony may think that having to provide a service 24 hours a day results in having to work unsociable hours, which is another construct.

Another means of eliciting more constructs from those initially listed is to ask, 'Which construct is more important, and why?' Of those above, Tony might select the third point, because for him the preservation of life is of paramount importance.

All this is telling us a great deal about Tony and his view of public service.

Having an idea of the theory, how does Harriet capture and analyse the results of data collection? Here's one way of doing it.

She writes each element (refuse collector, carpenter, etc.) on to a separate piece of card and numbers the cards (in this case 1–6). She takes three cards (either at random or in predetermined combinations of number, e.g. 1, 2, 3). She asks the question, 'In terms of their social value, what characteristics do two of the jobs share that distinguishes them from the third?' She would do this for various combinations.

When she has elicited the constructs, she can use the form shown in Exhibit 7.10 to capture the information. So in the first row is the construct 'Works outdoors' and 'Works indoors'. In doing this she should make sure that:

- the constructs are relevant. There are many similarities and differences, but the ones of interest are those in terms of their social value
- that she is using precise language, so that others will understand what is meant. For example, 'communicates well' is ambiguous; does it mean 'writes well' or 'makes good presentations'?
- she has not combined two different constructs on the same line; e.g. if the box on the left says 'works outdoors' and that on the right 'works with people', these are separate constructs and should be on separate lines

Exhibit 7.10 Repertory grid form

(Score 1)	*(Score 5)*	Element score					
In terms of their social value what does the pair of jobs have in common?	*In terms of their social value what makes the single job different?*	Fireman	Nurse	Classical pianist	Lawyer	Refuse collector	Carpenter
Works outdoors	Works indoors						
Works primarily with people	Works primarily with things						
Deals with matters of life and death	Deals with matters of little moment						
Etc	Etc						

She can now ask Tony to score each of the elements against each construct, using the top row of the table shown in Exhibit 7.10 (the use of the other two rows will be explained later). Shown is a five-point scale for each construct; the extreme described on the left-hand end scores 1 and that on the right scores 5. The score for each element depends where it lies between the two extremes, and the score is entered in the column for each element. For example, the first construct is 'works outdoors' — 'works indoors'. On this scale, a refuse collector would score 1 and a classical pianist would score 5.

Exhibit 7.11 shows the results as Tony might assess them for all the jobs.

Exhibit 7.11 Scoring for one construct

(Score 1)	(Score 5)						
In terms of their social value what does the pair of jobs have in common?	**In terms of their social value what makes the single job different?**	**Element score**					
		Fireman	Nurse	Classical pianist	Lawyer	Refuse collector	Carpenter
Works outdoors	Works indoors	2	4	5	5	1	3

Finally, Harriet needs to assess which are the really important or relevant constructs. This can be done by rating the elements according to overall assessment. Therefore, in the example, Tony would rate each job according to its social value, scoring one for low and five for high. (This ranking could be done by paired comparison (see later) if required.) The overall assessment is shown in Exhibit 7.12.

Exhibit 7.12 Overall scoring

(Score 1)	(Score 5)	Element score					
		Fireman	Nurse	Classical pianist	Lawyer	Refuse collector	Carpenter
Lowest social value	Highest social value	4	5	2	1	2	2

Next Harriet would need to see how well each of the constructs that she has elicited correlates with Tony's overall assessment of social value. A simple way of doing this is to sum up the differences in score. The smaller the difference, the more relevant the construct.

Exhibit 7.13 shows the differences for the 'Works outdoors – works indoors'.

Exhibit 7.13 Correlation

(Score 1)	(Score 5)	Fireman	Nurse	Classical pianist	Lawyer	Refuse collector	Carpenter	Total
Lowest social value	Highest social value	4	5	2	1	2	2	
Works outdoors	Works indoors	2	4	5	5	1	3	
Difference		2	1	3	4	1	1	12

Reverse correlation for overall value, but the scores for the construct remain the same

(Score 5)	(Score 1)							
Lowest social value	Highest social value	2	1	4	5	4	4	
Works outdoors	Works indoors	2	4	5	5	1	3	
Difference		0	3	1	0	3	1	8

Some constructs may have been written down in reverse order — i.e. the aspect of high social value will have been written on the left (e.g. 'deals with matters of life and death' in Exhibit 7.10), and will have scored only one. In order to detect constructs that fall into this category, you reverse the scoring (i.e. lowest social value scores 5 and the highest scores 1). This is also shown in Exhibit 7.13 under the heading 'reverse correlation'.

As you can see, the differences in the first case show a total difference of 12, while those for the reverse correlation show only 8. We can infer from this that Tony considers work outdoors to be of greater social value than work indoors.

Exhibit 7.14 completes the table shown in Exhibit 7.10 with scores for all the constructs. The overall value is shown at the top, together with the reversed value. The differences are shown in the two rows under each construct score.

Exhibit 7.14 Completed repertory grid form

(Score 1) In terms of their social value what does the pair of jobs have in common?	*(Score 5)* In terms of their social value what makes the single job different?	Element score						
		Fireman	Nurse	Classical pianist	Lawyer	Refuse collector	Carpenter	Total
Lowest social value	Highest social value	4	5	2	1	2	2	
Reversed score		2	1	4	5	4	4	
Works outdoors	**Works indoors**	2	4	5	5	1	3	
Difference		2	1	3	4	1	1	12
Difference with reversed score		0	3	1	0	3	1	8
Works primarily with people	**Works primarily with things**	4	1	2	1	4	5	
Difference		0	4	0	0	2	3	9
Difference with reversed score		2	0	2	4	0	1	9
Deals with matters of life and death	**Deals with matters of little moment**	1	1	5	4	5	4	
Difference		3	4	3	3	3	2	18
Difference with reversed score		1	0	1	1	1	0	4

This shows that the construct 'deals with matters of life and death' correlates well (a low difference of a total of only four). So Tony believes that the social value of a job is strongly related to whether it deals with matters of life or death.

As you will now realise, this is a laborious procedure! However, it can be useful when trying to capture and weight opinion based data.

DATA ANALYSIS TECHNIQUES

As has been mentioned elsewhere in this book, data analysis often provides a prompt to look for new or missing data. In this section we cover the following techniques for analysing data:

1. Pareto's principle;
2. Paired comparisons;
3. Force field analysis;
4. Cause and effect diagrams.

PARETO'S PRINCIPLE

Pareto was an Italian economist, who, examining the distribution of wealth, showed that a minority of the population owned most of the wealth. The graph in Exhibit 7.15 illustrates this distribution, plotting the cumulative proportion of wealth owned compared with the percentage of the population owning it, ranked from most to least wealthy.

Exhibit 7.15 Pareto's curve

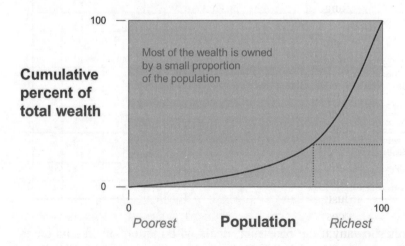

The curve, as drawn, shows that 20 per cent of the wealthiest individuals own 80 per cent of the wealth. So, if the Government wished to raise a tax based on wealth, it would be more fruitful to concentrate its attention on the 20 per cent most wealthy than to put in a lot more effort to raise tax from the remaining 80 per cent.

This kind of distribution is replicated in many situations and can be defined as a general principle (which, for convenience, we will call Pareto's principle):

> *In any series of elements to be controlled, a selected small fraction, in terms of number of elements, always accounts for a large fraction, in terms of effect.*

The comments on wealth above also illustrate some other names by which this (rather complicated!) definition is known:

* The 80/20 rule;
* The law of diminishing returns.

Examples of Pareto's principle abound in everyday life:

* A small range of causes account for the majority of fatal road accidents. Addressing the major causes (e.g. speeding) will help in getting value for money in terms of road safety.
* A small number of brewing companies produce most of the beer drunk.
* A small range of faults will create the bulk of rejects through quality control.
* A small percentage of customers will account for the greatest proportion of sales.

This principle is replicated in several management theories.

* *Management by objectives*: managers are required to identify 'key result areas' — those areas of their work where high performance is going to have the greatest impact on their results.
* *Critical success factors*: selection of the information needed to support managerial activities should focus on success factors. In most industries there are usually three to six factors which determine success and these key jobs must be done exceedingly well for a company to be successful.

This latter example draws us to the relevance of Pareto's principle to the consultant; it could be restated thus:

In a consulting project there will be a small number of key factors that the consultant must heed and control if it is to be successful.

The consultant therefore needs to identify the key dynamics involved — those aspects which will have a disproportionate effect on the outcome; for example:

- Those elements of production operations where the greatest savings can be made for given investment;
- The opinion leaders who have to be convinced of the recommendations;
- Those tasks which, when performed well, will significantly increase the consultant's credibility.

Once the consultant has identified the key dynamics, they should use them to decide what needs to be done and to set his or her priorities.

PAIRED COMPARISONS

Paired comparisons is a means of producing a rank order of items. It involves comparing each item with each of the others in turn and assessing whether it is of more, equal, or less importance according to a predetermined scale. As an example, imagine you have to collect views on the relative importance of a number of consultancy skills — for example, for assessing consultants. These skills might be:

1. Technical knowledge.
2. Project management.
3. Report writing.
4. Presenting.
5. Influencing.
6. Data analysis.
7. Commerciality.

Exhibit 7.16 shows a matrix for collecting this data which each judge completes. It is, in fact, half a matrix (because you do not need to compare B with A once you have compared A with B).

Exhibit 7.16 Relative importance of consulting skills

	PM	RW	Pre	Inf	DA	Comm	(d)	Total
Technical knowledge	2(a)	2	2	2	2	0(b)	10	10
Project management	(0)	2	2	2	2	0	8	8
Report writing		(0)	2	0	2	0	4	4
Presenting			(0)	0	2	0	2	2
Influencing				(4)	2	1(c)	3	7
Data analysis					(0)	0	0	0
[Commerciality]						(11)	X	11

Key points about the matrix are as follows.

1. Skills are written against each row leaving out the last skill. Then the same skills are written across the top in the same order as down the side, but starting with the second item. (In this way you avoid comparing a skill with itself.) Thus Exhibit 7.16 does not strictly need 'commerciality' at the bottom of the list, although it is included there for scoring purposes, and 'technical knowledge' is missed from the columns.

2. Award a 2 if the row is more important than the column. Award 1 if they are equal and 0 if the column is more important than the row. Thus, because technical knowledge is ranked more important than project management, box (a) has a 2 in it, but because technical knowledge is ranked less important than commerciality, box (b) has a 0 in it. Further down, influencing has been ranked equal with commerciality, so box (c) has 1 in it. Note that it is not necessary to be consistent; for example, although commerciality has been ranked *equal* to influencing, project management has been ranked *more* important than influencing and *less* important than commerciality.

Scoring is as follows:
1. Add up the scores in each row (the sums are shown in column (d)).
2. Add up each column, but take the reverse of each score in a box — thus a 2 becomes a 0, 1 remains 1 and 0 becomes 2. These column scores are shown in brackets against the row they relate to.
3. Add the row and column scores together. The item with the highest score is ranked highest and so on.

The result in the example is therefore as shown in Exhibit 7.17 below:

Table 7.17 Results of paired comparison ranking

Most important	Commerciality
	Technical knowledge
	Project management
	Influencing
	Report writing
	Presenting
Least important	Data analysis

Advantages
1. It is easier to do than by trying to rank all items in one go.
2. It allows judges to be inconsistent.
3. It enables you to combine the views of several judges by adding their scores.

Disadvantages
1. It looks complicated initially and needs careful selling to the client; sometimes the reaction may be that it is too complicated, but once they are familiar, clients seem very happy to use the charts.
2. Take care to set up the chart correctly — one item out of place ruins it.
3. The scoring is a little difficult to follow at first.

Operating hints
1. Be on hand to help client staff to fill in the chart on the first occasion they use one.
2. Do not let the client staff do the scoring unless they really want to.
3. Because of the complexity of scoring it may be preferable to set up a spreadsheet or web based system for this.

Applications
Paired comparisons is a means of obtaining not only a ranking but also a relative weighting for the elements under assessment. For example, in choosing the location of a new head office, a company may want to take into account the following factors:

- Access to motorway systems and airport;
- Access to mainline stations;
- Secretarial and clerical staff locally available;
- Office rents;
- Close to chairman's country house;
- Cheap housing for executives available;
- Grants and other incentives available.

Not all of these factors will be equally important, and a weighting can be attached by using the paired comparison method. Data on the relative merits of each prospective location could then be collected and compared for the more important locations.

FORCE FIELD ANALYSIS

Force field analysis (FFA) is a complicated name for a simple yet powerful technique. It presupposes that any situation is in a state of equilibrium at a given time and that the forces for change balance those opposing change. This is illustrated in Exhibit 7.18.

Exhibit 7.18 Force field analysis

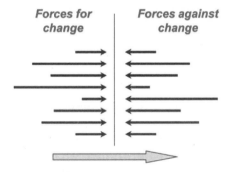

Direction of required change

The steps involved in carrying out FFA are:
1. Define the nature of the change required. This needs to be done with care and may involve breaking down change into a number of factors. For example, the key change may be to make more profit but there will be a large number of items that contribute to this and it would be more helpful to analyse each of these separately. Thus,

reducing the reject rate, increasing the selling price, increasing work rate, or reducing absenteeism could each be addressed using FFA, as each should contribute to increased profitability.

2. Identify what the forces are on each side. This is an activity which is probably best done with client staff, not only because of their knowledge of the situation but also because their participation should help in their recognising and accepting the need for specific changes. At this stage it is important to identify all significant forces and some of these will be human as well as technical. For example, a significant restraining force on increasing selling prices may be the opposition of the managing director.

3. Determine the relative magnitude of the forces. Plainly, change can be more effectively accomplished by altering the more significant forces. Almost certainly, too, there will be a number of major forces about which you can do nothing, and it is necessary to recognise which they are. (This is an application of Pareto's principle).

4. Determine an action plan based on changing the balance of forces, i.e. increasing those which favour change and reducing those which oppose it. Increasing some forces for change may create a reaction, however, so avoid increasing those that make people feel threatened or pressured.

FFA helps to elicit the important factors influencing change and provides a basis for planning action. As an illustration, consider the case of a smoker who wants to reduce the number of cigarettes they smoke each day.

Step 1: Define the nature of the change required; this can be quantified — it might be, say, to cut from 50 to 10 cigarettes per day (but would probably be best to reduce to nil).

Step 2: Identify the forces on each side: Exhibit 7.18 lists the forces that one group came up with.

Step 3: Identify significant forces you can do something about, and eliminate those you cannot. This step depends on who 'you' are: if you are the Government your capacity will be different from that if you are the subject yourself. So, if you are, say, a close friend or spouse of someone you wish to cut down smoking, you cannot do anything about advertising or the price of cigarettes.

Step 4: Determine an action plan. Increasing pressure to stop smoking may create increased resistance so you need to be more subtle.

Much depends on whether the individual wants to reduce smoking, but finds it difficult, or whether they have no interest in it at all. Assuming the former, you might have a bet with them: 'I bet you £100 you cannot reduce your smoking to 10 per day for one month.' This could harness the desire to show self-control.

Exhibit 7.19 Example of force field analysis

Forces for change ➔	⬅Forces against change
Desire to show self-control	Rebel against 'nanny knows best'
House and clothes smell	Cigarette advertising
Breath smells	Enjoys smoking
Discolours teeth	Friends do it
Heightens risk of cancer and other illnesses	Habit in certain situations
	Reduces stress
Aftertaste	Creates a good image
Health advertisements	Keeps hands/mouth occupied
Family pressure	Relieves boredom
Cost	Reduces food intake
Short of breath	
Sore throat	

Reduce from 50 to 10 cigarettes per day

Reducing the forces against change might be achieved by using an anti-smoking chewing gum. This not only keeps your mouth occupied but reduces the pleasure from smoking.

If, on the other hand, the individual does not want to reduce the number of cigarettes smoked, the problem is not that of how to cut down, but getting them to want to cut down in the first place — a quite different issue.

CAUSE AND EFFECT DIAGRAMS
Cause and effect diagrams are also known as Ishikawa diagrams, or fishbone diagrams because of their characteristic shape. They are a way of mapping information.

One such is shown in Exhibit 7.20, and illustrates an analysis of bad tasting coffee from a coffee machine. The effect is the bad tasting coffee from a coffee machine; the diagram shows the main possible causes of it.

The best technique is first to brainstorm a list of all the likely causes that might account for the coffee tasting bad, and then look for some uniting themes. In Exhibit 7.20 they are shown as:

- people and operation;
- process and design;
- materials;
- equipment.

So all of the causes could be subsumed under these headings.

Exhibit 7.20 Cause and effect diagram

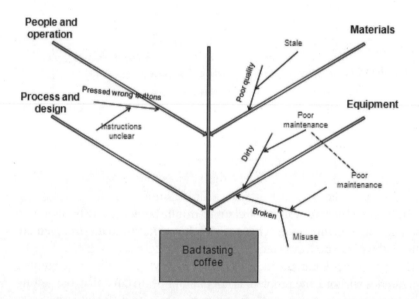

But causes can be related. So in the diagram, dirty equipment is a possible cause, and poor maintenance may be the cause of dirty equipment. The arrows allow the picture to be built up. And the same cause may be repeated — so poor maintenance is also a possible cause of equipment breakdown.

The diagram also has the benefits that when the first brainstormed list of causes has been mapped, it may stimulate further thoughts on additional causes.

SOME USEFUL MODELS

Models are a useful way of making sense of situations. A couple that conveniently might be covered at this point are *individual performance analysis* and *conflict analysis*.

INDIVIDUAL PERFORMANCE ANALYSIS

Force field analysis and Pareto's principle are generally applicable to situations of change, as they can be used to consider the technical aspects as well as the difficulties of dealing with people. Individual performance analysis combines a number of ideas to help in determining how the performance of an individual or group of individuals can be improved.

The analysis is based on two propositions.

1. Individual or group performance is a function of how well a series of separate tasks is performed; as well as technical tasks, these can also be process or managerial ones — for example, communicating with others, planning, motivating staff and so on.
2. The quality of performance of each task will be a function of:
    *   how clearly and well the task is defined;
    *   the individual's ability to do the task;
    *   the individual's motivation to do the task.

Change frequently involves new or different tasks, determining new priorities, learning new skills, doing things in a different way and so on. Individual performance analysis is helpful in situations in which performance is not reaching the standards required. Proposition 1 says that these new tasks and activities must first be identified, and Proposition 2 suggests that if satisfactory performance is not being achieved, it is because:

*   people do not know what they have to do; or
*   they are not able to do it; or
*   they do not want to do it.

This can be rendered as an equation:

$$\text{performance} = \text{direction} \times \text{ability} \times \text{motivation}$$

All three components are required; however well motivated I am, it is improbable I shall win the Olympic high-jump championship. On the other hand, although I may be capable of preparing a first-class report on a particular topic, if I am not interested or have other priorities, the report may be barely adequate, or late. Finally, I can be willing and able to do the wrong jobs very efficiently, but that does not lead to effective performance. For example, a department may produce a comprehensive monthly report, putting in a lot of effort to produce it on time, but if none of the recipients reads it, the task is efficiently done but totally useless.

Problems of performance attributed to poor motivation are in practice often caused by deficiencies in ability or lack of clarity about the nature or priority of particular tasks.

For example, some years ago I was invited to advise on a problem in a manufacturing plant. 'The difficulty', said the production director, 'is that although we have installed new processing equipment we simply are not reaching the levels of productivity we expected.' He wondered whether there was a problem with the first-line supervisors.

I had a series of meetings with the supervisors and it emerged that they were all concerned. What is more, they knew how productivity could be raised. The problem was not one of motivation or ability — it was that the important tasks of communication between supervisors and management were not being given the right priority.

The project opened up channels of formal and informal communication between supervisors and management. Shortly afterwards productivity was 50 per cent higher than before the project.

ANALYSING CONFLICT

There will be occasions when conflict arises — or at least is possible — as a result of a change project. Blake and Mouton (1964) suggested that when conflict occurs, people will believe that:

- conflict is inevitable and agreement is impossible; or
- conflict is not inevitable, yet agreement is impossible; or
- although there is conflict, agreement is possible.

These views will influence how people behave depending on the stakes involved, i.e. the importance they attach to the outcome. When the stakes are low, behaviour will be passive, but when they are high, behaviour will be very active. These types of behaviour are illustrated in Exhibit 7.21.

Exhibit 7.21 Conflict analysis

Behaviour	Conflict is inevitable, agreement is impossible	Conflict is not inevitable, yet agreement is impossible	Although there is conflict, agreement is possible	Perceived stakes
Active	Win-lose power struggle	Withdrawal	Problem solving	High stakes
↕	Intervention of third party	Isolation	Splitting the difference, compromise, mediation	Moderate stakes
Passive	Fate	Indifference or ignorance	Peaceful coexistence, smoothing over	Low stakes

From Blake, Shepard & Mouton

The 'worst' outcome of conflict is the win–lose power struggle, which is energy sapping to both sides and can be a Pyrrhic victory for the winner anyhow.

A point of significance to note about the model is that, when faced by conflict, it is what people *think* to be the case which determines how they behave. So, if participants think the stakes are high, and believe conflict is inevitable and agreement is impossible, then the result will be a win–lose power struggle. Similarly, you can infer these beliefs if a win–lose power struggle is taking place. If a win–lose power struggle is to be averted or stopped, then it is important that the beliefs of the participants about the nature of the conflict are changed — for example, that the stakes appear to be worth less, or that conflict is not inevitable or that agreement is possible. In this way the behaviours of the protagonists will become less destructive as they are modified as beliefs change.

Almost inevitably a consultant will be faced by conflict from time to time. Understanding the nature of the conflict as illustrated by the model can help in planning tactics to use to diminish disruptive consequences.

CHAPTER 8

REPORTING TO CLIENTS

I love being a writer. What I can't stand is the paperwork.

Peter de Vries

Sometimes when a speaker has his audience on the edge of their seats, they're trying to muster the nerve to get up and go home.

Anon

At a course for newly appointed management consultants, participants were asked what they had found most difficult in making the transition to consultancy. Each gave several reasons, but the group was unanimous that report writing was a major difficulty. That is consistent with my experience in training and supervising new consultants, and writing high-quality reports can be difficult for all consultants.

Moreover, if you ask consultants the most common reason why they might be working late at night, it will be because they are preparing a document or presentation.

This chapter is about reporting to clients. 'Report' can mean many things to consultants, so I will define my terms for this chapter as follows:

- A *report* is a communication to the client;
- A *document* is a report in written format;
- A *presentation* is face to face with an audience, led by the consultant, possibly supported by written or graphic material.

Nowadays the internationalisation of business and the people who work in it are such that you may be communicating with individuals whose first language is not English, and you need to allow for this. But most of the difficulties occur not because of infelicities of expression or style but from lack of thought about what is to be conveyed and how. Therefore much of this chapter is about preparation. First, however, let's review the occasions when documents or presentations are required.

REPORTS TO CLIENTS

WRITTEN MATERIAL
Consultants' written material includes:

- *Letters*: In fact nowadays these would be better termed *messages*, as with the growth of email in recent years the use of the post to communicate has greatly diminished. (I doubt that the number of letters I have received through the post from clients over the last 12 months exceeds single figures; in fact, it may well be nil!) Yet the number of written messages that we have exchanged is considerable. Email has influenced the style of written communication but like letters, the style of a message can be enormously varied and almost certainly will reflect the character of the sender, the nature of the relationship with the addressee and the subject matter.
- *Proposals* to undertake a particular contract or project. Sometimes these may be in the form of a relatively short letter confirming the key points of an oral agreement, but more often will be in report format.
- *Progress reports* reviewing the position of a project.
- *Position papers* intended to open or pursue a debate with the client on a particular topic.
- *Project or assignment reports* written at the conclusion of a project or the end of a phase of it, usually with recommendations for the future.
- *Manuals* relating to the operation of a system or a piece of equipment.

There are, of course, many other pieces of documentation that consultants may need to produce, such as training materials, questionnaires and other formats for data collection, as well as internal memoranda and the like if they work in a firm of consultants. These are not covered in this chapter, but the principles described can in some measure be applied to them.

As well as receiving these communications in written format, clients may ask consultants to present them face to face.

PRESENTATIONS

In our private lives we may be called on to make speeches — after dinner, at weddings and other family occasions or in some capacity in a society or public office. Practice and experience of these stand the consultant presenter in good stead, but there are special occasions required at all stages of the consultancy process — to colleagues, to clients, and to the public at large. Exhibit 8.1 illustrates some of the presentation occasions that occur, using a consultancy business process model.

Exhibit 8.1 Circumstances involving presentations

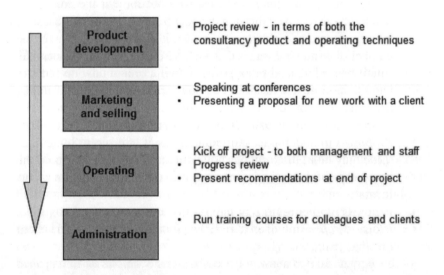

THE VIRTUOUS CIRCLE OF PERFORMANCE IMPROVEMENT

The three steps of the virtuous circle of performance improvement, illustrated in Exhibit 8.2, can be applied to improving performance in reporting to clients (and to many other practical skills too). The remainder of this chapter therefore deals with the three stages.

Exhibit 8.2 The virtuous circle of performance improvement

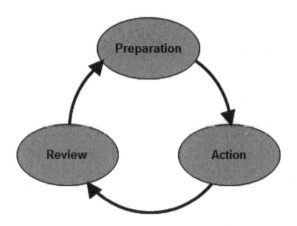

1. *Preparation*: the purposes of reporting to clients, deciding what to communicate and how.
2. *Action*: practical techniques for producing written documents and presentations.
3. *Review*: learning from experience.

PREPARATION

WHEN REPORTING IS REQUIRED

If there is a tomb to the unknown consultant, its headstone will be the contents page of a lovingly prepared and totally unread document. A client once complained: 'We did not want a report but the consultants appeared conditioned to produce a final tome.' Think carefully, then, whether a report is required to help the project along, or are you simply erecting a memorial for your own peace of mind? In some cases there is no discretion about whether a report is to be delivered, as when a client requires a written proposal, or the terms of reference for a project set out the timing of progress or other reports. Other circumstances in which a report should be considered are set out below.

There is something to report. Even on projects where there is no requirement for a project report it is worthwhile considering presenting a concluding review of progress. For example, in one case a consultant who had worked with a team of managers helping them — in an environment of considerable change — to redefine their objectives and roles, concluded the project with a paper that summarised what work had been done and what had been achieved.

Progress reports are an excellent mechanism for maintaining good client relations. Some projects may have progress meetings or reports scheduled as an integral part of the project plan, but even if this is not the case, they are worth considering as they can be used to:

- reassure the client that the project is proceeding well, even if there is nothing otherwise to report;
- engineer a meeting with the sponsor (the individual who commissioned the project) if the consultant is usually working with the sponsor's subordinates;
- provide a record of progress and a discipline for the operating consultant.

Position papers can provide a mechanism for thinking through a particular issue. The discipline of having to express a complex issue clearly to the client can help a project along.

For example, in a major study lasting more than a year, a number of independent outside consultants were seconded full time to the team and there were also inputs from specialist subcontractors. The output of the study was to be a single document (which ultimately ran to more than 2,000 pages!). Co-ordinating the various inputs and maintaining the necessary pace throughout the project were thus of major importance.

The project leader did this by getting the project team to submit a series of substantial position papers to the client, on subsidiary matters, throughout the course of the year. Not only was a series of milestones thereby created but also the means whereby the client could offer their own comments and contribution to the final product.

The difference between a position paper and a progress report is a nice but useful one. A position paper is a means of pursuing work-in-progress and perhaps airing a subject for debate. For example, a position paper during a strategic project might discuss the pros and cons of diversification into a particular business sector. It could serve as a mechanism for highlighting the issues critical to a decision on this matter as well as providing a means of eliciting the views and opinions of the key decision makers and influencers within the firm.

You can, however, fall prey to providing too many position papers.

> *On one particular assignment, which was on a part-time basis over many months, the consultant found himself volunteering to produce position papers more and more frequently, as this was the most convenient way of dealing with the client. The consequence was that he spent an increasing amount of time working on and revising position papers and less time with the client. This was a vicious circle: the client saw less of him and his contact became weakened; his papers became less attuned to the politics of the organisation and thus needed more time on revision. Eventually, the client terminated the project. The moral is: position papers are a means, not an end.*

The most common reports required of consultants, however, are *assignment or project reports*. These are produced at the end of a project, or perhaps at the end of a major stage of it. They are the documents which most new consultants (and often experienced ones) have greatest difficulty in writing. The emphasis on the project report is quite proper, however; often they are the only material manifestation of the work performed by the consultant and what the client has paid for. At the end of a project that has cost a lot in consultancy fees, the client needs to be presented with a document which does justice to that cost.

When to report using a presentation
The benefits of a presentation are:
- the personal contact enables two-way communication to take place; you cannot ask questions of a document;
- it allows you to invest the content with light and shade — you can emphasise important points in a way that is not possible in the written format;
- it allows you to bring the force of personality to the persuasion process — charisma if you like.

> *I would never have accepted the last point until an occasion when I lost my voice. I was running a series of one-week long*

courses for a particular client's managers, Monday to Friday. Arriving at my hotel one Sunday evening I found the cold I had had eventually caused me to lose my voice completely. I telephoned the colleagues who were sharing some of the sessions with me and told them (in a soft croak) of my difficulties.

They were not able to reschedule their sessions to the beginning of the week, so there I was, at 8.30am on the Monday morning with a new group of managers, about to start the course. Fortunately, the lecture room was equipped with a microphone through which I was huskily able to outline and start the management course. But I felt divested of power; it was not until then that I realised how much I depended on the use of my voice to project personality and hence to compel attention, to start to unfreeze course participants, to establish the right relationship between me and the managers, and the 101 other things that one has to do on a course, other than simply presenting the material, to make it work effectively. I got my voice back later in the week, but the course had one of the poorer ratings at the end of it.

Hence, consider using a presentation where you want:
- to be able to explain a complex topic;
- to provide the client with the chance to ask questions;
- to assess the client's reactions to what you are saying;
- to respond to the client's reaction by perhaps varying your approach.

PURPOSE

Having decided that a report is required, the first step is to clarify its purpose. Occasionally reports are to act as a source of reference only (e.g. the results of research, such as an opinion poll), but the majority of consultant reports are a means to an end — for example, to persuade a client to engage the consultant for a particular piece of work, or to accept particular recommendations as the result of a project.

This point is often overlooked by consultants — a report is meant to have some sort of effect within the client system. When considering the purpose, therefore, it is important to be clear about the nature of the effect the report is expected to have: how is the intervention of producing a report meant to advance the sales process (in the case of a proposal) or the progress of the project in which the consultants are engaged?

The report will be only part of a number of interventions in pursuit of these objectives. Indeed, in many instances, the report may be only a record of what has already been presented, discussed and agreed with the client.

In all cases, however, you must be clear about the purpose of this report: why is it being produced? What are the objectives it is intended to achieve and do they merit the investments of time and cost required?

Exhibit 8.3 shows the key aspects of thinking about purposes.

Exhibit 8.3 Purposes of a report

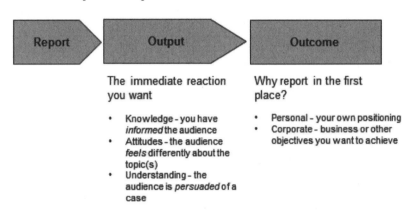

The Exhibit distinguishes between *outputs* and *outcomes*.

Outputs are the immediate results of the report. Typically they will comprise:

- knowledge — you have *informed* the audience;
- attitudes — the audience *feels* differently about the topic(s);
- understanding — the audience is *persuaded* of a case.

By contrast, outcomes are the longer-term effects of the report, which can typically be subsumed under:

- personal — your own positioning or that of your practice;
- corporate — business or other objectives you want to achieve.

It is always a good policy to start with thinking where you want ultimately to go before you plan how to get there. So in preparing a report ask yourself about the outcomes you want to achieve first.

You might, for example, choose to use a presentation:

- to introduce a new consultant to this client so that the client accepts him or her (so you might ask this colleague to take a key role in the presentation);
- to demonstrate personal insight and knowledge;
- to win further invitations to speak on the conference circuit.

At the start, therefore, it is worth reflecting on the purpose of the report. It is also worth bearing in mind that there are a host of other messages conveyed by a report — for example:

1. Its appearance: does the document look worthwhile?
2. Are the visual aids for the presentation well produced?
3. Its timeliness: (for example, if a proposal is delivered late, will this be a characteristic of consultant performance during delivery)?
4. The quality of the content: is it well presented and argued? Does it strike the right level and balance? Does it bring out the key issues? Does it add value to the client's views or merely reflect them?

These are features of all reports and help the client to form an impression of the quality of the consultant. Similarly, the astute consultant will manage these aspects carefully to give a favourable impression, particularly with proposals, when clients may have relatively little other evidence on which to form a judgement.

Ideally, you will have met at least one of the intended audience for the report; a useful technique is to prepare a report with an image in mind of a typical member of its audience. This has several advantages, in that it enables you:

- to take account of what the client knows or does not know already;
- to couch the report in language which is familiar to the client;
- to set the right level of treatment;
- to allow for particular sensibilities.

Having decided that a report is required, and what its purpose is, you should consider how much time it is going to take to create. A rule of thumb in creating a document is that from start to finish you should allow one day for each ten pages. This is obviously very approximate — some will be written far more quickly, whereas an inexperienced consultant may require much longer to produce a complex report to an acceptable standard.

Likewise, a good presentation is like an iceberg — the bit you see is supported by a vast amount of preparation you do not see. So do not stint on preparation. Almost certainly you will need to spend more time on preparation than the duration of the presentation; some consultants use a rule of thumb which allows an average preparation time three times the length of presentation. If the material is in readily presentable form (the contents of a report that has already been written, say) or the content is very familiar, then the time required will be less. On the other hand, the rule breaks down, in my experience, for short presentations; a first-class ten minute speech may take several hours to prepare!

Remember therefore to allow time for report preparation in a project plan or in preparing a proposal.

ORGANISING AND STRUCTURING THE MATERIAL
It may be that the content of your report is already determined. For example, if you are presenting a proposal, it may well be that the client has already been sent a copy of the document and the presentation is to highlight the key points and answer questions.

We will assume, however, that you are starting from scratch. What follows is a personal approach to creating a report; it works for me and I hope, perhaps with some adaptation, it may work for you.

Step 1: 'Brain dump'
Firstly, I make a lot of notes of my thoughts on what might go into the report. These thoughts are based not only on reflection but are also stimulated by reviewing relevant material, which might include earlier project reports (on this or other similar projects), the proposal (in the case of a project or progress report), previous progress reports, working papers and so on. The brain dump is not in any particular order — it is a series of notes without structure, of varying levels of detail and so on.

Step 2: Look for the outline structure
Having made these few pages (not too many) of notes, the next step is to look for an outline structure. Exhibit 8.4 shows the typical structure of some different types of document.

These, of course, are very general and the structure of every report has to suit the material being presented, but above all, the structure of the report must be logical and help the audience absorb what is being put across. A good structure will also make it easier for you to create the report. A report is a bit like a story and it is sometimes helpful to think of it as such. To this end there are some golden rules.

1. Start off with what the audience knows before moving on to what they do not know.
2. The report should lead the audience naturally to its conclusions or recommendations. You should imagine the audience nodding their head in agreement as the argument unfolds. It is a good idea to frame the recommendations first and then structure the rest of the report to lead naturally to those recommendations.
3. Put similar material together. Bearing in mind the content of most consultancy projects, reports are often about complex subjects. You can complicate understanding still further by mixing up all the topics. Two tips to help the audience, then:
   - Include in your introduction a few words about the structure and contents of the report;
   - A summary of the report at the beginning (i.e. a synopsis of the principal points, trends in the argument, main conclusions and recommendations) can provide the audience with a bird's eye view of the report. I think of the summary as a map with which the reader can find his or her way through the report.

I find it helpful to think of a road atlas in how a report should be structured. A road atlas will have route planning maps at the front: large scale maps that will allow an overview of a whole country in a page or two. Next follow the road maps, all at the same scale, which guide you from town to town. Then as appendices you have extremely large scale maps that are of towns and guide you through them. The road maps do not need to be at the same scale as the town maps; likewise, the appendices in a report go into detail on specific aspects.

In reviewing your notes consider whether the material fits any of the structures suggested in Exhibit 8.4 or whether an alternative structure might present the material better. Exhibit 8.5 shows some different ways of structuring a project report. In all cases, however, there should be a logic underlying the structure.

Exhibit 8.4 Typical contents of different types of report

Proposal

1. Introduction
2. Appreciation of present situation
3. Scope and objectives of the project
4. Method of approach
5. Programme of work required
6. Prospective benefits arising from the project
7. Resources required (from the client as well as the consultant)
8. Expected timescale and costs
9. Reasons for using us as your consultants in this project (including previous relevant experience)

Terms of business might be included as an appendix

Progress report

1. Progress (against forecast programme of work)
2. Significant achievements and problems
3. Points on which you wish to consult the client (e.g. issues for approval or decision)
4. Plans for the future

Project report (see also Exhibit 8.5)

1. Summary
2. Introduction
3. Findings
4. Discussion of and commentary on the findings
5. Recommendations
6. Appendices

Exhibit 8.5 Two alternative project report structures

Basis of division	Contents
By business structure (e.g. factory site, business division, or functional area) or topic	Introduction Topic 1: Findings, conclusions, recommendations Topic 2: Findings, conclusions, recommendations Topic 3: Findings, conclusions, recommendations Summary of key recommendations
By recommendation	Summary of recommendations Recommendation I: rationale leading to this Recommendation 2: rationale leading to this Recommendation 3: rationale leading to this Summary of key steps required for implementation

Step 3: Prepare a more detailed structure

Sometimes an outline structure is sufficient — I found it so for this chapter — but in dealing with a report you need to break the material down into convenient chunks. If the report is a big one, you will need to have sub-sections as well. Some ideas about the subsections will undoubtedly arise in preparing the outline sections; alternatively, the nature of the project may determine the structure. Exhibit 8.6 shows the contents of a report on management training and development in a multi-divisional company: each of the major sections is concerned with a separate business division, but is structured in broadly the same way as the others.

Other ways in which a project might determine the structure of a report are:

1. *Operational procedures:* Dick's report on stock control (using the example in earlier chapters) might follow production processes by dealing with raw materials, work-in-progress and finished goods separately.

2. *Project work packages:* for example a proposal for advice on the choice and installation of a new telephone system might cover:
    *   determining user requirements;
    *   defining selection criteria;
    *   review of suitable systems and method of choice;

Exhibit 8.6 Example contents of a project report

Executive Summary
Introduction
1.1 Background
1.2 Methodology
Overview of the group
Division one
3.1 Nature of the business
3.2 Development and training focus
3.3 Selection of recruits
3.4 Reduction of staff turnover
3.5 Sales training
3.6 Selection of managers
3.7 Manager training
4.   Division two
4.1 Nature of the business
4.2 Development and training focus
4.3 Professional staff utilisation
4.4 Commercial staff performance
4.5 Training management staff
5.   Division three
5.1 Nature of the business
5.2 Development and training focus
5.3 Making the new organisation effective
5.4 Management development system
6.   Summary of recommendations

- installation;
- commissioning.

3. *Conceptual framework:* a report on profit sharing-bonus could include sections on the key elements of how bonus is calculated, the operation of the scheme and how bonus should be distributed.

If all else has failed, think about your recommendations — how are they structured? This structure can be replicated earlier in the report. (And do not fall into the trap of starting to produce the report before you have decided what your principal recommendations are! You may hope that by the time you get to that section, they will emerge. But the preceding part of the report will be a mystery tour for the reader and simply demonstrate the confusion of your own thought processes.) So, if your report on a post-merger organisation concludes with recommendations for each function (marketing, production, etc.) then earlier parts of the report on findings and conclusions might be divided up into sections dealing with each function.

Step 4: Organise your material
So you now have your notes and a detailed structure. The next step is to organise your material under the headings you have chosen.

Here, the concept of the storyboard is useful.

With a large report, I allocate a half page to each subsection and rewrite the key points from my notes under each heading. With a shorter document I use the initial 'brain dump' and put a section number against each note so that I can pick up the relevant comments when I get to the appropriate section.

Most frequently, however, I use a single sheet of paper to produce a 'storyboard'. I divide it into eight sections and allocate material to the main headings. (I use more sheets of paper if there are more than eight sections.) I find this technique particularly helpful with preparing presentations. Exhibit 8.7 shows the storyboard for a progress review presentation I made recently to a client.

Word-processing packages often have an 'outliner' facility, which enables you to organise material on screen. But whether you use pen and paper or a computer, allocating the material under headings is essential in preparing a report for two reasons. The first is that it enables you to test out the structure. If you find it difficult to allocate material to different subsections, it may mean the structure is not quite right. This is the time for fine tuning.

The second reason is if anything, more important: you are taking decisions on the content of the report — what it is to convey.

Exhibit 8.7 Example of a storyboard

1. Opening 'Rendezvous' – recap on the original objectives of the project and the key design features	5. Propose a project structure that would support the achievement of these objectives
2. Review the project to date – show that we have been very successful in the work that we have done so far	6. Indicate the nature of the support that we could give, and how much it might cost
3. Recap on our perception of the changes in their circumstances that have occurred since we started	*7. Closing* Summarise key points and what the next steps are that we propose
4. Set out what we see to be the new priorities that need to be pursued	

At this point, pause:

Have you really thought through the contents of your report?

The problems of report preparation stem primarily from lack of clarity of thought. So, for a project report, for example:

- Will the report satisfactorily meet the terms of reference (you should refer back to the original proposal)?
- Are you identifying and addressing the really important relevant issues (which may only partially be covered by the terms of reference)?
- Are your recommendations sound? Do they follow from your assessment of the situation? Do they make sense (ask a colleague) and are the priorities balanced correctly? Are they feasible — what is sound for one enterprise may be impossible in another?

Do not gloss over these points of self-examination; a little time invested here can save time later. Too often, however, this point is acknowledged only after bitter experience, having failed to do it.

Step 5: Decide what is to go into the report

The last stage is about deciding what is to go into the report — and what is not. Sometimes there is some confusion between a report and a record; a former colleague of mine had not made the distinction and as a result his reports were diffuse and full of extraneous details. They became a lot better once he used the report as a means of conveying selected information rather than a total record. (And should he have wanted to record details, these could have been confined to appendices in the report).

What must not be put in a written document is material that should not be committed to paper. This in particular covers criticisms of individuals; remember that, almost certainly, people other than the intended recipients will have access to your report in the client organisation.

It is also important that there is a homogeneous level of detail in the report; it would be inconsistent in a report on corporate strategy to deal with details of canteen menus (and vice versa). Similarly, the nature of the reader for whom you are writing should be consistent throughout in terms of assumed knowledge and the level of treatment of the subject.

In a written document, the appendix is a useful way of dealing with details. In deciding whether material should be in the body of a report or in an appendix, consider, does the reader need to study these facts now, or can they be taken on trust for the time being? If they can be left, then they are material for an appendix. For example, statistical tables may be summarised in the text to support the main conclusions with the full data reproduced in appendices. On the other hand, do not condemn all supporting information to the appendices; it is very irritating to have to turn continually from the body of a document to refer to a table in an appendix.

By the end of this step you should have completed the preparation for your report. You should have decided on its major divisions and sub-divisions and the main points you will make in each.

It may seem that the preparation outlined above is laborious; so it may be, but it is not unduly time-consuming and can save a lot of time later. It can be completed in an hour or so for short reports and even for major reports I have found it rarely takes more than a day. It is brief compared with actually writing a report, because writing entails not only considering what to say but also how to say it. Deciding how to express a particular point well can be time-consuming and is time wasted if the point does not merit inclusion in the report.

Inexperienced consultants (and experienced ones too) may find the completion of the preparation stage a good point at which to discuss the structure and content of their report with a colleague.

After this comes the time-consuming part — expressing your thoughts in writing.

WRITING REPORTS

By the end of the preparation stage — organising and structuring the material — you should have decided what it is you want to put across and in what order you are going to do it. In this section we consider written reports. This is not a book about style or grammar (there are plenty of books about those) but there are some important points for consultants to consider in expressing themselves on paper.

IS THERE A CONSULTANCY STYLE OF WRITING?
Inexperienced consultants sometimes think there is a particular style of expression that they should use when writing as a consultant. I have come across reports constructed to include a particular turn of phrase because the writer considers it compelling. But the rule is, write to express, not to impress.

If there is a consultancy style of writing, it is a style of great clarity. The task of a consultant in communicating with clients is to clarify rather than to obscure.

As with all communication, writing has to be attuned to the receiver; this does not mean that it must be written in the same way that the client would write it, but it must be comprehensible if it is to serve any purpose. It can be useful therefore to have in mind the person who is going to read it.

By way of example, Exhibit 8.8 illustrates alternative section headings for the same report, geared to different audiences. The first is perhaps more suited to a staid, traditional organisation; the second style might appeal to more radical clients.

PHRASEOLOGY AND EXPRESSION
These ought to be controlled to reinforce the message. It does not always do to call a spade a spade. I have even come across a client who, in effect, said, 'We recognise our performance in this area as appalling; we don't need you

Exhibit 8.8 Alternative titles

A study of the feasibility of introducing a performance appraisal system	Performance appraisal: a management priority
1. Introduction	1. A history of impoverished performance management
2. Findings of this study 2.1 The need for performance appraisal 2.2 The acceptability of a formal appraisal system 2.3 The design of the system	2. Views of the executives 2.1 We need to manage our people better 2.2 We don't like appraisal but we ought to do it 2.3 Use appraisal for taking salary and development decisions
3. Recommendations 3.1 Design of a new system 3.2 Implementation plan	3. The way ahead 3.1 Introduce a new appraisal system 3.2 Do it now

to tell us this and we do not wish to see a report cataloguing our failures. We are confident in your judgement and want only your recommendations.'

I have always tried to use a delicacy of phrasing when referring to a client's deficiencies — part of the skills of regarding a half-empty bottle as being half-full. (Although a cynic has commented that a consultant would never say this, but conclude that the bottle was twice as large as it should be.) So, instead of weaknesses, one refers to 'areas where there is scope for improvement'. Weasel words, perhaps, but ones which convey the same meaning without loss of face for the client.

On the other hand, there are a few clients who take an almost masochistic pleasure in being told how awful they are.

LANGUAGE

Language — the words that you use in writing — must be used well. Short words are preferable to long, if they are equivalent, but use the language which comes most easily to you. It is probably easier to get the points down on paper first, in a way which you find comfortable, and subsequently check that the language is clear and simple, rather than strain for a different writing style. Practice should aid improvement.

Exhibit 8.9 shows the well-known formula to determine the so-called 'fog factor' in writing. What this shows is that the more words used on average per sentence and the longer the words used, the more difficult it is to comprehend what has been written.

Exhibit 8.9 Fog factor

An empirical formula used to assess the complexity of writing measures, the so-called 'fog factor' of a piece of writing: $Y = 0.4$ times $(W + X)$ where: $Y =$ number of years of full-time education required to comprehend the writing. $W =$ average number of words of three or more syllables in a sentence. $X =$ average number of words in a sentence.

Every business, industry, or profession has its own language to describe specialist aspects of it; this jargon (and I am using the word in this particular sense) is helpful to those in the know but can be unintelligible to the outsider. It would be laborious to have to express everything in layman's terms — just imagine how difficult hospital doctors would find discussion without using the specialist terms they are taught. I therefore do not believe that the use of jargon is a bad thing.

Indeed, for consultants one of the signs of proficiency in a business sector is that they learn its jargon, and can therefore use it with their clients. The use of jargon is wrong when it does not apply to the client's business and particularly when it is used as a smokescreen to try to impress. Fortunately, most clients have the sense to cry 'Foul!' in the latter case and the consultant should learn the lesson.

Finally, on the subject of language, there is the use of verbs in the active or passive voice; the difference is illustrated below:

* Active: 'We carried out a survey';
* Passive: 'A survey was carried out'.

Those with a scientific schooling will have been strongly influenced to use the passive voice ('a test tube was taken ...') in reporting their experiments, but the constant use of the passive voice makes for dull reading. Exhibit 8.10 illustrates the same passage written wholly in the passive and active voices.

Exhibit 8.10 Active and passive voices

Passive: 'At the start a survey was carried out. Respondents were asked to complete a questionnaire. Key features of the product were listed in the questionnaire and had to be placed in order of attractiveness by respondents. Design and colour were considered most important.'

Active: 'At the start we carried out a survey and asked respondents to complete a questionnaire. We asked them to place key features of the product, listed in the questionnaire, in order of attractiveness. Respondents considered design and colour most important.'

A feature of the passive voice is that it is impersonal — 'a survey was carried out' — we need not say by whom. Conversely, the active voice is personal — we need to say who carried out a survey.

Normally, this is dealt with by using 'we', even when a single individual only was involved with the work. The danger then is too many 'wes' — we this, we that, etc. So a balance between active and passive voices is desirable.

THE USE OF ILLUSTRATIONS

Although a cliché, a picture can tell a thousand words. So it is worthwhile thinking how you can illustrate the points you are making in a report. There is a host of ways of doing this, but remember that illustrations are meant to help rather than hinder understanding. The most frequent cause of the latter is presenting too much information or irrelevant data. The key question is, 'Does this illustrate the point I am making, simply and clearly?'

Illustrations are often used to make qualitative points — to show trends, relative sizes or relationships — and thus great precision is not required. A *bête noire* of mine is the use of numbers to six significant figures — rarely needed — and even more heinous is to derive those figures from ones that are not as accurate themselves. (For example the average of 55, 57 and 58 is better presented as 56½ or 56.7; 56.6667 implies accuracy to the fourth decimal place, which may not be true at all.)

REVISION

When you have written the report, read it through. This is not just to check grammar and spelling; it is also sensible, metaphorically, to step back to examine your handiwork. Provided the preparation has been done well the contents should cover the topics that need to be addressed, but revision should include cutting verbiage, and simplifying wording. Above all, ensure that you have expressed simply and clearly what you are trying to convey in your report.

REPORT PRODUCTION

As part of a consultant induction training course, I used to run a business appraisal case study, which required consultants to prepare a project plan for a hypothetical project. Without fail, they always forgot to include the time for producing the final project report in their plans.

It is as well to remember that there are several stages between completing the final report and its delivery to the client:

- Typing, if it is not already in soft copy format;
- Proof reading and correction;
- Quality assurance;
- Amendments and approval;
- Preparation of final version;
- Printing and binding if it is to be delivered in hard copy.

So the first important lesson about report production is that it needs time, and sufficient time should be allowed for it.

The list above also shows quality assurance and it is vital that this happens — at the very least on the physical production of the report. So it is worthwhile asking a colleague to read through the report for typing errors and for comprehension. A consultant close to a particular problem can easily fall into the trap of believing that others will see things as they do. The consequence could be passages in a report which are at best ambiguous or at worst incomprehensible or libellous. A colleague who has some understanding of what you are writing about should be able to point these out. If you are a sole practitioner it is still worth getting someone — your partner or a professional colleague — to help out if at all feasible.

In large firms, quality assurance may go beyond this, covering the structure, content and writing in the report as well as its presentation. If this is the case, it is sensible to start the quality assurance process before setting pen to paper — get agreement to the structure and content of the report in principle before writing it. Alterations at an early stage are far easier to accommodate and less time-consuming than attempts to recast the 'finished' product.

Finally, there is the question of presentation of the document itself. Quite a lot of expense may be justified in the case of a project report, which may be the only tangible evidence of the work the consultant has done.

Large consulting practices may have a house style — a typeface, paragraph numbering, report covers and so on which are standard. Small firms or sole practitioners may have a de facto house style. In any case, I would suggest the following priorities for production of a project report.

1. The content of the report: irrespective of how glossy the report is, if the content is obviously poor, then you have failed.
2. The editing of the report: it should be laid out well and free from typographical errors.
3. It should not be delivered late. The delivery of a report is a very clear manifestation of the performance of a consultant, and late delivery counts against you.
4. Packaging and presentation: a good typeface, and high-quality paper (not an obvious photocopy), robustly bound and with an attractive cover can help a lot.

A note on draft reports

All written material presented to a client must be of satisfactory quality. There can be no compromise.

A pitfall for the new consultant is the so-called 'draft' report. A consultant might submit a substandard draft report to a client in the expectation that he will then subsequently have the chance to amend and upgrade it before issuing a final version. If, however, the client accepts the draft, the consultant will have delivered a product which is substandard. The use of the heading 'draft' on a report is to allow a client the opportunity to make an input — for example, by suggesting more persuasive ways of presenting recommendations. From the consultant's view it should be able to stand as a finished product.

MAKING PRESENTATIONS

One of the best presentations I have ever seen was during a training course for consultants. Each had to make a five-minute presentation on the subject of his choice. Gerald's was on the economic cycles following decolonisation in Africa — an impossibly large subject to tackle in the time. He illustrated his talk with sheets of scrappy flip-chart paper spread round the room; his delivery was a sustained gabble; his language was from a political stance slightly right of the Daily Telegraph. Despite these

apparent offences against the 'rules' of presentation, his was a
tour de force, which I remember years after the event.

Why does this presentation stick in my mind? Despite breaking the rules of presentation it had style, it was informative and humorous. It kept our interest and was memorable, and this style was appropriate for the occasion — a training course, when many of the other presentations were simply worthy. So, despite the apparent breaking of the rules, it achieved the main objectives of a presentation.

Of all the topics in this book, making presentations — public speaking — is therefore the one about which it is least advisable to be doctrinaire. Part of the art is entertainment and stage management: the aim is to attract and retain the interest of an audience for a period of time and leave it with a favourable impression. As with entertainment, there is scope for considerable variation in making presentations, and it is a mistake to force people into the wrong style of presentations. I remember one individual whom I persuaded to use very conservative slides for a presentation. The next time I saw him present he used his own highly-stylised slides: not only were the slides better but they also improved his presentation and it was far more memorable.

So, regard this section as a primer only. It will not teach you to make brilliant presentations, but it should provide a guide to making satisfactory ones and help you to avoid the more dangerous pitfalls. With growing confidence and experience you will be able to decide which techniques are most helpful — and which to disregard — in your own presentations.

PRESENTATIONS V DOCUMENTS

The main difference between presentations and written reports lies in the capacity of the audience to absorb what is being presented. Harold Macmillan was disappointed with the reception his maiden speech received in the House of Commons when, as he commented to a fellow member, he had included 14 good points in it. He was told that any good parliamentary speech would have only one point in it if it was to have any impact.

It is difficult to follow this dictum as consultants, but the principle remains that it is generally more difficult for an audience to absorb orally presented information than written; similarly, most people retain what they see rather better than what they hear.

Chapter 10 deals with designing and presenting training sessions and workshops. The reason for segregating these as a special form of presentation is because presenters usually have far more freedom in determining structure, timing and so on than in other types of presentation, and can control these to their advantage.

The importance of presentations to management consultants is that their business success can depend on how well they are done. The most significant occasions when a consultant needs to make a presentation in this context are a sales presentation at the beginning of a project, and a concluding project presentation.

In both cases, the object is that the client will accept the consultant's recommendations: to proceed with the project using the consultant's support (in the sales presentation) or to proceed with the next stage of work (in a concluding presentation).

Presentations may also be needed during the course of a project for disseminating information, reporting progress, and so on. In all cases the client will be influenced not only by the validity of the consultant's arguments, but also by the quality of the presentation. It is essential therefore that a consultant learns the mechanics of making good presentations at an early stage. What makes for good presentations?

Exhibit 8.11 sets out the questions that presenters need to ask.

SPECIFICATION

There are three elements to specification: purpose (which has already been dealt with under preparation); format; and constraints.

Format

Format relates to the type and formality of the event.

The first thing is to understand the nature of the event. Large audiences make for more formal occasions. The conference presentation to 250 delegates has to be different from the boardroom presentation to three directors. The size of the audience determines the nature and extent of the interaction you can have with each individual — for example, on the simple matter of eye contact. It is a good thing to establish eye contact with individuals in the audience but with an audience of 250, all you can do is let your eyes range over them.

Exhibit 8.11 Some initial questions to ask

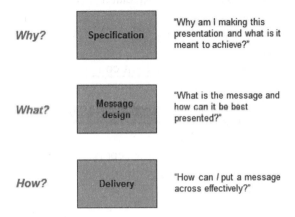

Why?	Specification	"Why am I making this presentation and what is it meant to achieve?"
What?	Message design	"What is the message and how can it be best presented?"
How?	Delivery	"How can *I* put a message across effectively?"

The larger the audience, the more inhibited most people will feel about asking questions or making points from the floor (leaving aside hecklers at political meetings!). Although you have greater control as a presenter, the amount of two-way communication will be very limited. The size of the audience will therefore condition the form of the presentation.

There is a range of different types of presentation events — both social and working — as illustrated in Exhibit 8.12.

Exhibit 8.12 Freedom of presenter to define content

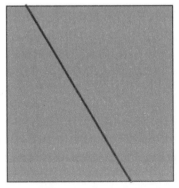

Presenter orientated

- After dinner speech
- Lecture
- Formal presentation
- Informal presentation
- Discussion in workshop
- Everyday conversation
- Questions after a presentation
- "Any questions" panel session
- Interview

Audience orientated

This shows the power of the presenter to define the content of the presentation. For example, an after-dinner speaker may not normally expect any questions, so can plan exactly what they are going to say. At the other end of the spectrum, if you are interviewed by a journalist, you may have a general idea of what is going to be asked but no control over the details.

It also shows the proportion of time you are expected to speak continuously without interruption and the degree of control you have over the content.

In a presenter-orientated event, the onus is on the presenter to keep things going; an audience-orientated one is much more at the dictate of the audience, perhaps under a chairman, as exemplified by a panel session in which the presenter must respond to the audience's questions.

Working at either extreme of the scale is difficult; a lecture may require careful and extensive preparation for fluency but, equally, responding to questions needs the ability to put your thoughts in order very rapidly and to be able to express them well immediately.

The middle of the scale is easiest — everyday conversation in which we all engage — so if you have any control over form then it is worth pushing the form of the presentation towards the centre of the scale where it is easiest to operate. Many presenters do this instinctively; for example, the management trainer may choose to have a participative discussion session on — say — 'skills of recruitment interviewing' rather than deliver a lecture.

Constraints

There is rarely complete freedom in making presentations, so before beginning to prepare your presentation, it is worthwhile thinking about the constraints and how you can work effectively within them. The different types of constraint are illustrated in Exhibit 8.13.

Exhibit 8.13 Presentation constraints

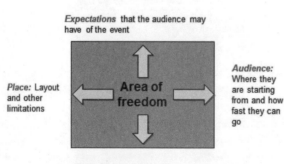

Expectations

Consultants' presentations are usually subject to the expectations of the intended audience — often a client. Expectations may be partly logistical — e.g. what time the presentation will start, how long it will last, the supporting documentation — and partly to do with the presentation itself — its purpose, content, form and so on.

Of course, some presenters engage their audience's attention by deliberately not meeting their expectations. It is probably unwise to contravene logistical expectations (no point arriving on the wrong day or speaking for three hours when only half an hour was required) but you perhaps have rather more latitude as far as the content and delivery of the presentation are concerned. Even so, consultants have less freedom than others. (Once I heard a certain member of the House of Lords speak after dinner and he gave an amusing account of life in the Upper House. Six months later I heard him again, when he was billed to discuss the attitude of central Government to a particular aspect of business. He gave the same speech as before and it was equally well received.)

Audience

As mentioned already, it is useful to have an image of a typical member of the audience in mind when thinking about the content of a presentation. Points you might consider are:

- What do they know already?
- What will they understand easily? (This is particularly important not only in terms of their education, but also when working with audiences whose first language is not English.)
- What is their frame of mind likely to be when they enter the room?

The answers to these questions will help in deciding where you should start, how fast you can go, and the style with which you conduct the presentation.

Time of day and duration

It is curious that after lunch or dinner are regarded as appropriate times for speechmaking but are avoided by formal presenters. Maybe that is because the average presenter, assisted by audio-visual gadgetry, is not half as interesting as a good after-dinner speaker.

Sometimes scheduling a presentation at an unusual time may cause interest. Breakfast meetings are not unknown but the only time I have been invited to make a presentation at midnight was to a team of nightshift workers.

If you want to limit the amount of time spent on discussion (in circumstances when discussion might expand to fill the time available) you could schedule the presentation to start in the necessary time before lunch or finishing work for the day.

A frequent question is, if involved in presenting a proposal for new work in competition with other firms, is there any advantage in presenting first or last? The advice of an experienced (and successful) consultancy salesperson to me was, 'Don't be first. Aim for last, but avoid the end of the day.'

My own view is that there are pros and cons to each. The first presenter catches the audience at their freshest and can also have a high impact. On the other hand, being the last presentation means that the audience has a clear idea of the questions to be answered, which they may not have asked the first presenter.[2], Other factors, however, such as the quality of the proposal, its presentation and the rapport struck between consultant and prospective client will probably influence the outcome far more than the timing of the presentation.

Ideally you should be able to have the time you require to make a presentation (and you should guide your client on the amount of time you may need) but often you will have to present within a given timetable. For example, if competitive presentations of bids for a particular project are scheduled at 90-minute intervals you will need to work within this limit. If no timescale is given, it is worth a telephone call in advance to find out what is expected. If presenting to a board of directors, say, it is likely that your sponsor will know the amount of time to be put aside for the presentation. If no time limit has been proposed, you will have to work to your own timetable. My experience is that presentations of proposals for prospective work usually last between one and two hours, but could be much shorter if the purpose is simply to meet the operating team. Progress reviews can vary considerably in duration, as can the presentation of recommendations at the end of a project. In these latter cases, the length of the presentation has to be determined by the material you are trying to put across.

---

2   In a study of parole reviews among judges conducted in Israel, reported in 2012, it was noted that the rate at which parole was granted fell during the course of a morning, went up again after the judges returned from lunch, and then fell again during the afternoon. Extending this to the judgement of buyers, it would therefore seem to be best to be on first thing in the morning or afternoon – provided the panel has been given lunch! (Reported in Kahneman, 2011).

Allow time for questions and discussions as well as your delivery. Remember, too, that the audience will lose interest if a speaker goes on a long time without interruption, so interspersing your presentation with opportunities for audience participation can be a good way of breaking it up.

Some clients take a while to get organised. It is not unusual to go to a client's office and have to wait 15 minutes whilst the audience is rounded up. This does have its advantages — it gives you a chance to familiarise yourself with and relax in the surroundings where you are to make the presentation and to get your notes, visual aids, etc. organised. You can also be introduced to the audience as they arrive. So, though tardiness on the part of the audience can be irritating, it can have its advantages over walking into a strange room, facing a sea of expectant and unknown faces and having to jump straight into a presentation.

Layout and other limitations
You will rarely find yourself presenting in the ideal setting. When speaking at a conference, with luck you will have good facilities but when presenting on a client's premises the chances are that you will present in an office or meeting room. You will have to make the best of it. There may be little flexibility in arranging where people sit and the scope for visual aids will probably be limited.

Every consultant has their own particular horror stories about disasters with visual aids; almost everybody has suffered because a projector failed and there was no spare. One of mine was the occasion many years ago when we were bidding for a particular project and had some 35mm slides prepared at short notice (and great expense) to illustrate our presentation. We were assured that a 35mm projector would be available at the hotel where the presentation was to be made. To be on the safe side, however, we decided to take a projector of our own too. As we went to the taxi, laden down with briefcases, slides and projector, we took a last-minute decision not to take our projector. Needless to say, the one promised was not available and our presentation therefore suffered. So with media, remember Murphy's law — if anything can go wrong, it will.

MESSAGE DESIGN
Some general guidance on what is to go into a report has been given earlier in this chapter, but there are additional factors to be considered for presentations.

A sound structure is vital for a good presentation. Bearing in mind the difficulties of oral as opposed to visual communication, good structure is even more important to a presentation than it is to a written document. It is like telling a story, and the reason structure is so important is that, unlike a report in which a reader can flick back to check a point or re-read something they have found difficult to understand the first time, a presentation is in 'real time'. (As someone said, 'A book allows immediate action replay'.) Once you lose the comprehension of your audience, you will have lost their interest. So it is important to start off from what they know or can reasonably be expected to know and develop from there.

An old adage is, 'Tell them what you're going to say, say it, and then tell them what you've said'. There is some merit in this advice if used carefully; presentations should seem natural rather than overly prepared and an undue emphasis on technical structure detracts from professionalism.

> *A former colleague of mine suffered from this; his presentations were faultless — and boring. They were carefully structured and meticulously prepared but they were tedious. What had happened was that he had effectively removed any imprint of his own personality from the presentations, so they were lifeless. On the other hand, there are entertainers who can make a recitation of the London telephone directory exciting.*

These reservations notwithstanding, the adage does remind us that presentations have a beginning, middle and an end. For the time being I will concentrate on these and then come back to opening and closing presentations.

The beginning

At the start of a presentation it is worth making some allusion to what is to come. I often do this by using a slide of the structure of the presentation — for example the topics to be covered.

It is sometimes helpful for the listener if you recap where you have got to in the presentation between major topics, so you might show this slide again between sections.

Another major function of the beginning is to bring everybody to the same starting point. How you do this depends on the audience and purpose of the presentation. If, for example, you are reporting progress to a client whom you see routinely, the nature of the introduction will be different from a sales presentation to a group of strangers.

Finally, your introduction should make clear the ground rules for the audience. Are you expecting them to participate, interrupt, ask questions, keep silent until permitted to speak, or what? You can deal with this by explaining how you wish to handle questions.

The choices are:

- As you go along;
- At the end of each section;
- At the end of the presentation.

Which you pick depends on the circumstances. For example, if there is the risk that questions simply anticipate material to come, then it might be sensible to defer them. Allowing questions as you go through helps comprehension better, but has the risk of disruption; it can play havoc with time management as it can be very difficult to keep questions and answers within the time allowed.

Much also happens in terms of group dynamics at the start of a presentation, and this is covered under 'opening and closing', below.

The middle

The middle of the presentation is its core. Structure here applies both to selecting the content and to the order in which it is delivered.

The best way of structuring the delivery of a presentation is as a story.

A novelist does not introduce significant characters without at some stage explaining (or at least enabling the reader to infer) who they are and their relevance. The writer of whodunits would get short shrift from readers if, on the last page, the culprit was a character unmentioned before. The same principle applies to a presentation: the audience must understand not only what you are saying, but also why you are saying it and what they are to make of it.

The conference presentation is often akin to a lecture; there is usually a continuous presentation from the speaker rather than one punctuated by interruptions and questions. The presentation must again be logical. In many respects the conference presentation demands even more care than the others: you know less about the audience — they are likely to have varied starting points of interest, knowledge and ability — and you are less likely to get feedback on the clarity and quality of your presentation, as questions may be less forthcoming.

The end

The end of the presentation is often used to recap on what has been said and in particular to re-emphasise the main points made. The end of the presentation will have more impact than the middle (and sometimes adroit speakers claim attention by indicating the talk is about to finish, by phrases such as, 'Finally, then . . .'). If there has been some discussion during the course of the presentation, a skilled presenter may include some relevant points arising from it in the conclusion.

Do not neglect the end of a presentation. The whole presentation can be thought of as being like a piece of orchestral music, with an introduction, middle and end. An orchestral piece does not simply fade out — it has a clear and deliberate end. It may even have a grand finale!

Preparing visual aids

You will notice that we have assumed the use of visual aids in a presentation. Research shows that people learn better if you use a visual channel as well as an aural channel to communicate.

But there is one vital thing to remember — that visual aids are meant to be *aids*. Too often presentations are supported by visual handicaps! Most visual aids used are screen projections and the common failings of these are lack of visibility — the audience is not able to read what is on the screen — and too much information being compressed on a single slide. Make sure that the headings on your slides are meaningful, like newspaper headlines. Ideally, members of the audience should be able to follow your narrative if they read only the headings on your slides.

Worse still is the poor use of visual aids, where they are simply the speaker's notes rendered as a series of bullet points. Remember that visual aids are meant to support and illustrate what the speaker is saying.

Having said this, it would be nice to think that presentations are prepared in a totally logical order; in practice, however, the process is iterative, as shown in Exhibit 8.14.

Exhibit 8.14 The process of preparation

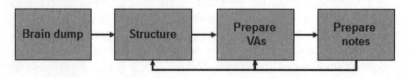

What this shows is that during the course of preparation other ideas may emerge which affect earlier stages. Indeed, for presentations which are repeated (as in a training course) there will be further refinement following the delivery of the first one or two presentations, and indeed continual fine tuning thereafter.

In theory you should decide what you want to say then decide which bits need illustrating. Some people may even prepare good presentations like this; but the practical fact is that consultants are working under time pressure and have to take a few short cuts.

One such is to prepare the visual aids first based on your storyboard and use them as a framework. Indeed, it is good practice to ensure that if you are using PowerPoint, say, you prepare slide headings that tell the story of the presentation rather than simply being titles for each slide.

You can use hard copies of the visual aids as a basis for speaker's notes by annotating them with the comments you wish to make about each. Do not do the reverse, however, reproducing your notes as visual aids — the only person they will be aiding is you!

Preparing what to say
Speakers' practice varies from using no notes at all to using a complete script. Which you choose will depend on the circumstances and your own personal preferences.

The circumstances influencing the choice of detail on notes are:
- The formality of the occasion: if you are making a speech, for example, which is likely to be recorded or widely quoted, you may prefer to use a script or detailed notes. Unless you are very skilled, however, a full script means gaining precision at the expense of spontaneity. Rarely is the trade-off worthwhile. Consultants often use brief headings as a prompt — it is rare to need a detailed script or (in a client presentation) to use no notes at all. (Although, the appearance of using no notes at all can be given if the visual aids can be used as a prompt.)
- Co-ordination with visual aids: it may be necessary to work on cues if control of the visual aids is not in the hands of the speaker; this can be better done by using a script.
- The lighting: in the days of slide projections, I once had to make an internal presentation at short notice to substitute for one of my colleagues. I wasn't prepared for the lecture room to be cast in

darkness so the slides could be seen; the result was that I couldn't see my notes — I had to make the presentation from memory!

Personal preference will depend on:
- Familiarity with the material: you may make a presentation on a particular topic on more than one occasion and, although the context may be different, as you gain greater familiarity with the material you will need less extensive notes on later occasions.
- Your experience and confidence in making presentations. Less experienced or less confident presenters may prefer more extensive notes. A word of warning, however: spoken language is not the same as written, and good expression on paper does not sound so compelling when spoken.
- Your fluency: some individuals have great skill in speaking to few notes — others need more prompts. At the other end of the scale, there is the need to have a certain acting ability to impart life to a full script.

The use of humour
The person who makes a living telling jokes is called a comedian. Unless you are a comedian, there is no need to make a presentation entertaining by telling jokes. Humour, however, is quite different from telling jokes, and it is more appropriate to consider the use of wit.

A good rule is that if you cannot think of something humorous to say, then don't say it. In a presentation you are presenting something of yourself, and an audience is quick to spot someone who is attempting to be something different from what they truly are. So, if it is in your nature and ability to tell a good joke, then you can do that in a presentation; if you are not a natural humourist, it will stick out like a sore thumb and your audience will be embarrassed to have to respond to a poorly told joke. (All of us have been part of an audience on some occasion when this has happened, so we know how embarrassing it can be.)

The subjects about which to be humorous need to be chosen carefully. The presenter has the privilege of the attention of an audience and has an advantage over them. The poor use of humour abuses that privilege, and tempts the reaction, 'Why do we have to waste time listening to this?' So humour should at most be a leavening to the presentation, not a major part of its content.

Opening and closing

The opening and closing of a presentation have particular features unrelated to content.

The opening is the most important; it is the point at which the audience is forming an impression of the speaker, which will affect their reception of the content of the presentation. It is important therefore to be in control of this process.

The first thing to consider is your appearance — what you wear and your grooming. It is not unlike a job interview, when again you are trying to create a favourable initial impression. As a consultant, you need to look smart and business-like. It is a debatable question what you should wear: it is not always a good idea to dress as your clients do, because they don't expect you to look like them; they expect you to look the part of a consultant.

Next, remember that the audience is assessing you, and thus may not be paying as much attention at the start of the presentation as later on. It therefore pays to start at a slower pace and increase as you go on. It also makes sense to defer getting right into your presentation at the start; it is better to concentrate on putting the audience at their ease and arousing their interest. Many speakers do this by introducing their presentations with a relevant anecdote or story.

Some presenters do the opposite of making the audience relaxed. I attended a conference at which a noted QC and parliamentarian began by asking delegates questions in a very aggressive fashion. His questions were akin to a cross-examination, and good answers were awarded a House of Commons key ring. He kept everyone's attention, it was instructive and entertaining, but it would be untrue to call his session relaxing!

Closing is important because it leaves a final impression with the audience. It does not have to be a climax, but the most common difficulty of inexperienced presenters — especially at conferences — is running out of time. This can give the appearance of a hasty or ill-thought-out end to the presentation. It is as well, therefore, to pace yourself through the presentation — to have some idea of at what point you should have half your time allocation left, and so on. (Pacing is far more difficult during an informal presentation when questions may interrupt and disturb your own time schedule.)

To this end when preparing your speaker's notes it is useful to divide your material as follows:

1. Must include: vital to the argument.
2. Should include: important supporting material.

3. Could include: useful padding (e.g. humour or anecdotes) but
                       no harm if not included.
If you are running out of time, you can then concentrate on the 'must' items.

Rehearsal
In theory, all presentations should be rehearsed; in practice, time has a measurable cost to consultants and therefore the practical opportunity for rehearsal will often be limited. Exhibit 8.15 suggests a rule of thumb to decide whether to rehearse or not.

There are different degrees of rehearsal and the most comprehensive is the dress rehearsal when the presentation is made as it will be 'on the day'. Dress rehearsal is <u>vital</u> for an important presentation with inexperienced presenters, and is <u>desirable</u> in all cases where the presenters are not experienced.

Experienced presenters, however, are less likely to need a rehearsal, but on important occasions a 'walk-through' rehearsal is useful. This checks the stage management and is particularly helpful on those occasions when a team is presenting. During the walk through, you can agree on the programme and how questions will be handled, ensure that visual aids are used consistently and so on; i.e. make sure that the details run smoothly.

Exhibit 8.15 When to rehearse

	Low	High
High	Don't bother	"Walk through" rehearsal
Low	Rehearse if time	Vital to rehearse fully

Experience of presenters

Importance of presentation

In rehearsals of all presentations you should check:
*   timing: not only the duration of the whole thing, but the balance between sections too — remember that presentations almost always take longer on the day than in rehearsal;
*   the visual aids: they are available, work and can be seen;
*   continuity: between the sections of your own presentation or those of colleagues, if presenting in a team.

If you are rehearsing a presentation, it is as well to do it with an audience. An audience helps to supply a degree of realism (which mirrors the real thing) and they can often make helpful suggestions afterwards for improvements.

DELIVERING PRESENTATIONS

You have prepared what you are going to say and rehearsed it. The great day (or, more likely in the case of a consultant, the day) has arrived: what now?

Whether you like it or not, presentations are a form of entertainment; on the day you have to think about stage management and performance.

Stage management

Stage management is visible only when something goes wrong. At the theatre, stage management goes unnoticed unless the safety curtain refuses to rise, the lights fail or some similar disaster strikes. The same applies to presentations: the horror stories told by consultants almost invariably involve some failure of stage management. It is very evident if a projector breaks down or you arrive late. So what follows is a checklist covering points of stage management before and on the day.

Before the day:

- Be sure you know where the presentation is to be held, when and for how long.
- Ensure that any equipment you need (projectors, etc.) is available if being supplied by the client. With projectors, also remember you need a screen (not always remembered by the client's staff). If you are taking your own equipment, you can be sure that if you do not take an extension electric cable, the one on your projector will not reach the electric point. And if presenting in a different country, make sure a plug socket adaptor is available.
- Check how many people are coming; this will affect the number of handouts required (if you are using them) as well as the form of the presentation.

On the day:

1. Arrive early. This allows time to organise yourself and visit the toilet.
2. Try to get to the presentation venue before the audience (not always possible, particularly if the presentation is at a conference). This will give you a chance to reorganise seating arrangements if you need to (so that, for example, everybody has clear sight of the screen).

3. Check that all equipment is working. If using a flip chart, check there is clean paper on the stand (I have known occasions when you may be given a pad with only two clean sheets on it), and that you have markers which work. (A favourite trick of presentation course tutors is to put the caps so tightly on flip chart pens that they cannot come off. This certainly reinforces the point to students.)
4. Make sure your speaker's notes are to hand and in the right order. If you are using cue cards, then make sure they are tied together in some way, or at least numbered. If not, you could have considerable difficulties if you drop them.

Performance

Some years ago, I came across a consultant who had a monotonous voice. He knew his voice was monotonous, but it was the way it came out and there was nothing he could do about it. He could give witty and entertaining presentations, but his voice remained a distinct disadvantage.

By the time you become a consultant, your speech and accent are probably set; besides, the attempt to make them something other than they are will be transparent and to your disadvantage. So this section deals with delivery as a series of simple rules. They will not make you a good presenter, but they may help you to avoid the most common pitfalls.

- *Speak so that you can be heard.* This will sometimes require you to raise your voice. You can ask your audience if they can hear you.
- *Speak naturally.* Oratory is rarely appropriate or necessary in business, so use the tone and language with which you feel comfortable. For most people, however, it is worth slowing down the speed of delivery.
- *Look at the audience* — not over the tops of their heads. You may be trying to communicate a vision, but do not pretend it is behind the audience. Eye contact helps to make people feel included; looking at the audience enables you to observe their reaction. Let your eyes move from one individual to another — continuously looking at one member of the audience can make them embarrassed and cause the rest to wonder whether you have a special relationship! If you are holding your speaker's notes, hold them well up, so that you keep your head up. (We all know people who make presentations to the floor.) If you are using visual aids, avoid spending long periods turned to the screen.
- *Control what people see.* This does not mean only visual aids but keep them visually interested. When you watch a play, you will see

that the actors on stage other than the one speaking will remain still — particularly during a long speech; then, when it is time for another to speak, they will move with a flourish to attract attention. So it is with a presentation — your movements will attract attention (so will the movements of members of the audience and the arrival of refreshments). If you want people to concentrate on a picture, keep still; move when you want them to pay attention to you. Again, if you are holding your notes, do so in your less dominant hand, to avoid waving them around.

- *Do not devote great chunks of your presentation to explaining how you come to be giving it,* commenting on its mechanics or the process of its creation ('When I was asked to give a presentation on "congenital idiocy" I looked it up in my dictionary . . .') or apologise for being there. These will make the presentation seem amateurish in the hands of anyone but a talented professional.
- *Prepare for questions.* In some presentations, it is possible to have a few planted amongst friendly members of the audience, so that you can shine by your prepared response. The audience at a rehearsal can also be used to identify questions that might be asked.

Obviously the best technique is to answer questions honestly and say when you do not know the answer. Sometimes you may need to buy time whilst you think of an answer, and a technique for doing this is to ask a question in return ('I wonder if you could elaborate on that a little...'). A further technique, much favoured by politicians, is to answer a different, easier, question.

If you are faced by a hostile questioner, do your best not to be more aggressive in return. If anything, try to be demonstrably helpful and courteous; at best it may mollify their hostility. There is a good chance that many in the audience will sympathise with you but you will lose that sympathy if you respond aggressively.

INFORMAL PRESENTATIONS

Thus far the image of the presentation has been of the consultant standing in front of an audience to deliver a presentation, but many times the need to present information is less formal – for example during the course of a round table meeting. In this situation there may be only a small number of participants and the formal delivery of a presentation may not be possible, or unsuited to the dynamics of the meeting.

Preparation is still needed, but rather than conveying the visual messages through slides on screen, you can prepare paper based graphics that you can give to the participants; this is sometimes called a 'panel presentation'. This has the advantage that you can put a lot more information on a single page – detail that would not be legible when projected onto a screen. The disadvantage, however, is that if you have several pages and give them out at the start of the presentation, others at the meeting may well look ahead; you have no control over what they are looking at, and indeed cannot so easily direct their attention as you can when delivering a screen-based presentation.

REVIEW

Reporting is a skill and, like most skills, improves only with practice. It is unrealistic, therefore, to imagine that on concluding this chapter you will create reports which are a vast improvement on what you have achieved in the past. There are a lot of pitfalls in writing and presenting, however, and avoiding those highlighted should create some improvements.

The greater part of this chapter has been given over to preparation. This is because preparation needs time but, as with all communication skills, improvement only comes about through analysing carefully after the event:

- what went right;
- what went wrong;
- what I will do differently and better next time.

It is best to do this analysis shortly after the delivery of a document or presentation. If the reception has been notably good (or bad) then it will be self-evident but most of the time your performance will be mixed. Comments can be solicited from colleagues and informally from individuals in the audience.

And then you need to act. Reporting is a craft skill and like others — such as playing sport or a musical instrument — it will improve only with critical practice.

CHAPTER 9

INFLUENCING CLIENTS

Persuasion: a species of hypnotism in which the oral suggestion takes the hindering form of argument or appeal.
Ambrose Bierce, The Enlarged Devil's Dictionary

Persuasion is how we get other people to undertake an act or make a decision that we want and is required in situations when the person you are trying to persuade — the listener — has the option of saying 'no'. This is always the case for consultants who, by definition, do not have management authority to mandate things to happen within the client system. They therefore have to persuade the client's management, who do have this power.

There are numerous occasions when a consultant attempts to persuade a client, from the mundane to the momentous:

- to adopt particular recommendations;
- to fix a meeting on a particular day;
- to second a member of staff to a project;
- to agree to extending a deadline;
- to sanction additional expenditure.

Of course, persuasion is an art we use throughout our life, with family, friends and colleagues, and much of the time we use persuasion unconsciously. We encounter different styles of persuasion every day:

- The six-year-old child who says, 'If you won't let me play with that toy, I won't be your friend,' is using an emotional threat in order to negotiate; adults do the same but (usually) rather more subtly;

- Individuals may compel acceptance of their views simply through their status, force of personality, or another sort of power;
- Our relationship with an individual may be very trusting; they have been sympathetic and supportive to us in the past, and we will agree with their proposal simply because we trust them;
- We are influenced by others' opinions and actions; if common behaviour in an organisation is to work on a Saturday (even though it is not a working day) we may feel compelled to do the same;
- We can be inspired by someone communicating an appealing vision (a method often used by orators).

In this chapter we look at influencing an individual both through building a persuasive case, and through processes of social influence.

First, however, it is important to note that persuasion is not manipulation and it is very difficult, if not impossible, to persuade someone whose mind is made up to the contrary. If the other person is not open to persuasion, it may be best to avoid wasting your time! So in what follows, we are making the assumption that you are not pursuing a hopeless case.

THE POWER OF THE CONSULTANT

Let's start by considering what power consultants have to influence clients. Whatever role consultants are performing, they need influence to be able to create change. Influence is the exercise of power and is underwritten by it. It is important for consultants to understand whence they draw their power, and also to recognise where power lies in the client organisation and of what sort it is.

A helpful analysis of different types of power has been provided by Hersey, Blanchard and Natemeyer (1979) in connection with their studies of leadership, under the seven headings reproduced in Exhibit 9.1.

The availability and usefulness of different sorts of power will vary according to circumstances. It is rare to have only one kind of power or to exercise influence through only one kind.

There are some points of particular interest to consultants arising from this analysis.

1. Although an internal consultant usually has some defined position within the organisation and thus has some *legitimate power* this is usually of little use in influencing change. By definition the external

consultant rarely has any legitimate power. This is in distinct contrast to a line manager or executive, accustomed to using legitimate power to get things done. Managers or executives who transfer to a staff role, or that of external consultant, need to adjust their approaches to influencing to take account of this change in their power base.

2. The foundation of consultants' power is their *expertise*. If working for a firm of consultants, it is probably this for which they have been hired and almost certainly it will be what the client buys. Even so, the consultant has other power bases available, and *connection power* is particularly useful in influencing change. Most consultancy projects are commissioned by senior management, and the consultant thus has influence over more junior staff because of the connection with senior management. This can present a problem to the consultants having been hired by middle management but who have to influence senior management — they have no connection power.

This was illustrated on a project after the go-ahead had been given by the personnel manager commissioning it. It involved working in factories at different locations, all under the control of the operations director. He felt he had not been adequately consulted by the personnel manager about the project and stopped it shortly after it started. It could not be restarted until the operations director had satisfied himself on the details.

One of the features of expert power is that it is situational; thus the plumber has expert power over the lawyer when the central heating has broken down. Expert power does, however, diminish in the presence of a greater expert. For example, new consultants could find that their expert power diminishes in client meetings at which they are accompanied by more senior people from their own firm.

Legitimate power must be underwritten with other types of power if it is to be meaningful. For example, line managers may need access to all of the power bases in some measure to do their jobs. From the consultant's point of view, it is interesting to consider the power bases of senior individuals in an organisation to find out who really has influence, particularly 'ministers without portfolio' — are they has-beens with high-sounding titles or are they the power behind the throne? (See also stakeholder analysis in Chapter 7.)

One kind of power has not been listed in Exhibit 9.1 and that is negative power — the power to say 'no'. Given that the job of a consultant is

Exhibit 9.1 Types of power

Coercive power is based on fear. A leader high in coercive power is seen as inducing compliance because failure to comply will lead to punishment such as undesirable work assignments, reprimands, or dismissal.

Connection power is based on the leader's 'connections' with influential or important persons inside or outside the organisation. A leader high in connection power induces compliance from others because they aim at gaining the favour or avoiding the disfavour of the powerful connection.

Expert power is based on the leader's possession of expertise, skill, and knowledge, which, through respect, influences others. A leader high in expert power is seen as possessing the expertise to facilitate the work behaviour of others.

Information power is based on the leader's possession of or access to information that is perceived as valuable to others. This power base influences others because they need this information or want to be 'in on things'.

Legitimate power is based on the position held by the leader. Normally, the higher the position, the higher the legitimate power tends to be. A leader high in legitimate power induces compliance or influences others because they feel that this person has the right, by virtue of position in the organisation, to expect that suggestions will be followed.

Referent power is based on the leader's personal traits. A leader high in referent power is generally liked and admired by others because of personality. This liking for, admiration for, and identification with the leader influences others.

Reward power is based on the leader's ability to provide rewards for other people. They believe that their compliance will lead to gaining positive incentives such as pay, promotion, or recognition.

to promote change rather than prevent it, they are unlikely to use it often. More significant is the fact that negative power is widely distributed in an organisation; the factory hand and office clerk both have considerable negative power; both can make life difficult for a manager or executive. If negative power is the only source of influence available over organisational matters, it will be used. Consultants should remember this in introducing change and should provide consultative procedures that avoid the need for staff to exercise negative power.

Consultants need an acute sense of the nature and distribution of power — both their own and that within their clients — if they are to be successful. Although their power lies in their expertise, at more junior levels in the client organisation it is their connection power which enables consultants to get things done. It is therefore important for the consultant to maintain links as high up the organisation as possible. To a lesser extent, referent and information power are also available to the consultant to influence change.

THE RESPONSE TO CONSULTANTS' INFLUENCE

It is worth considering the possible responses to the consultant's attempts to influence a client. Leaving aside rejection, Charles Handy (1981) has suggested that responses to influence fall into the following categories:

- Compliance — 'I'm doing this because I have to';
- Identification — 'I'm doing this because it is you who has asked me';
- Internalisation — 'I'm doing this because it is my choice'.

All of these responses imply that the change has been accepted; all are therefore effective, but each has pros and cons.

Compliance requires that there is sufficient power behind the change to ensure a positive response. Thus the change must be backed by — for example — the legitimate power of a line manager within the organisation. For instance, the introduction of a new accounting procedure may only require the chief accountant to authorise it, following which the accounting staff will use it. The consultant, too, may have sufficient connection power to ensure a compliant response.

The drawback of compliance is that as soon as the pressure for change has disappeared, things may revert to the way they were before. A similar difficulty applies to the *identification* response — once the consultant withdraws, the changes introduced may be undone. Referent power is required by the consultant to effect the identification response.

The *internalised* response is generally regarded as the most enduring and is required for any change of a fundamental nature (i.e. in the goals or culture of the organisation). It does not require a particular power base, but it does require time and skill on the part of the consultant to introduce changes using participative processes that are most likely to lead to an internalised response.

From a commercial point of view, the identification response is more gratifying and rewarding than internalisation. Internalisation implies 'we changed because we wanted to', and very possibly the consultant may be seen as irrelevant to the change. This is not the way a consultant can demonstrably earn their keep and so there is a strong temptation to prefer identification!

PREPARING AND PRESENTING A PERSUASIVE CASE

Rational persuasion is the basis which consultants use most often to analyse and present a case persuasively. The key elements are shown in Exhibit 9.2.

Exhibit 9.2 Factors influencing persuasiveness

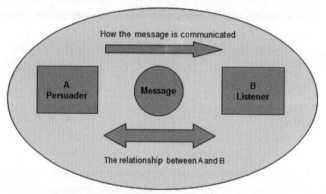

1. *The message* will affect the reaction of the listener. Any message which B perceives as having a bad net outcome is going to be poorly received. Such messages might be:
   - 'Please work late tonight';
   - 'You owe me £2,000';
   - 'We want you to work in our Timbuktu office'.
2. *How the message is communicated* will affect how it is received. There is an old joke about the Army sergeant who was asked to break the news to Smith, one of the corporals in his platoon that his father had died. After some thought, the sergeant formed up the platoon on parade and gave the command 'All those with fathers, one pace forward ... where do you think you're going, Smith?' Insensitive communication can create resistance to a persuading message; for example, contrast the appeals:
   - You will work late tonight;
   - Could you please work late tonight?

   ...both of which (despite the apparent diffidence of the latter) could be orders.

3. The *relationship* between the persuader (A) and listener (B) is crucial and will depend on B's perception of A. At an extreme, if A is an untrusted enemy of B, it will be very difficult for A to persuade B of anything, but there does not need to be a historical relationship between A and B for there to be difficulties. For example, if B has a totally irrational and baseless dislike of red-headed Glaswegians and A happens to be one, then A will start with a disadvantage.
4. The *circumstances* in which the message is communicated. We are much more likely to be persuaded to climb down a drainpipe from a third-floor window in the event of a fire than simply for the sake of it.

It is unlikely that you will have total control of all these items; nonetheless, there will be occasions about whose outcome you may be particularly anxious, and in which you wish to maximise the chance that your persuasive attempt will be successful. In this chapter we concentrate on the first two items above — namely, the nature of the message and how it is communicated. With most communication, success starts with careful preparation. The issue for a consultant is therefore how to present a proposition in the most persuasive way.

Outlined below is a practical approach to preparation which has three stages.
1. Develop an acceptable proposition.
2. Analyse your case.
3. Prepare your presentation.

DEVELOPING AN ACCEPTABLE PROPOSITION
If the listener is likely to be totally agreeable to the proposition, there is little point going through an elaborate routine of preparation. Conversely, if the proposition you are making is totally unacceptable, persuasion will not be successful. There is little chance of acceptance of an unacceptable proposition except by misrepresentation or manipulation, both of which involve deceit. For example, a confidence trickster uses deceit to persuade someone to part with money for nothing in return.

There are three steps to developing an acceptable proposition.
1. Clarify your objectives.
2. Define the listener's objectives.
3. Define the proposition.

Clarify your objectives

The first step is to know what you want to achieve. Simple persuasion objectives for a consultant in the course of operating might be:
- to defer the progress review for a week;
- to replace Dick with Tom on the project;
- to start work on Phase 2 in February.

It is also important to know why these objectives are necessary, i.e. the ends to which these are the means. The reasons, related to the examples above, could be respectively:
- to complete more work prior to the next progress review;
- to provide Dick with sufficient time to undertake a new assignment which requires his particular skills;
- to allow sufficient time for this phase to be complete by July.

Having defined these ulterior objectives, alternative means of meeting the same ends could be defined by asking 'how' of them. Taking the first example, asking 'how?' of 'to complete more work prior to the next progress review' could lead to the alternatives of:
- work weekends and evenings;
- add additional people to the team; as well as the original proposition of 'to defer the progress review for a week'.

The process is illustrated in Exhibit 9.3.

Exhibit 9.3 Generating alternative objectives

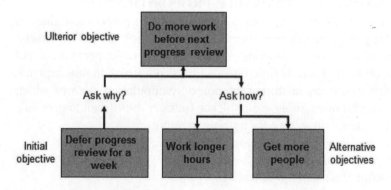

If the first proposition is not acceptable, this process could lead to alternatives that are acceptable. It is also a useful process in deriving alternatives if negotiation is to take place.

Define the listener's objectives
You will have noticed that each of the ulterior objectives shown above has benefits for the consultant. Although the client may be sympathetic to these, they are in themselves unlikely to be persuasive. Persuasion is listener-oriented communication and the process that has to be followed is to show how the required act or decision can help the listener meet their own goals. This means that the persuader has to have some idea of what the listener's goals might be.

If we know the listener, then we will probably have some idea of what his or her goals might be in both general and specific terms, for example:

- To avoid risk taking;
- To go home at 5pm on Tuesday;
- To complete the project before the end of the year;
- To keep control.

Some years ago the tutors in a training college had to convince two directors to sanction expenditure on an interactive video system. One — Barry — was keen on anything new, whereas Alan — the other — was very conservative. The tutors knew that they would have to appeal to them separately. With Barry, it was along the lines, 'Barry, interactive video is new in training. If we want to be ahead of everybody else, we've got to have it.' Barry's reaction was, 'That's exciting — let's have it!'

With Alan, the presentation was different. 'Alan, interactive video has been around for some time now; it represents the next natural step from the investment we have made already in computers and video.' Alan's reaction was, 'That doesn't sound revolutionary — why don't we go ahead?'

It would have been impossible to appeal to their contrasting innovative and conservative motivations simultaneously, but tuning the approach separately worked.

How do you infer the objectives of a listener you have never met? One way is to be briefed by someone who knows them already. For example, a client's subordinate can help you to work out their boss's objectives. Other than this you have to guess, but this is not difficult, as most people's general objectives are those of self-interest or the interest of groups or institutions to which they belong. In these cases, it is probably worthwhile assuming fairly general objectives until the initial conversation with the listener provides you with more information. You therefore have to listen very carefully at the start of the conversation to what the listener says to pick up any clues about their goals.

Define an acceptable proposition
Having clarified your own and the listener's goals, you need to define a proposition that meets them both.

Take the example given earlier: to defer the progress review by a week. This may be totally acceptable to the client, so there is no problem — they could not care less. But if they had to make a report on the project to their board of directors the day after the scheduled date they will be averse to any deferral. The proposition would not be acceptable and an alternative should be sought.

Whereas persuasion is a process whereby the listener accepts a particular proposition in preference to all others, negotiation is more complex. It involves a number of propositions, quid pro quos, bargaining and so on. A model often used by negotiators to describe the negotiation process shows the range of propositions on a spectrum of best, expected and least acceptable results from our point of view. Likewise, the other side may also have a rank order of attractiveness — but in the opposite direction from us.

Take a simple example — bartering in a Middle Eastern bazaar for a carpet. The pricing expectations may be as shown in Exhibit 9.4.

Exhibit 9.4 Bartering for a carpet

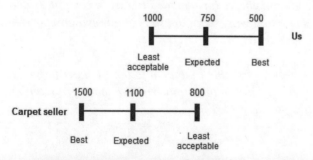

In the example, we reckon on a price of up to 1000 rials for the carpet; the carpet seller will not accept less than 800. Fortunately there is some overlap, and the final price settled on will be a result of the relative bargaining skill of the two parties. (Of course, the matter is made more complicated because we do not necessarily know the range expected on the other side. The first time I went into a Middle Eastern bazaar, I didn't bargain — I paid the price asked. The shopkeeper looked amazed, and a little disappointed.)

If the two ranges of position do not overlap, then it may not be possible to resolve matters by negotiation. In a shop, this may not matter; in business if a resolution is needed, the conflict analysis model described in Chapter 7 can be helpful in planning a resolution strategy.

ANALYSING YOUR CASE

Insurance salesman: 'Dick, this is a really good policy. I recommend it to you whole-heartedly because it gives me the best commission.'

Not a particularly compelling sales message, is it? It aims to persuade by showing how the listener can help the persuader achieve their objectives. Persuasion must be listener-orientated and needs to show how the proposition can help the listener achieve their own objectives.

'So what?' analysis is a technique that helps, and an illustration is shown in Exhibit 9.5. The listener's objective (relevant to this case) is written at the top, so as to keep it in mind. The 'so what?' analysis can be applied to both our proposition and the principal alternative. The alternative may often be, 'do nothing', or there could be several.

Exhibit 9.5 Example of 'so what?' analysis

Listener's objective: to ensure that the project is completed on time		
Proposition: to put back the progress review meeting by a week		
Benefits	Features	Disadvantages
Recognise that the consultant is being honest	**Client is told of need to put back the meeting by a week**	
	Later than planned	Seems as if the project is falling behind
More progress to report at review	**Allows more time for work prior to review**	
	Other members of the panel will need to be told	They will wonder if there is a problem

In each case, the analysis is the same; a list is made of the principal features of the proposition, in the centre column. Features are the objective facts about the proposal but a recital of these is not compelling by itself; what is more attractive is interpreting the facts in the context of how they will help achieve the listener's objective or not. These are the benefits and disadvantages of the proposal.

If you want to translate a feature into a benefit or disadvantage, you ask 'so what?' of it (and hence the name of this form of analysis).

This approach is more straightforward for material items than for ideas or concepts, but is applicable to the latter. There may also be a complex mass of objectives, so the first step must be to simplify objectives and features. This is done in the example in Exhibit 9.5. Once completed for the objective quoted, there may be other objectives which are also relevant; the first feature is also relevant to the (client's) objective 'to be able to trust the consultant'.

Once complete for the proposition, a similar analysis could be done for any alternative propositions, the most likely of which is 'keep the meeting at the same time'. (This is not quoted here because it is in the main simply a reversal of the benefits and disadvantages shown in Exhibit 9.5).

This form of analysis helps you to look at your proposition (and the alternatives) from the listener's point of view. Remember that persuasion is listener-oriented communication.

Having analysed your case, you have then to decide how to present it.

PREPARING YOUR PRESENTATION
Persuasive presentation needs to be structured in this order:
1. Engagement.
2. Discussion.
3. Action.

Engagement
Initially the listener needs to be convinced that there is a problem which merits their attention and needs action — or a decision — from them now. You have somehow to engage their attention and to do so:
- the problem or issue must be recognised and accepted as such by the listener;
- the solution of the problem must be a matter of priority for them;
- they must believe that a solution *is* possible.

In matters of complex persuasion, the process of engagement — getting the listener to 'buy into the problem' — may be a separate step in the persuasion process.

> *A personnel manager was having great difficulty in administering the company's car scheme. The boss, the personnel director, whilst accepting the problem, did not accept the personnel manager's view of its nature and urgency. What the personnel manager then did was to stop protecting the boss from all the queries and problems on the car scheme.*

> *Soon thereafter, the personnel director began to see the problem from the personnel manager's point of view.*

Attempts at persuasion will be successful only if the engagement step has been completed. Failures in persuasion are often due to entering at the discussion or action stages without having completed the engagement stage satisfactorily. Thus, for example, starting the discussion on the proposition 'Put the review meeting back by a week' with a question about to what date it should be postponed, is starting at the discussion stage.

Discussion
Having accepted there is a problem or issue, which must be addressed now, the listener's next question may be, 'Well, what do we do about it?' Indeed, they may immediately put forward propositions of their own. (Incidentally, this latter behaviour is a sign that the engagement stage has been satisfactorily completed.)

This is where the preparatory analysis is used. In describing your proposition you highlight its benefits and the disadvantage of the alternative. Thus:

- *Consultant*: 'By deferring the progress review meeting by a week, we shall be able to report much more significant progress than if we held it as scheduled.'
- The client may respond with objections; these will be based on the disadvantages of your proposition and the benefits of the alternative, thus:
- *Client*: 'Deferring by a week will create some concern among panel members that the project is falling behind schedule.'

The preliminary analysis will have shown up this as a potential objection and you should be prepared to deal with the most likely objections. A possible response is:

- *Consultant*: 'It may cause more concern to have the meeting at the original time if we have not completed the action agreed at the last meeting.'

Note in this exchange that they are talking about how to avoid creating concern among panel members — not whether the meeting should be deferred. This could be because either the client is articulating their own concerns, or has accepted the consultant's proposal and is now thinking how to implement it to best effect.

The consultant might confront this by using a technique known as a 'trial close'; it is a form of '...if...then...' statement:

- *Consultant*: 'If we can put the other panel members' minds at rest, then are you willing to put the meeting back a week?'

The response to this will help direct the subsequent discussion; is it concerned with convincing the client to defer the meeting, or is it about helping them to implement it effectively? Further trial closes can be used to identify other objections or concerns the client might have. If the consultant cannot find the answer by using the trial close they must still try to find out the client's real concern from the nature of the discussion, so they can direct their efforts in the most effective way.

This may seem a trivial point but in my experience it crops up over and over again; the barriers to a proposal are often not those of 'why?' but 'how?' In other words, there is a concern about means rather than ends.

So discussion consists of the debate about the possible ways in which the problem or issue might be addressed and the pros and cons of each. This should culminate in an agreement on action or a decision — hopefully the one you wanted.

Action
Action, however, does not automatically follow from discussion. You may have taken the horse to water but it will not always drink. The ideal response might be:

- *Client:* 'OK, I'm happy to postpone the meeting by a week. I'll call up the other members of the panel to let them know and make sure they don't get worried.'

In practice you might get responses like:
- 'I'd like to think about this';
- 'I'd like to talk this over with . . .';
- 'Let's stick with the original date for the time being and review closer to the time'.

Now, the face value of these statements may be what is meant and if it is you have to treat them as such. Alternatively, what is being said might mean, 'I'm still not convinced but don't want to continue this conversation.' Another possibility is that the client does not like to commit to a decision. In both the latter cases further pushing may be needed.

Techniques you might use when being put off:

1. If the listener is putting you off for *genuine reasons*, you have to respect those reasons: further pushing would simply irritate them. What you can do, however, is to confirm what happens next. A response such as, 'Fine; when should we get together again to decide what to do?' gives you the chance to try again if you have heard nothing. So, although you do not have a firm commitment to the action or decision you want, the steps leading to it will be clear.

2. If the listener is still *unconvinced* you need to find out what is bothering them. There may still be a misapprehension which you have failed to address satisfactorily, or they have a piece of relevant information unknown to you, which is their reason for procrastinating. You have to run over the steps in the persuasion process to find out what the sticking points are:
   - 'We agreed this was a problem which required a decision now';
   - 'We have reviewed the range of possible solutions';
   - 'We have agreed that this is the best solution';
   - 'So, let's go ahead'.

3. Some people *dislike taking decisions*: a favourite ploy for avoiding decisions is to seek further information. Again, it is essential to distinguish circumstances in which more information is truly required from those when it is a procrastination ploy. In these latter circumstances, you need to emphasise:
   - the adequacy of the data already available;
   - the urgency of taking a decision.

Once the listener has agreed with your proposition, close the discussion. Continued discussion may result in their rethinking their position and you will have gone backwards in the persuasion process.

THE PERSUASION MEETING

In this section we consider some of the features of a persuasion meeting and some of the techniques you can use to increase success.

Winning and losing

What are your feelings about being persuaded? Are you easily persuaded? If so, are you a person of little strength of character or have you taken to yourself the wisdom of Andrew Carnegie, whose epitaph on himself was said to be, 'Here lies a man who knew how to enlist into his service better men than himself'?

Difficulties arise in a persuasion event when it is seen by either side as a contest in which the winner will be the one whose view prevails at the end of the day. The danger of persuasion becoming a contest is that the listener can always win: they can say no. So as a persuader you need to avoid circumstances in which it becomes more important to win the debate than discuss constructively. The route to win/lose comes from a polarisation of views and is like an oral tennis match with two sides hitting the conversational ball at each other from opposite sides of the net. It is characterised verbally by a lot of 'Yes, but . . .' statements as each protagonist puts their point of view counter to the other. Argument usually reaches an unsatisfactory conclusion.

A technique to deal with this is to say, 'Let me see if I understand what you are saying' and going on to summarise your understanding of their position. This has the benefits of demonstrating listening, checking comprehension and breaking out of the altercation. No one is a fool in their own estimation and they will believe the point they are making is a good one. In debate, concentrating on what you are going to say next means that you are not listening as carefully as you might to what is being said and there is a breakdown in communication.

Another technique is to give the listener positive 'strokes' — showing respect for them and their opinions. This can be done by emphasising points of agreement; the graduation of 'degrees of agreement' shown in Table 9.1 is helpful in recognising not only whether you are for or against a proposal but the degree of feeling you have for it either way.

Table 9.1 Degrees of agreement

Sharing	'I feel as committed as you do on this issue.'
Supporting	'I will help your efforts on this issue.'
Sympathising	'I applaud your efforts but do not feel obliged to help.'
Acquiescence	'I couldn't care either way.'
Rejection	'I cannot support you.'
Opposition	'I will act against you.'

It is useful to be clear where each of you stands on an issue by estimating where you are on the scale.

Of course, it is important to maintain your position if you do not agree with a proposal. It is not always possible to reach a satisfactory compromise. As one client remarked, 'I admire a consultant who makes different recommendations from those I wanted.'

GOOD NEWS OR BAD NEWS FIRST?

Sometimes the question arises, 'Should I deal with the disadvantages of a proposal before its advantages, or vice versa?'

My rule of thumb, based on experience, is to start with the advantages of a proposal you want accepted, and start with the disadvantages of a proposal you want rejected. Experimental evidence tends to back this up (reported in Handy, 1981); a group of subjects was told that an individual was intelligent, industrious, impulsive, critical, stubborn and envious. A second group was told the same, but the adjectives were read in the reverse order. Each group was then asked to characterise the individual, and the first group (where the 'good news' came first) came up with a more favourable evaluation than the second.

Avoiding the answer 'no'

In the same way as the listener may wish to defer a decision to avoid the answer 'yes', you may wish to do the same to avoid the answer 'no'. Once a decision is made, it is more difficult to undo; the listener, for example, will have made an emotional commitment to the decision once taken. (Happily, the same process, however, works in reverse; having taken the decision in your favour, it is emotionally painful to undo it.)

So, if it looks as if your persuasion attempt is failing and there is no satisfactory alternative to fall back on, then aim for a deferral. Taking the example of wanting to defer a progress review meeting, you might say, 'Well, obviously you're not very happy about this. Why don't I do some more sounding out and come back to you in a couple of days?' Although this sounds wishy-washy, it gives you a breathing space and allows you to continue to canvass support. This latter would be politically difficult to do if a decision had already been made not to defer.

This is but one aspect of negotiation.

Negotiation
Negotiating is not the same as persuasion in that:
- persuasion is between unequal parties — the persuadee can say no and that is it; in negotiation, the power is more evenly balanced as both parties have agreed that they want to reach an agreement;
- the roles are also more balanced on each side; the object is to find mutually satisfactory ground by bargaining so a process of movement rather than intransigence is expected on both sides.

Having pointed out the differences, however, it is worth summarising some of the more useful negotiating tactics.

The process of adjournment has already been described in the previous section. As well as avoiding the answer 'no', it can be used to allow tempers to cool or consultation with other parties to take place. (The latter may be apparent only; for example, a manager negotiating with a union may have given their 'final' offer; they cannot revise it further without losing credibility, but a pretence of consultation with superiors may enable them to do so.)

There are problems when there is no common ground between opposite sides, i.e. there is no overlap between the least acceptable points on each side (see Exhibit 9.4). The consequence depends on the stakes involved; if the stakes are low you can simply agree to disagree but if they are high, then each side will try to get the other to change its negotiating position by raising the stakes. For example, a union may threaten strike action to encourage the management to increase a pay offer, the argument being that it is worthwhile settling at the higher figure to avoid the potential disruption and loss.

Asking for more than you want can be useful in two ways. Firstly, if it is a matter of scale, then you can be negotiated down to what you wanted originally, whilst the opposite party will be satisfied too. (So, asking to defer the meeting by ten days could result in a compromise of five days, which is certainly better than none at all.) Secondly, a number of minor proposals could be included amongst the major ones. The minor ones can be used to obscure the critical ones, or be sacrificed to secure the key results sought.

Sometimes experienced negotiators make a large concession at the start and use that to win a disproportionately more valuable number of smaller concessions from the other side by continually reminding them of the large concession made originally. (The counter to this is to insist that once a concession is made, it is no longer part of the negotiation.)

Listening is particularly important in negotiating, particularly reading between the lines to understand what is really being meant. If you and the other side are representatives who have often negotiated, you may have developed ways of communicating which the superficial observer would not notice. For example, both of you will know for certain when the other has truly reached his final offer. With a stranger it may be difficult to know whether the statement that the offer is final may be simply a strategic ploy.

Sometimes negotiators try to upset the other side in the hope that they may get some information or other advantage thereby. For example, there was a barrister who, when he wished to put witnesses off balance, called them by the wrong name.

A further variation to this is to introduce a personal element to the negotiation. The negotiator introduces emotion by (implicitly) claiming that tough negotiation is being tough with them as an individual. Do not fall into the trap of confusing the two — it is possible to carry out tough negotiation whilst still maintaining a pleasant personal relationship.

From the above, it will be seen that negotiation can be thought of as a form of 'game', with rules, rituals, specialised forms of words — and this is exemplified in the ritualised bargaining which goes on between employers and employee representatives.

PROCESSES OF SOCIAL INFLUENCE

Robert Cialdini has analysed influencing processes extensively (Cialdini, 2001), and identified six principal ones. These are shown in Exhibit 9.6, together with a summary of the key features.

Exhibit 9.6 Processes of social influence

Reciprocation	Obligation to return a favour, even if unwanted, works with concessions
Commitment and consistency	Once a small commitment has been made, others will be won over because of the need for consistency
Social proof	We watch others then copy
Liking	We say yes to people we like
Deference to authority	Authority derives from symbols as well as reality
Scarcity	Scarcity increases perceived value

Cialdini notes that these processes are conditioned — we tend to follow them almost automatically. They are involved extensively in product marketing and selling, and apply in all aspects of our lives. So, for example:

- *Reciprocation:* if someone buys you a drink in a bar, you will feel obliged to buy them one in return;
- *Social proof:* TV comedies often use canned laughter to increase the comedic value of a programme;
- *Deference to authority:* someone well dressed, arriving in a chauffeur-driven car, will be assumed to be pretty important.

The reason we are amenable to these processes is that they usually work in our best interest. So reciprocation, for example, is a good way of getting on with your neighbours. But there are occasions when they result in people behaving in what to us seems an irrational way — and in what to them, on reflection, would also seem to be irrational. Cialdini, for example, tells the story of his brother who as a student was very successful at buying and selling cars. He would place an advertisement for the car he wanted to sell in a local newspaper and then invoke the principle of scarcity by inviting all prospective buyers to view the car at the same time. This put pressure on them to take a quick decision, as each knew that if they didn't buy there and then, they could not get the car. The principle of scarcity made possession of the car more important than simply its functionality.

The following sections consider a couple of areas where the use of social influence, notably commitment and consistency, and social proof, apply to the work of a consultant.

GETTING CLIENT COMMITMENT

There will always be client staff whose attitude is, 'If you're so clever, go on and prove it!' But unless they are acting in an executive role, a consultant will be creating change via other people, who will therefore have their part to play and should be clear about and accept their responsibilities.

Clients should identify with the success or failure of consultancy projects for which they have engaged the help of consultants; it is far easier to create change in an organisation which accepts joint responsibility for success or failure than one in which the project is totally identified with the consultant. The consultant from Smith Associates should therefore avoid the project being labelled as the 'Smith Associates Project'. The consultant should position themselves as assisting in the client's project, so that the client accepts responsibility.

Quality circles are problem-solving groups set up and led by supervisors from among their own teams. A feature of quality circle programmes is that they are voluntary. In the programmes I have been involved with, first-line supervisors are invited to attend a training course as a circle leader, at the end of which we would call for volunteers to start their own circles. If no one volunteers, then there can be no circles.

Obviously we make as sure as we reasonably can that those who attended the training programme are likely to volunteer but the end of the course, when volunteers are requested, is always a nail-biting point for the consultant.

Needless to say, on one occasion, through an unfortunate combination of circumstances, I got no volunteers.

The group was then confronted with the consequences of its decision in respect of the programme and the effect on the company. We had agreed earlier in the course on the value of the goals the programme set out to achieve and these would be lost if the programme folded.

Because of this, one supervisor changed his mind and said that he would have a go, and others followed suit. But no such result

would have been achieved if they had not accepted their personal
responsibility for ensuring the success of the programme.

Commitment to a project and acceptance of its outcomes is best achieved amongst client staff by giving them opportunities to participate in it. Consultancy projects are joint endeavours between consultant and client and there is a better chance of achieving acceptance if client staff have been able to contribute to determining the changes required. A participative approach is essential if there is to be an internalised response from client staff.

The level of commitment must reach a critical mass if change is to endure. Many initiatives wither and die because commitment has not been built up to this critical level. Not only are numbers important but also who is committed. In every organisation there will be easy 'converts', but they (unfortunately) are not always the opinion leaders. Every change project should include a plan for identifying the key client staff who might make up the critical mass (and that could be as few as one person) and obtaining their support.

MANAGING EXPECTATIONS

Even before you set foot on a client's premises, there will be expectations about you and the project you are going to undertake, if held only by senior management. When working with a wider constituency of client staff, they too will have expectations. Sometimes these can be counter-productive; for example if there is little trust between the top and the bottom of the organisation, then there may be great suspicion about you as an emissary of top management.

Expectations are managed by managing communications. With a few notable exceptions, communications within organisations are not particularly good and so it does not take much effort on the part of the consultant to improve on the regular channels. If solid information is not available, rumour — probably ill-informed — will take its place. So it is important that within all projects the consultant actively controls the information which is disseminated.

But managing expectations goes beyond this; consultants also need to ensure that they do not themselves create unwarranted expectations. This is particularly easy to do at the data collection stage of a project. You can imagine the reactions of client staff who are asked questions such as:

- 'Are you happy with your remuneration?'
- 'Would you relocate if the office were to move to Wales?'
- 'Where is there scope to cut staff numbers?'

The obvious inferences from these questions are respectively, 'Pay is going to be improved;' 'The office is to be moved to Wales;' and, 'There are going to be redundancies.' The consultant has to decide whether rumours along these lines are helpful and, if not, avoid creating them.

Expectations are also an important factor in motivation, as shown in the equation:

motivation (to do something) = **desire** (for the reward promised if I do it) *times* **expectation** (that if I do it, I will get the reward)

For example, suppose you were stopped in the street by a man who offered you £100 to borrow your expensive watch for an hour, payable on returning the watch to you. Most of us would consider £100 for an hour's hire of a watch a very generous payback. Equally, however, we would be concerned that once we parted with the watch we would not see it or the man again, let alone the £100. Notwithstanding our desire for the reward, our expectations would lead us to turn down the man's offer — irrespective of whether it was genuinely made.

A similar process can occur during a consultancy project: everybody may subscribe to the goals the consultant is trying to achieve, but still not be motivated to co-operate. Often this occurs because of lack of trust or cynicism about the intentions of senior management. 'We tried this before, but management went back to their old ways after three months,' or 'They say there'll be no redundancies, but they said the same five years ago, and 50 people had to go within the year.'

Irrespective of the truth of these, if they are what people believe, they constitute a problem for the consultant trying to create change. Those involved with the change have to be convinced to put in the effort required to make it happen — otherwise the consultant will be faced with a self-fulfilling prophecy of failure.

Sometimes reassurances from top management can be adequate, but the principle of social proof can also be invoked. Clear demonstrations of support — such as senior executives chairing project meetings or speaking at training sessions — can serve to convince doubters of management's bona fides. A pilot trial is also useful for showing the workability of a project.

IMPROVING YOUR INFLUENCING SKILLS

The same process applies to improving influencing skills as with any other form of communication: preparation precedes action. After action, there is a review to see what lessons can be learned and applied to preparation on the next occasion.

You must therefore review each influencing occasion to see what can be learned from it: what went well, what went poorly? How successful were you? Were you adequately prepared? It can be helpful to go back to the analysis stage and check out how well you did it. Did you assess the other person's objectives accurately? Did you remember all the arguments in favour of your proposal and had you anticipated all the objections that were raised?

It is also sensible to review the meeting itself; how would you behave differently — for example, did you find yourself side-tracked onto an unimportant or irrelevant issue? Did the discussion degenerate into an argument?

The process of review should result in some clear lessons to be applied next time — to both preparation and action.

Try it. Success following trying out the techniques covered in this chapter will be even more persuasive than the text!

CHAPTER 10

DESIGNING AND PRESENTING TRAINING SESSIONS AND WORKSHOPS

Education is an admirable thing, but it is well to remember from
time to time that nothing that is worth knowing can be taught.

Oscar Wilde

Most consultants have to run a training session at some time. This chapter is thus not aimed at the professional trainer — or the consultant who regularly presents training courses — but at the consultant who has to run a training course as an adjunct to the project being carried out. Instances when training might be required could be on introducing new systems (computer or manual), teaching client staff new specialist techniques and so on.

There are at least two key differences between presenting a training session and presenting in the other contexts described in Chapter 8.

- Training is directed towards enhancing a skill so that individuals should be able to do something different or better as a consequence. By contrast, other presentations could be aimed more at informing or persuading.

- You should have fewer constraints on training than on a presentation. More flexibility enables you to fashion the session so as to be able to achieve the training objectives better.

A lecture at a conference could be construed as a form of training but I have in mind the occasion when you have a small number of people — 25 or fewer — whom you have to train, and it is up to you to decide how you will do it.

Workshops are yet another kind of gathering aimed at developing performance. They have many characteristics in common with training sessions, but some important differences too. These are covered at the end of the chapter.

CREATING A TRAINING SPECIFICATION

A training specification is a useful bridge between the outline of a training programme and its detailed design. If you are designing a training programme for a client, you can use the training specification to get client input or agreement at an intermediate stage. The contents of a training specification are as follows:

1. Description of the programme:
   - The learning objectives;
   - Its style (e.g. a series of exercises based on a case study; a participative workshop, etc.);
   - The number and nature of participants for whom it is designed;
   - Its duration and structure (e.g. four days, two two-day seminars, residential or non-residential);
   - The resources required (trainers, equipment, films, etc.).
2. Timetable, setting out the timing of each session.
3. Session outlines: for each session:
   - *Rationale*: why this session is included in the event;
   - *Objectives:* the teaching objectives for the session;
   - *Key learning points* to be covered in the session;
   - *Session outline* describing what will happen in the session.
4. The basis on which the training is to be evaluated.

DEFINE THE TRAINING OBJECTIVES
You must start off by deciding what the purpose of the training is: what participants should know or be able to do at its conclusion.

It is particularly helpful to think about objectives in terms of behavioural or testable outcomes. Exhibit 10.1 shows the objectives for a session on the techniques of 'brainstorming'.

Exhibit 10.1 Objectives for a brainstorming session

At the end of the session participants should be able to do the following:
1. Define brainstorming.
2. List the characteristics of a brainstorming group.
3. Identify the guidelines for a brainstorming session.
4. Participate constructively in a brainstorming session.
5. Recognise possible applications of brainstorming back at work.

When you are dealing with easily testable skills or outcomes — such as those illustrated in Exhibit 10.1 — then the need for the training should be fairly clear, as should be the method of carrying it out.

Where training is less specific — for example, management training — there is often a 'syrup of figs' mentality: participants are subjected to it on the grounds that whatever it is, it will probably do them some good! This is probably true, but it does represent an ineffective use of time and resources. In these circumstances, it is sensible to carry out some detailed training needs analysis. This might be carried out by getting precise answers to the following questions.

1. In what way are we trying to improve business performance?
2. What requirements does this place on improving individual or group performance?
3. What do people need to do differently or better to achieve this improvement?
4. What support do they need to accomplish this?
5. What role does training have in this?
6. How should this be delivered?
7. What conditions need to be created so that the training is applied effectively at work?

Very often the consultant is invited in only at stage 6. This is not necessarily a problem provided the causality back to stage 1 is clear. If it is not, then perhaps this indicates some work that the consultant needs to carry out beforehand, to clarify the model of performance applying to the business.

If the subject you are teaching is complex it may need a series of sessions to put it across — in other words, a training course.

You will then need to define the objectives for each session.

DESIGNING TRAINING SESSIONS

Having defined learning objectives, you will need to design a session to achieve them. To this end you need to have some basic guidelines on how people learn.

There is a saying often quoted by trainers:

Hear and forget, see and remember, do and understand.

It underscores the point that in general people's visual memories are better than their aural ones, but personal experience has a more profound effect than either. People have different preferences in the way they learn. Some learn best by observation; some by actually doing. Some like to understand the theory and others the practical application of what is being taught.

Groups of people being trained will have a mix of these preferences and so a mix of activities is used. Inevitably, therefore, sessions popular with those who have one preference will leave those with another indifferent.

The choice of method of putting material across also depends on what is to be learned. Exhibit 10.2 illustrates a relationship between the nature of what is being taught and the method used.

Knowledge-based learning — as the name suggests — is directed towards increasing a participant's knowledge. An example of this end of the spectrum is training client staff in, say, the implications of a new piece of legislation. A skills-based subject is related to doing something. This covers all operative skills — for example, how to operate a new telephone system — but it also covers a lot of managerial skills (for example, making a presentation).

Exhibit 10.2 Training method used

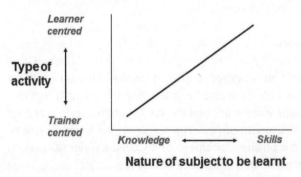

A trainer-centred activity is focussed on the trainer (e.g. a lecture) whereas a learner-centred activity is based on the trainee (such as a practical exercise). Skills training is effective when done on the job, as well as away from work. In this chapter however, we are concerned with training sessions away from the job; Exhibit 10.3 lists some of the most used methods of training. Also shown is the relationship between the type of subject to be learnt and the training method most appropriate. If the trainee has no knowledge of a subject, it is probably best for the trainer to tell them about it first and thus the trainer-centred approach is appropriate. On the other hand, the use of, say, a new piece of software is best learned by practice.

Exhibit 10.3 Spectrum of training methods

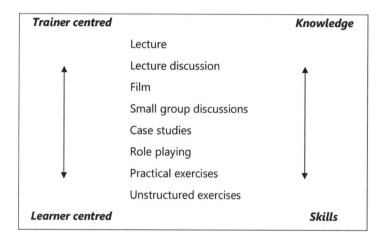

It is essential to remember that learner-centred activities involve the trainer in different forms of activity rather than sitting back and watching what happens.

With learner-centred training you should consider how trainees are to get feedback. If they are undertaking a practical exercise, for example, how will they know what they are doing right or wrong and how will they judge the quality of their performance?

The trainer has therefore to organise the feedback process. It can be done by the trainer or through other members of the group. If the latter, group members must feed back only that data which they can reasonably be expected to be able to collect. (For example, in training in recruitment interviewing, trainees may take the roles of interviewer and prospective recruit: the 'recruit' could quite legitimately comment on how they felt during the course of the interview.) If they are to give feedback, group members should be coached in the skills of observation and they need to be able to recognise the difference between effective and ineffective behaviour or performance. Video recording can often help in the feedback process.

The amount and rate of feedback must be regulated; too much feedback is indigestible and can result in a deterioration of performance.

So, in designing a training session you should consider the structure of the topics to be taught and where they fall on the knowledge-skills spectrum. Almost certainly there will be a mix and you should use the appropriate method for putting across each element. In my experience, consultants tend to err towards the trainer-centred end of the spectrum in terms of the content of a training session. There is usually more scope for learner-centred activities and it makes it more interesting for participants too.

DISTANCE LEARNING
Distance learning on an increasing number of topics is available to those who have access to the internet. The marginal cost of providing it and participating is low, and study can be scheduled at times to suit the learner, who also can go at their own pace. Good distance learning programmes are interactive and multi-media, and hence engaging.

There are, however, definite benefits from getting learners together for training in a classroom, notably the social interaction and the dedication of attention wholly to the training. For this reason blended learning, which combines distance learning with face to face sessions, combines the advantages of each.

(This of course is not new; any schoolchild will recognise the combination of school lessons with homework!)

SIZE OF THE AUDIENCE
The size of the audience you choose should be a function of administration, organisation and the need for personal interaction. So it will depend on:
1. How many people are to be trained?
2. How many can be spared for a training session at a single time?
3. How many can be comfortably accommodated in the training room?
4. How are they going to be involved? (If, for example, you want people to join in a discussion, the average 'air-time' available for each participant in a group of 30 is 2 minutes per hour.)

5. What constraints are there on the physical facilities? For example, if trainees are to use computers, how many are available?
6. What are the constraints imposed by your teaching structure? If there are practical exercises involving sub-groups, how many people should be in each? Does this put a minimum or maximum number on the course participants? Similarly, if groups are to work in separate rooms, how many can be accommodated and does this place a maximum number on the participants?
7. What is the need for interaction between you and each participant? If individual coaching is required in part of the session, how many people can you deal with? If this is a major limitation, is it worthwhile having a colleague available for this part so you can have more people on the course as a whole?

Project management or commercial constraints will often influence a training session as well and cause departures from the ideal approach.

FORM OF THE PRESENTATION

A lecture is only rarely an appropriate form of training. Almost always some form of audience participation is necessary to maintain interest. It has been said that people can concentrate only for eight minutes at a stretch without some involvement. I am not convinced that eight is the right number but I do believe that audience participation enhances interest and learning.

Audience participation can be achieved by asking questions, soliciting opinions, and allowing people to air their knowledge. Answers can be posted on a flip chart (and the sight of a trainer poised, ready to write down comments on a flip chart, can often help to elicit responses from an audience). Remember that open-ended questions (starting with how, why, where, etc.) will prompt more comment than close-ended questions (starting 'do you . . .', 'have you . . .', etc.) which simply invite a yes or no answer.

EXPECTATIONS OF THE AUDIENCE

It is the trainer's job to fashion the expectations of the audience. The trainer may have been responsible for an initial briefing beforehand — perhaps by an email with an outline of the course content — which will influence expectations before arrival.

The first part of a training course (or session within it) will set the tone for the whole. At the start of a course a trainer may give a short briefing about what is to come, but will usually be giving a lot of verbal and non-verbal signals about the style of the course. Typically, nowadays, the style of a training course will be:

- *informal*: it is not run as a formal conference or meeting;
- *relaxed*: allowing participants to behave naturally rather than being on their best behaviour;
- *low-risk*: it does not matter if participants make mistakes or are wrong;
- *business-like*: notwithstanding the comments above, participants are there to learn and this involves hard work and effort.

A technique I use at the start of a training session, which helps to unfreeze groups, is to get them to do something counter to their expectations. For example, if they expect a lecture, with their bottoms stuck to their seat for half the day, try to start with an exercise in which they have to move around the room.

The trainer will set the norms of behaviour for the session. For example, sitting behind a desk with your jacket on will convey a completely different impression than sitting on the edge of the front of a desk (nothing between you and the audience) with your sleeves rolled up.

Again, the way you talk to the audience will influence their attitude; making fun of questions may inhibit other questioners; criticising their contributions may create an adversarial attitude.

Thus the presenter's behaviour, although nothing to do with the content, can profoundly influence the quality of a training presentation; controlling behaviour carefully leads to better sessions.

WHAT TIME OF DAY SHOULD YOU CHOOSE?

More often than not the time of day chosen for a training presentation will depend on administrative limitations. Consider whether the training is best given at a single session or two (or more) sessions. It might be better, for example, to have two half-day sessions than one whole day. If the session is not to last a whole day, the timing may be constrained by the availability of participants. It may be easier to release them at one particular time than another.

It is important that a consultant considers the implications of timing on participants' perception of the importance of training. If it is clear that it is being squeezed in around a host of routine matters then it will not be rated as very important. On the other hand, if participants have a three line whip to attend (from their bosses, not the consultant) then they will rate the importance of the training more highly.

DURATION OF TRAINING

Training should take as long as it needs; a training session, however, will need in most cases to allow for breaks in mid-morning, lunchtime, and mid-afternoon unless there are strong reasons why it should not. The ability to judge how long a session should last comes with experience, but making a session plan helps. Exhibit 10.4 illustrates this for a half-day training session on making presentations.

Remember to pace yourself through a training session. If you are falling behind, you can perhaps cut some of the 'could' or 'should' material from later sessions. Work longer hours and have shorter breaks only as a last resort.

Exhibit 10.4 Timetable for training session on presenting

Time		
9.00am–9.30am	Plenary	Lecture/discussion on how to prepare and deliver presentations
9.30am–9.55am	Individual	Put finishing touches to five-minute presentations (prepared in advance)
9.55am–12.00pm	Two syndicates	Individual presentations, video recorded (inc. coffee break) 5 min presentation 5 min discussion 3 min replay 2 min contingency =15 min total per person 7 people in each syndicate
12.00pm–12.30pm	Plenary	Film – 'Making presentations'
12.30pm–1.00pm	Plenary	Discussions of key learning points arising

Participants in training events also get tired: the physical activities involved in training may be quite different from their day to day work; there is the need for sustained concentration. There is no point in getting through the training agenda and finding that the participants left you mentally hours ago!

PHYSICAL ARRANGEMENTS

The first requirements of the physical arrangements are that they should be comfortable and free from distraction.

For longer training courses and to avoid disruptions, it is worth considering taking participants away from their place of work, for example to a hotel or preferably a specialist training centre. However, this has the disadvantage of expense.

Room layout can also be managed to good effect. Practical considerations, such as being able to see visual aids, will strongly influence layout, but tables and chairs can be arranged in different ways. Exhibit 10.5 shows the main layouts.

Exhibit 10.5 Alternative seating arrangements

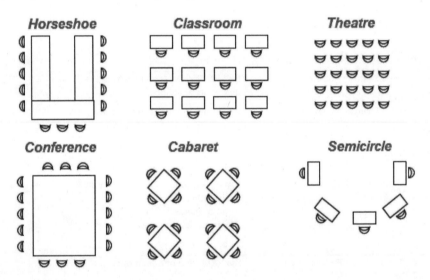

In choosing a room layout consider the dynamics of the event. For example, do you want all the participants to be able to see and communicate with each other? If so, seated in a circle (for example, around a boardroom table, or less formally simply seated in a circle with no table) is best. Alternatively, you may want people to attend to you in the whole group, and then to have discussions or exercises in small groups, in which case the cabaret style layout is best.

REMEMBER ADMINISTRATION

If you are running a training course, the administration of the whole course may be your responsibility. If this is the case, then give it the high priority it deserves. My experience is that delegates on a course will put up with poor trainers but not with poor administration. Failures of administration are far more apparent than those of training, so do make sure that the administration works. A poor speaker will create far less havoc than no lunch!

IMPROVING TRAINING PRESENTATIONS

You can use the same approach to improving a training presentation as for any other. On formal training courses, however, there is usually some attempt to collect participants' views at the conclusion and this can provide helpful feedback on the quality of presentation.

The quality of the training, however, is often more difficult to assess. Some aspects will be easily assessed but others will be less susceptible to assessment, and may require some time to become apparent. If you are making a training presentation as part of a larger project you may be able to follow up to see how effective the training was.

The question to be answered in any assessment is, did the training achieve the desired objectives? Remember that a highly-rated presentation does not mean that the training objectives were necessarily achieved but you can be fairly sure that a bad presentation will lead to poor training.

Increasingly clients will ask for some means of assessing the impact of training. A common method of doing this is the Kirkpatrick levels of evaluation, which are as follows:

1. *Reaction of student*: what they thought and felt about the training (traditionally measured in the evaluations at the end of a course in what are called 'happy sheets'!)
2. *Learning:* the resulting increase in knowledge or capability.
3. *Behaviour*: extent of behaviour and capability improvement and the effect on personal performance.
4. *Results*: the effects on the business or environment resulting from the trainee's performance.

RUNNING WORKSHOPS

A simple distinction between a training session and a workshop lies in the role of the consultant. The consultant as trainer is required to be fairly directive — the trainer has the information, skills or knowledge and needs to impart it to the trainees and is therefore in the best position to define how it must be done. This does not necessarily apply at a workshop, and so the consultant has to act more as a facilitator. These two roles are therefore at different places in the spectrum of consultancy behaviour defined in Figure 2.1.

A workshop nonetheless has to be planned as carefully as any training session. The following are amongst the points you should consider.

1. What is the purpose of the workshop? You might also consider whether the first item on the workshop agenda should be to reaffirm its purpose, its importance, and to define some criteria of success at its completion.

2. Who should attend? What agendas are they coming with and what processes will need to be put in place to deal with these?

3. What should the workshop agenda be? In a training course, the trainer can set an agenda in some detail; by contrast, in a workshop the participants may well have strong views on the way the agenda is to develop. Even so, you will need to think through each item on the agenda. Training might feature on it — e.g. teaching participants a problem-solving technique applicable to the work being done. You may also need to have contingency plans to cater for the different directions in which the workshop might properly go.

4. What logistics should be put in place? For example, a one-day session on creating a new strategy might work better if people are away from work, in an unusual environment, wearing casual clothes, etc. as these differences may prompt them to think in different ways.

In many ways, a workshop is a halfway house between a training session and a meeting; a consultant must be competent in handling all three to be effective.

CHAPTER 11

MARKETING AND SELLING CONSULTANCY PROJECTS

It is better to know some of the questions than all of the answers.
James Thurber

Consultancy projects rarely appear out of the blue. Before any project can be carried out, it must first be sold. Increasingly, organisations are augmenting their own resources with consultants and becoming experienced in using them. However, they need to know of you and your services if they are to buy them, and hence the need for marketing and selling in consultancy.

This can be challenging for consultants, many of whom when they chose a career struck off any options involving selling. Often they believe that in order to sell they have to change their personality to that of a stereotypical 'high-pressure salesperson'. Moreover, rarely in operating consultancy do you get such black and white outcomes as winning or losing a sale, so there can be a real fear of failure.

So the first thing is getting your mind-set right and if, when you saw the heading of this chapter, you strongly felt the need to avoid this topic, then this section is for you! Many professionals feel uncomfortable about selling, and we know — for example from sports coaching — that if you feel uncomfortable about a task, you are less likely to perform it well. So it is essential that you approach marketing and selling consultancy with the right mind-set.

As we shall see in this chapter, being a high-pressure salesperson is counterproductive. On the domestic front, each of us makes hundreds of purchases each year, and each one of those purchases was sold to us. Now, if you look back over your personal purchasing experience, particularly over items of major expenditure, how often did you experience a high-pressure sales technique, to what extent was it successful and, if it was successful, would you happily deal with that salesperson again?

The fact is that most people's memory of being sold to is bad; the buyer experiencing a good salesperson does not even feel they are being 'sold to'. The good sales person should be a facilitator of the buying decision.

David Maister has written extensively on professional services, and with Charles Green and Robert Galford has developed a 'trust equation' (see *The Trusted Advisor*, The Free Press, 2002). This equation (see Exhibit 11.1) shows that the greater the self-orientation, the less the trust. The person aiming to achieve a sale at any cost has high self-orientation. And, although, this may be effective in the short term, it will destroy any chance of a long-term relationship. Most business in a professional firm is repeat business, so even if you win the battle for a single sale, you will lose the war for an ongoing stream of business from this client.

Exhibit 11.1 The trust equation

$$T = \frac{C + R + I}{S}$$

Where

> T = Trustworthiness
>
> C = Credibility (what you say)
>
> R = Reliability (what you do)
>
> I = Intimacy (the sense of security you inspire)
>
> S = Self orientation (your motives)

Research (and probably your personal experience) shows that the salespeople who succeed are:

- those who listen to what you want;
- those who take an active interest in helping you to find the right product to meet your needs.

These are good rules for a consultant salesperson, and should help to raise the confidence of any professional specialist called on to sell, i.e.:

- Listen carefully to what the client says and try to identify clearly what they want;
- Show an active interest in their problems, and work out what you can do to help.

This is what is meant by facilitating the sale. It also follows that if you cannot help, you should say so.

The second reservation that consultants have about selling — fear of failure — depends entirely on how you define failure.

The senior partner of a large firm of consultants told of a major sale they had recently lost. 'We had put tremendous effort into this bid and were, obviously, very disappointed that the project had been awarded to a competitor. I and my two partners who had led the bidding team sought a meeting with the client to review what had happened. The client was apprehensive about the meeting, and visibly relieved when we conducted an objective review of why we had not been chosen. The way we conducted this review encouraged this client to offer us more business thereafter.'

The point of this story is that although the transaction was lost, the relationship was strengthened. The relationship between consultant and client is like a bridge, whilst separate sales are like the traffic passing over it. If there is no bridge, you cannot have any traffic; conversely, there is little point in having a bridge with no traffic either! So winning a sale should never be at the expense of the relationship. If you lose a sale, do two things:

- Find a way of using this to strengthen the relationship with the client;
- Use it to learn — what will you do differently or better next time?

THE MARKETING AND SALES PROCESS

Marketing and selling consultancy projects are pre-contract activities.

Marketing finishes and selling begins in consultancy once a specific prospect is identified, so the process set out in the Introduction, shown in Exhibit 11.2, involves both marketing and selling.

Exhibit 11.2 Selling consultancy projects

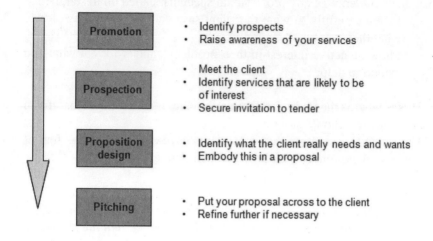

The first stage of *promotion* is to identify suspects — those organisations you wish to pursue as potential clients. As it is unlikely to be a good investment of time, or even possible, to meet every prospect, there needs to be some basis for selecting which you follow up. Indeed, the whole process of selling consists of whittling down intelligently at each stage, a process known as qualification.

The next stage is to raise the suspect's awareness of your consultancy and the services you have on offer. How you do this depends on what sort of consulting practice yours is. If it is a household name, then it may well be an individual will know of your practice, but not of your specific services and how they might be of value. A large practice might want to promote itself in a sector through large scale promotional activities – an advertising campaign, web casts, running a conference or seminar. Smaller practices may not have the resources to do this, nor the benefit of name recognition, so might simply contact the target, perhaps sending them some promotional material. It is unlikely that any sales will result directly from this activity; the purpose is to create an awareness of your services and a dialogue between you and the potential client.

Prospection is conducted usually as one or a series of meetings. The outcome of this phase is to secure authorisation to put in a proposal for carrying out a consultancy project — but not at any cost! There is no point in submitting a proposal if there is no chance that the client will buy it.

At early meetings the salesperson has to listen very carefully to find out what the client wants. A rule of consulting is, 'Sell them what they need in terms of what they want'. There may well need to be more than one meeting before the authorisation to put in a proposal is given. This can take some considerable time; for example, I have a client with whom I had meetings intermittently over the course of three years before being asked to submit a proposal.

The purpose of the proposal is to secure the sale. A proposal is the written specification of the work that is to be undertaken by the consultancy and the terms on which it is to be carried out. It may also contain the arguments for conducting the project and the benefits that might accrue by doing so. But the construction of what goes in the proposal is not a trivial matter, which is why *proposition design* is separated from pitching. Proposition design is about finding the key elements that are going to distinguish your proposal, not just in meeting the basic requirements of the client, but in going beyond this – for example, taking into account the political context, or recognising the cash flow challenges that undertaking the project may present to the client. In some ways, the process of selling consultancy is a process of product specification. The art of high quality proposition design is to identify, articulate and clearly meet clients' needs precisely.

Pitching is about putting your proposition across to the client. It is usually embodied in a written document — the proposal. The proposal may be in a number of formats: a text-based document (which itself could be a letter or report); a graphic presentation; or a combination of these. Very often, pitching might consist of sending a document (nowadays usually expected by email rather than hard copy by post)[3] and then making a face-to-face presentation.

If the sales process to this point has been conducted well, the proposal document may simply be the written confirmation of what has already been agreed. Similarly, if you are submitting a compliant response to an invitation to tender, the content of the proposal may have been prescribed. In other cases, there may be quite a bit of work involved after the proposal has been submitted. For example, there may be questions to answer; the proposal may need to be modified or refined to reflect more closely what

---

3   When sending a document, do so in pdf format. Sending in Word means that you are also sending a lot of other information. I've had a lot of fun looking at document properties in word documents sent to me to find out how they originated. So make sure, if you have to send in Word and are cannibalising an earlier document, that you check the document properties and modify as required.

the client wants. Some may have elaborate procedures for deciding whether or not to accept a proposal and, indeed, the proposal may prompt a client to reappraise the nature of the project involved.

Finally, you hope, the sale will be made. However, in reality, the process is much like a leaky pipe: not all the suspects that enter at one end emerge at the other as clients. At each stage there is a loss. The proportion of prospects that finally provide you with business is usually very small — a few per cent at most — so you have to approach quite a lot of targets before you get a sale. This leads to two messages of hope for those who are new to selling consultancy.

1. Don't be depressed by suspects who don't get to the meeting stage, or meetings that fail to lead to proposals. This is all part of the normal process.
2. Provided you have identified the right targets (and your sales technique is not disastrous!) eventually some sales will emerge from the pipeline.

It also indicates the priorities for salespeople in using their time: sales effort is best put in at the point closest to making the sale.

In the following sections we look at other aspects of each of these phases.

PROMOTION

PRODUCT DEFINITION

Consultants of all kinds have to be able to describe what they do for their clients, and product development consists of refining the details of these descriptions. Descriptions may be concrete (e.g. 'We are a firm of recruitment consultants; we generate a shortlist of candidates willing and able to fill a vacancy.') through to the abstract (e.g. 'As a process consultant, I engage with your people to help them carry out their work more effectively.')

The services a consultancy might offer depend on the skills and experience of its consultants. The 'product' is the method by which an individual consultant's capabilities are delivered to a client. A sole practitioner may have a narrow range of simple products, whilst a large practice may combine the capabilities of many consultants to conduct long-term, complex projects. The choice of product will also influence the size of a sale; a small practice may sell a few consultant-weeks each sale, whilst a large one might sell many work-years in a single sale.

Equally important is defining what you are not going to do.

A new client approached me: 'We have been given your name by XYZ, who have been doing some excellent work for us in team building. XYZ no longer wish to do this work, and have suggested you could help.' XYZ is a major practice which is following a focussed strategy. This means defining clearly what they will and will not do. The piece of work they were doing for this client was excellent, and seen to be so, but it now fell outside their chosen area of business so they turned it down. I admire them; in implementing strategy, the difficult task is declining promising opportunities outside the area of business chosen.

One of the most effective ways of developing new products in any business has been the sponsorship of a 'product champion'. A product champion is an individual who believes in a product concept and is enthusiastic and energetic enough to develop an idea into a marketable reality. So, in a consultancy an enthusiastic product champion is much better than a half-hearted individual who sees the task as a chore.

Having decided on your products, promotion is aimed at raising awareness of the firm and its services more generally.

PROMOTIONAL ACTIVITIES

It is important to define the services that you offer; if you cannot explain your services, it is unlikely that clients will understand them. For this reason, it is particularly helpful for a newly formed consultancy to produce a brochure. (I am not convinced that a brochure functions as anything more than a substantial calling card; the value of preparing one lies, however, in the discipline of having to define your services clearly and the needs they address.)

Some organisations may be excluded as clients once the service has been defined. For example, a company with no international business is unlikely to be interested in international marketing, nor is a services organisation likely to be interested in manufacturing control systems. You need, therefore, to identify a suspect profile that defines the characteristics of the sort of organisation that might be a client for the services on offer.

These suspects will be made aware of consultancy services through the promotion to publicise them. Promotional activities include:

- advertising and publicity material — e.g. brochures, website;

- mailshots — both postal and via e-mail;
- publicity about the firm and its work (including the use of social media);
- speaking at conferences;
- running seminars;
- publishing articles in journals and newspapers;
- other publications — e.g. books, manuals, software, periodicals.

The efficacy of each of these varies considerably, and you need to build up experience of what works for you.

At the most basic level, you need to be able to respond to an enquiry, and provide useful information to a prospective client. You, therefore, need some promotional literature. Nowadays, of course, you can create a website quite easily (and, being relatively cheap, even the smallest practice is expected to have one).

But the main purpose of promotion is to generate enquiries in the first place. Your website should be set up so that it appears when appropriate key words are used on a search engine.

More generally, you need to decide what you should be famous for and then direct your professional efforts to achieving this in your marketplace. Good quality enquiries arise because a prospective client has a need and recognises that your firm could be the right one to help.

NETWORKING
As well as broadcast activities, such as those shown above, there will be face-to-face opportunities to promote the firm and its offerings; these are generally categorised as 'networking'. Opportunities for networking arise on occasions when you can come into contact with prospective clients informally. Attendance at a conference may lead to this, but there will be social occasions — for example, through membership of a sports club — which will bring prospective clients into contact. And of course there are many networking groups that have been set up specifically to facilitate this; for example, almost every large town will have a breakfast club of some kind.

An important group of people to include in a network are 'connectors'. These are third parties who can introduce business to your own firm. For example, an accountant may be asked to recommend a consultant who can advise on the selection of computer systems, or a banker asked to recommend a consultant who can give sales training. And of course past clients are a rich source of referrals. The object of marketing, therefore, is to raise awareness of your services amongst not only clients but also connectors, so that they will contact you when they know of an organisation needing the service you offer.

PROSPECTION

Prospection is panning for gold. It is an evolving dialogue with a potential client to see what scope there is for working together to mutual benefit.

The chances of initiating contact with a client on the very day they have a need for consultancy services are low. The promotional phase will serve to establish some familiarity between consultant and prospect; it should establish whether, in principle, they might work together. The consultancy practice will lay out their services, and (you hope!) at the same time the client will respond and say, 'Yes, I am interested.'

So, the prospection phase is characterised by the start of a substantive dialogue between consultant and client about the scope for working together. It is at this point that the consultant salesperson realises that there is a complementary buying process within the client.

The reality is that a consultancy project is a joint venture between consultant and client, and the selling/buying activity is directed to sorting out the details of the joint venture. This concept is often of help to those new to selling consultancy, many of whom think that selling involves persuading people to buy things they don't want. This is certainly not the case in selling consultancy; if you sell a client a project they don't need, you run the risk of:

- engaging in a project doomed to disappoint the client;
- ruining the client relationship.

Selling consultancy involves identifying an overlap of interest between consultancy and client to your mutual benefit.

Consultants have capabilities which their clients do not have, or have in insufficient measure. Conversely, the client has a whole bundle of issues or problems which consultants could help to resolve, but which have to meet several criteria before the client is receptive to the idea of outside help.

1. The problem must be recognised as such and the client must have decided that they want to do something about it. Problems can be broadly categorised as remedial (putting something right that is going wrong) or developmental (advancing the enterprise in some way).

The problem concept may have arisen within the organisation. Alternatively, the consultancy may approach the client organisation with some ideas about areas they might usefully address.

2. The resolution of the problem must be a matter of priority — the client has to do something about it, now.

3. The client must believe the problem can be solved. Marketing by consultants can help in both meeting this and the previous criterion: the possibility that a problem previously thought to be insoluble can now be solved can make it become a matter of priority. For example, a certain level of absenteeism is accepted in all organisations; however, if it became known that it was possible to halve it easily, many previously content organisations would seek to do this.

4. The client recognises the need for outside help — whether it is expertise, experience or the objectivity of a professionally qualified outsider.

Part of the process of selling a consultancy service consists of getting the agreement of purchasers that these criteria are met. In the selling situation you are trying to get the prospective client to acknowledge that the issue:

- is relevant to their business and needs to be addressed;
- merits attention now;
- can be resolved with outside help (provided by you, the consultant!)

Note that the client's perspective is from the issues that concern them. (And it is worth noting, at this point, that today's priority can easily be forgotten tomorrow. All consultants have suffered from clients who, one day have asked for help on a project and the next have found the priority has disappeared!) The salesperson's task is to establish a link between these issues and the services the practice has to offer.

Once the client has decided to launch a project and seek outside help, a consultant will need to be selected from those the client knows or who have a reputation in the required specialism. If you have helped the client to identify the issue and launch the project in the first place, you will be well placed to secure the assignment. If not, winning the project will depend on whether the client knows of you and your reputation.

WHERE TO SPEND YOUR SALES EFFORT

For this reason, the attractiveness of any prospect can be ranked in the following order (the least attractive first).

1. *Cold calls*: here the consultant takes the initiative. Consultant and client will be personally unknown to each other. Although cold calling is unattractive by comparison with the other sources of prospects set out below, it can still be worth doing and has to be done if there are no opportunities in the other categories. Moreover, it can provide useful market data; even if they do not want to buy, you can have valuable conversations with those you contact. Moreover, it is far better if suspects make it clear early on that they don't want to buy rather than your putting a lot of effort into pursuing someone who has no serious intention of buying.

2. *Introductions* to new clients: existing clients can provide introductions; there are also 'connectors' (other professional firms, banks, etc. as mentioned above) who can provide introductions.

3. *Leads*: the difference between a lead and an introduction is that with a lead a probable need for consultancy services has been identified. Leads can again arise from clients, contacts, connectors and so on.

4. *Extensions*: this is the further work you might conduct with existing clients. Note that one of the outcomes of doing a consultancy project is a different — closer — relationship between consultant and client. This means that you have an inside track when bidding for work with existing clients.

Domestic experience confirms the validity of this ranking. If a house painter calls at your door, the chances of your needing some painting doing and wanting him to do it straightaway are small; likewise, so too is the probability of success from a specific cold call. Friends might be using a painter to decorate their house and recommend him — this is an introduction. The lead would be if you wanted some painting doing and you asked friends who had recently had their house redecorated to recommend a painter. Finally, an extension occurs when you ask the decorator, with whom you are satisfied, to quote for doing a couple more rooms.

Sales statistics in consultancy practices reflect the relative ease of each of these sales techniques. Business with current or recent clients can account for two-thirds or more of sales. So, the best opportunities for selling are amongst existing clients, either by extending projects or spotting opportunities in other areas. An extension to a project might come about by repeating the work for another part of the company. For example, a firm may call on a consultant to help in designing and introducing cost control procedures in one subsidiary. Having succeeded there, they may be asked to repeat the process in other subsidiaries. Extension work might also occur within a project, evolving from help in planning to help in implementing. Extension sales have to be dealt with carefully, however.

> *At the start of my consulting career, I saw scope at a client's to start a new project. A senior colleague stopped me: 'I realise they can do this, and it is needed,' he said, 'but it is not amongst their present top priorities as a business. We would lose face as a consultancy practice if we were to advise them to undertake a project of low priority.'*

Because large firms of consultants offer a wider range of services, there is usually more opportunity for them to be able to offer help in areas outside the scope of existing projects. In this respect, therefore, a small practice spotting a client need that it cannot itself address, might act as a connector for a different firm, hoping perhaps for a quid pro quo eventually.

Referrals (leads and introductions) will account for most of the balance of sales in all cases; only a small percentage of sales will come from cold calling. And, as cold calling is the least fruitful — and hence most time consuming — of sales activities, it follows that you have to put a disproportionate amount of time into selling if you are launching a new consultancy practice.

The important point to emerge from this is that an important asset for any consultancy is its network of relationships — the contacts it has with past and present clients, connectors, and so on. A job for every consultant is to create and maintain a network.

DEVELOPING A SALES CONVERSATION

The first contact from a client might be by letter, email or telephone. Some organisations may issue a general invitation to tender containing carefully thought out terms of reference and a background briefing; in the public sector there may also be an obligation to publish this on a web site if the size of the contract is more than a set amount. Let's look at the phone conversation.

In Chapter 3 we introduced Dick, of TDH Ltd who was working on a stock control system for ABC Ltd. Let's go back to the sales process that might have preceded starting when Dick receives a telephone enquiry from a director of ABC Ltd, who is a new prospect. After introducing himself, the director might continue:

Director	'I'm told that you might be able to help us with a problem we have on our stock control system. We're thinking of installing a new computer-based system and want some external consultants to work with us. I gather you can help.'	*Dick might query how the director knows about TDH Ltd, e.g. was it from a web search or a reference from another client? This information could help in planning future marketing.*
Dick	'We've done a number of projects of varying scales for a wide variety of clients in this area. Perhaps you could give me some background on your firm and the stock control system.'	*Dick establishes in principle that TDH is able to help. He may never have heard of ABC Ltd, so he needs some background information.*

So, they discuss the nature and context of the problem and the selling process has started. For example, the client will be forming an opinion of TDH Ltd by how well Dick demonstrates his understanding of the problem and the quality of his questions.

At this stage, it is not necessary for Dick to suggest possible solutions — quite the reverse; even if the problem is technically easy to solve there may be serious barriers to getting acceptance within the organisation.

The conversation could conclude:

Dick	'I think the next stage is for us to meet. Shall we fix a date now?'	*Dick is fixing the next step in the selling process.*
Director	'Can I come back to you on that — I'll call you in the next day or so.'	*Not a particularly well-organised director but the point is to illustrate Dick's response . . .*
Dick	'Fine; can I contact you next week if I've heard nothing in the meantime?'	*Which allows Dick to take the initiative in contacting the director again should it be necessary.*

They will need to arrange a venue for this meeting; a visit to a client's office or factory can tell you a lot about the business, so I try to arrange that at least one of the early meetings takes place on the client's premises.

PROPOSITION DESIGN

Sometimes clients have a clear definition of the project they are initiating and the nature of the consultancy support they want. Frequently, however, they may have only a broad idea of what is needed, and use their conversations with consultants to refine their view both of the project and of the role that consultants might take. Work on proposition design, in practice, often starts before the invitation to tender is offered.

The consultant's performance in the course of these discussions will influence the client's predisposition whether or not to invite them to tender. Sales meetings provide a client with a first experience of what it is like to work with the consultant.

GATHERING INTELLIGENCE FOR PROPOSITION DESIGN

Prior to contracting to work on a particular project, a consultant will carry out a preliminary investigation or survey to assess its nature and scope. It is a mini-project in itself to:

- collect data about the problem as defined;
- analyse it to identify the key issues;
- decide the type of approach which will lead to resolving the issues;
- plan how the project is to proceed;
- determine the consultant and other resources required;
- find out something about the politics and other contextual aspects.

In some projects, this may already have been done by the client — for example, if the consultant is required to make a defined contribution as a specialist to a complex project already being undertaken. In other cases, a preliminary investigation might be the first stage of a multiphase project, for which the consultant might charge fees, particularly if diagnosing the problem is of value in itself.

Continuing the example above, however, we will assume that the consultant is involved in defining all of the stages above before the project starts and so Dick arranges to carry out his survey. Prior to visiting the prospective client he might do some more research on ABC Ltd by looking at its web site, getting hold of the company report and accounts, plus publicity material on its products. Dick could also ask the client to provide additional information that might be available and helpful. He will thereby be able to learn something of ABC Ltd in advance and to focus his enquiries during his visit rather better.

Dick will have a mental, if not a written, checklist of points he will want to cover during his first visit. He may want to tour the relevant factory/offices/stores and be introduced to key people. But remember that this is not always appropriate; it is an intervention into the organisation and, therefore, has to be considered in the context of the project's goals.

Where matters of opinion (rather than hard data) are concerned, he may wish to talk to more than one person to distinguish between commonly held and individual views.

It is vital during a preliminary survey to try to identify the real problem rather than the symptoms. Consultants have a touching faith in their own abilities and some cynicism about their clients' skills in separating symptoms from causes. That this endures is because it is often borne out by fact. Thus, Dick will find the superficial description of the stock control problem is:

- they want a new computer-based stock control system;
- the current system, installed two years ago, has been outgrown, and, indeed, has never worked satisfactorily.

On further probing, he will probably find that:

- production and sales do not talk to each other and ...
- ... the only thing they agree on is that they hate the IT department ...
- ... who hate them equally, because they do not provide the data required, or it is inaccurate or late and ...
- ... the computer system *is* inadequate.

Now, whether or not he expresses it to his client, Dick is not going to get very far with the project unless he gets everybody working together. There are people issues involved as well as technical ones and the approach Dick adopts has to allow for both dimensions of the problem.

MEETING THE NEEDS OF *THIS* CLIENT
Dick will also need to assess, at the survey stage, what sort of client he is dealing with and the nature of the working relationship they will have.

He will need to rate how good a client the organisation is; is it accustomed to using management consultants and able to manage consulting projects? If not, Dick will need to provide more project management support than otherwise and guide the client in using a consultant effectively. Is the project likely to be complex – for example, breaking new ground for this client? Again, this will determine the amount of time needed from the consultant

There will be assumptions, on both sides, about the nature of the client–consultant relationship, and Dick should consider the following points in particular.

1. What is the relationship of the member of client staff commissioning the project (whom I call the 'sponsor') to the overall project? Is it their brainchild or have they been deputed to look after it? If the latter, who is the real client? How committed are they to its success and what personal objectives might it be meeting? Are there any 'unwritten expectations'? Beware of taking on projects to which the sponsor is uncommitted; more junior staff will sense this with the result that the project will be a low priority for them and the consultant will have a tough job carrying out the project. Again, beware the sponsor who is initiating a project as a personal crusade in the organisation. Others may be interested in seeing the project fail and, if it does, the sponsor may find it politically expedient to blame the consultant.

2. What will the sponsor's involvement be after the project starts? If they are not going to be the principal point of contact, who is? What will your reporting relationship be to the organisation? As a strategic ploy, you should keep the reporting relationship as high as you can. In practice, this means that even if the sponsor delegates day-to-day contact to a subordinate, you should make sure you continue to deal with the sponsor as your client. The reason for this is that your power to get things done will depend, in part, on the level of your connections in the client organisation.

3. Which client staff will be available to work with you? At the very least, it is helpful to have a 'Mr/Ms Fixit' who can act as your guide to the organisation, arrange meetings and make internal information available to you. Beyond this, you may need advice about the nature of the business and the industry; after all, clients should be experts about their own business! In short, therefore, consultants need support from client staff to help them work effectively. It is important that the client understands this, and provides the necessary help.

4. How should the project be publicised within the client organisation? Who needs to be told, and in what detail? This will depend on the nature of the project but it is better to take the initiative in informing staff rather than having to react to rumours and gossip.

These points need to be resolved before starting the project and should, at least in outline, be taken into account in preparing the proposal.

PITCHING

PREPARING THE PROPOSAL
Having carried out this survey, Dick should have collected enough data to prepare a proposal, which is the document embodying the terms of reference for the project.

On the first occasion of working with a client the proposal will probably need to be written out in some detail, but once a good consulting relationship has been achieved a client may be happy with a short confirmatory letter covering the key points which have been orally agreed.

In all cases, however, the key points below must be considered in detail by the consultant and agreed — at least in principle — by the client, whether or not they are written down, so that the expectations of both the consultant and the client are the same.

1. Your *appreciation* of the problem: at the very least this is simply feeding back to the client the data that has been given to you. Much better, however, is to interpret the data with insight, so that the problem is seen by the client from a different, more helpful perspective than before. Do this particularly if you have a standard approach to a problem; this allows you to differentiate your proposal.

   For example, a client was seeking to appoint recruitment consultants and briefed two firms of consultants, both of whom impressed the client at the initial meeting. The choice, therefore, had to be made on the basis of the proposals they put forward. One consultancy provided a standard proposal; it reflected nothing of the briefing and could have applied to any client. The other provided an appraisal of the business issues relating to the appointment, developed from the briefing they had received. The latter firm was appointed.

Thus Dick's appreciation of the problem at ABC Ltd might emphasise the technical problems as manifestations of the need for better teamwork (a point he will need to express sensitively).

2. The *scope and objectives* of the project. These set the boundaries for the project and what is to be achieved within them. If ABC Ltd is a multi-site company, Dick may limit the scope of the project to one site — or even one product group — as appropriate.

The objective may be to have a new stock control system working well but Dick may suggest more precise measures of this, such as the requirements of the new computer system and when it should be installed and running.

3. The *method of approach*: there may be a totally standard, off-the-shelf approach to carrying out the project. There is nothing wrong with this. (Indeed, taking an example from another profession, whilst under the surgeon's knife on an operating table, we much prefer they use a standard, well-proven approach.) On the other hand, consultants should not fall into the trap of fitting clients' problems to their solutions. Innovation, therefore, is not a *sine qua non* — it must be introduced wisely.

So, Dick might use a standard approach to stock control in ABC Ltd, but be innovative in introducing it so as to achieve better team working.

4. The *programme of work* entailed. This is getting much closer to planning and, at this stage the principal tasks should be described, at least in outline. A project might fall into a number of discrete phases of work and in the case of ABC Ltd, consist of:
   - specification of the new system;
   - delivery and introduction of the new equipment;
   - parallel running with new and old systems;
   - complete transfer to the new system.

   In this section you should explain what the client will be getting for their money — i.e. the deliverables — and when they should expect them, for example, when a new system will have been designed, or when a report will have been delivered and the points it will cover.

5. A *summary of the prospective benefits* arising from the project. This is particularly relevant in written proposals, which may be used for selling the project concept as well as your firm's services to your sponsor's colleagues. Thus, in this proposal Dick may quantify the reduction of working capital, and the consequent savings in interest payable resulting from the expected reductions in stock levels.
6. The *resources required*. This will cover the time required from the consultant and the consequent fees. With a multi-stage project, the size of later stages may be contingent on the first; even so, it is helpful for budgeting purposes to give a client an indication of what future costs might be. As almost all consulting projects involve input from the client's staff, there should also be some indication of the resources required from the client.

An outline plan may also be included but for the purpose of this example we will assume that detailed planning is done after the survey stage, when the programme of work will be elaborated and set against a timescale.

You will probably also need to state why you believe you are qualified to carry out the project. This may relate to academic qualifications but, in most cases, will consist of a history of relevant project experience. In Dick's example, he will cite similar projects on which he has worked involving stock control issues. A large firm of consultants may quote a summary of the jobs it has carried out and add brief CVs of the consultants expected to work on this particular assignment, tailored to show why each consultant is qualified to work on any particular project.

The need for previous experience of a similar project or knowledge of the business sector will depend on the nature of the work being undertaken by the consultant. In all cases, however, clients should ask sufficient questions to reassure themselves that the firm and/or consultant has appropriate experience and professionalism. Reputable individuals or firms of consultants will be equally anxious to do a good job — if they fail they will lose their reputation. One bad job can cost 100 good ones.

References from other clients may be useful in validating the reliability of consultants new to a client. High-risk projects should, of course, not be entrusted to any consultant in whom the client does not have complete confidence.

THE PROPOSAL AS A CONTRACT

The proposal is also the basis of the contract between client and consultant; it should therefore specify:

- the work to be done by the consultant and the deliverables (and, where otherwise there may be ambiguity, note any work specifically excluded);
- resources which the client must provide;
- the timing and duration of the project;
- the basis on which fees will be charged.

Sometimes, these may change during the course of a project. If this happens, it is as well to document the changes, e.g. in a letter to the client confirming them.

You will also need to tell the client your terms of business, including:

- how long the offer remains firm: you may want to review the fee estimate if the client does not decide for six months or if the consultants originally assigned are no longer available;
- whether fee rates are to be subject to revision during the course of the project;
- the terms on which the fees will be paid;
- the conditions under which the project may be terminated by either side;
- what is covered: does it include expenses and VAT, or are they separate? If separate, how are they to be charged? Are secretarial and other services to be provided by the client or by the consultant? If the latter, is a separate charge to be made for them?

In these litigious times, it is as well to put in a clause which disclaims responsibility for achieving particular results or for any consequential losses. Whether it will provide total protection is arguable but at least it will help in removing any ambiguity on this point. Some professionals, such as architects, are not able to disclaim this but management consultants are, and probably rightly so, as much of their work does depend on the effective co-operation of the client's staff. It is rare for a consultant to be able to guarantee the benefits arising from a project and written proposals should reflect this, e.g. by using 'should' instead of 'will' in referring to future events.

Clients may also want some guarantees of confidentiality. Other clauses might cover matters such as rights to copyright, patents, royalties and other intellectual property and any restrictions applying to consultants — such as taking up employment with the client, or doing similar work on sensitive matters for other clients within the same sector. (It would be clearly unethical for an individual consultant to prepare a marketing strategy for a company with a particular product range, having just done the same for their major competitor.)

WHO SHOULD MAKE THE PITCH?

In some larger firms of consultants the job of the salesperson has historically been separated from that of the delivery consultant. Nowadays, because of the degree of specialisation often involved and the insistence of clients, operating consultants are usually involved in the selling process, at least in the final stages. Consultancy salespeople may take responsibility for managing the client relationship; they will be the first point of contact for a client, but will then involve an appropriate specialist who will carry out the project.

If the consultant who has worked on selling the project is to be involved in its execution, there is no problem of transition. In some circumstances, particularly in a large firm, however, there may need to be a handover from a sales executive to the operator.

One of the deadly sins mentioned most often by clients of consultants is the gap between the expertise of the impressive senior consultant who wins the contract and that of the consultant who does the work. This is not a new gripe; Anthony Jay commented in a *Harvard Business Review* article: 'Rate yourself as a client' (Jay, 1977):

> *There was a famous London management consultant in the 1950s whose craggy face, bushy eyebrows, deep perception and penetrating analysis were almost hypnotically irresistible to the boards of large corporations. But once the corporation was hooked, he was never seen again. For the next 18 months the offices were overrun with hordes of fresh-faced business graduates completing their management education at the corporation's expense.*

In the current world the same has been said of a major global consulting practice. 'Invite them in,' said one client, 'and it's like opening a box of frogs – within no time they are all over the place!'

If there is to be a transition, part of the handover process should be a thorough briefing about the client and the project. Early in my career I had to start a project with totally inadequate briefing; in particular, I did not know exactly what expertise the client's chief executive was expecting from me. We had the following exchange during our first meeting:

Me: (fishing for a clue), 'I'd be interested in your view of how you expect me to contribute to the project.'

Chief Executive: (not helping in the slightest), 'I'd like you to use your own particular expertise to help us.'

Fortunately things were sorted out eventually, with no ill effects — but a good briefing would have avoided that dangerous corner.

Typically, the problems of handover are not only lack of briefing, but also:
- being committed to an approach which the sales consultant knows and likes, but with which the operating consultant has little sympathy;
- after a rather more extensive investigation, finding the situation is fundamentally different from that assumed when the project was conceived.

The message is simple: the consultant who sold the assignment must remain in close contact with its execution.

CHAPTER 12

THE BUSINESS OF CONSULTANCY

Annual income twenty pounds, annual expenditure nineteen nineteen six, result happiness. Annual income twenty pounds, annual expenditure twenty pounds ought and six, result misery.
Mr Micawber in *David Copperfield* (Dickens).

I was once involved with a specialist consultancy (not a management consultancy) staffed, in the main, by individuals with formal professional qualifications — largely barristers and accountants — and the occasional chartered secretary. Each was an expert in their field and the firm provided first-class advice to its clients.

The chief executive had a problem, however. 'Our profits are falling,' he confided one evening after work, 'what is more, our cash flow is poor and the amount of work-in-progress we have is far too high.'

When I looked into the problem, I found that although the professional staff were immensely capable within their own fields of expertise, they were far less effective at creating new engagements or invoicing their clients. It was not a problem of ability but one of willingness. The professionals would put these tasks at the bottom of their lists of priorities; other tasks would almost always supervene.

I have seen this frequently replicated in professional firms — not only in firms of lawyers and accountants, but also in medical practices, research

laboratories, stockbrokers, chartered surveyors and management consultants
— and it is, I believe, a universal truth:

> *Professional people do not like administration. They will give it
> low priority and avoid it whenever possible.*

Why is this? It is probably because professionals have been schooled for
a long time in their specialisation. The emphases are on quality of advice
and breadth of experience in the area of their expertise. The professional's
reputation grows because of specialist ability, not because they do administration well! But if a professional firm is to survive and prosper, it is vital
that its business is managed to an adequate standard.

The purpose, therefore, of this chapter is to illustrate some of the important commercial aspects of running a consultancy business: for example,
in the way that you organise your work.

You need to keep a record of how you spend your time and this can be a
chore. The need to achieve results within tight deadlines can also be difficult,
particularly if the consultant is fascinated by the technical ramifications of
the problem. The commercial imperatives of running a consultancy business
can, therefore, conflict with the inclination of consultants to avoid administration and become preoccupied with the projects they are undertaking.

THE CONSULTANCY BUSINESS PROCESS

Exhibit 12.1 The consultancy business process

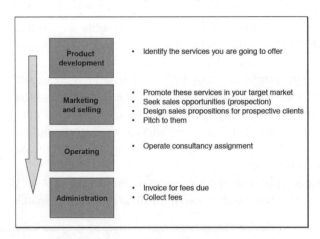

Exhibit 12.1 shows the main tasks involved in a consultancy business, already covered in more detail earlier in the book. Time must be spent on all of these activities. A consultant's stock in trade is time; it is the raw material of a consultancy business and accounts for the greatest proportion of business costs. So, managing time allocation and how it is charged to the client is at the heart of managing a consultancy business effectively.

If new consultants understand this, they should be able to appreciate — though not necessarily enjoy — some of the pressures to which they are subject. If, alternatively, you are planning to set up a consulting business, it is vital that you understand how it works. A capacity to provide professional advice is rarely sufficient by itself to ensure commercial success!

We have met TDH Ltd in previous chapters, a practice of three consultants, Tom, Dick and Harriet working together, and they are supported by an administrative assistant. They are based in a small office they rent outside London. They try to keep their commitment to expenditure to a minimum, so use outside services to supplement their own where required. The administrative assistant raises invoices, keeps the books, deals with enquiries (the consultants are not often in the office) and provides secretarial support to the consultants. Temporary staff are used when the assistant is sick or on holiday.

Tom has prepared a budget for the forthcoming year. Exhibit 12.2 shows the breakdown of the costs expected.

Tom has budgeted basic salaries of £60,000 p.a. for himself, Dick and Harriet, which will be supplemented by a share of the profits at the year end. As far as possible, expenses incurred in carrying out their work are recharged to their clients. But there are other expenses in carrying out their business that they cannot recover — for example, in connection with attempting to sell to prospective clients who do not buy — and these are also shown.

Exhibit 12.2 TDH Ltd: fixed costs

	£ p.a.
Consultants' salaries (3 × £60,000)	180,000
Pensions, National Insurance (25% of above)	45,000
Non-recoverable expenses	5,000
Office expenses	25,000
Administrative assistant (includes benefits, etc.)	30,000
Other costs (marketing collateral, etc.)	15,000
Total	300,000

The budgeted expenses of the business, therefore, amount to £300,000 and, at least, this amount of revenue needs to be generated to break even. In fact, Tom, Dick and Harriet would be disappointed if the revenue was as little as this, because they would like incomes more than £60,000 p.a. To do this, they need to follow three key rules in running a consultancy business; they are as follows.

1. Maintain the proportion of time earning fees (the utilisation).
2. Carefully invest the time not earning fees.
3. Control the cash.

RULE 1: MAINTAIN UTILISATION

Tom, Dick and Harriet get their revenue by selling their time — they do not provide product-related services. So, they do not sell the results of research as reports, organise conferences or sell proprietary software for computers, which are some of the other ways in which a consultancy firm can generate revenue. Rather, when making a sale, TDH Ltd estimates how many days work it will need and multiplies it by a daily fee rate to estimate the price.

Their revenue is determined by how many days they work on fees multiplied by the daily fee rate. *Utilisation* is the time spent on fees as a percentage of paid days and covers all the fee earners in the firm. Therefore, in the case of TDH Ltd, the administrative assistant would not be included in this calculation.

Now, although consultants are paid for the whole year, not all of this time is available for consulting activities. Tom has estimated how many days could be available for consulting activities and Exhibit 12.3 shows his calculations. Out of a total of 260 days, only 212 are left after allowances for holidays, illness and training.

As shown in Exhibit 12.1, this time cannot be spent entirely earning fees; it has to be allocated to selling, marketing, administration and other activities throughout the year. Consultancy firms that do not reserve time for these can alternate between feast and famine, and this can particularly afflict small firms or sole practitioners. Consultants engaged full time on a project for several months have no time for developing further business and at the end of the project, therefore, have nothing to do. There is then a period of no revenue whilst they sell the next engagement, which then occupies them full time. This effect diminishes with increasing numbers and independent professionals sometimes associate formally or informally to smooth it out.

Exhibit 12.3 TDH Ltd: working days available per consultant each year

	Days	
Total days available: 52 weeks × 5 days		260
Statutory holidays (8 days)	8	
Annual holidays (5 weeks)	25	
Illness	5	
Continuing professional development (CPD)	10	
Total time unavailable		48
Net time available		212

The level of utilisation will depend on the nature of the consultancy business. In recent years, large consultancy practices have undertaken very large projects where they are, in effect, acting as subcontractors. This enables them to achieve very high levels of utilisation for members of the teams involved, who may be assigned to the same project for years at a time. Management consulting is different and has somewhat lower levels of utilisation. A good rule of thumb for a management consulting practice is to aim for an average utilisation of about 60 per cent over all professionals, from the most senior to the most junior. This is 156 days per year per person (60 per cent × 260 days = 156 days). More than this means more revenue, but you have to take care that the remaining time is sufficient for the non-fee-earning activities.

With a large consulting practice, of course, the work is not uniformly distributed; more senior people may spend more time in selling and marketing than their junior colleagues, who will spend most of their time earning fees. Thus, in a large firm, senior people may spend only a few days per month earning fees, whilst junior consultants might be engaged full time on doing this.

By contrast, sole practitioners getting no work as a subcontractor to other consultants typically find they work 100–140 days per year on fees.

DETERMINING FEE RATE
Tom also has to decide what fee rate to charge; he knows that consultants can charge from £500 per day to more than £2,000 per day. He, therefore,

has to analyse how total revenue might vary according to different fee rates, assuming that Tom, Dick and Harriet each earn fees for 156 days in the year.

The result is shown in the graph in Exhibit 12.4, which shows how annual revenue varies with different fee rates. Also shown is the estimate of total cost from Exhibit 12.2 — £300,000. The breakeven point, where revenue equals cost, is at a daily fee rate of just over £640. So the fee rate must be more than this.

Exhibit 12.4 Breakeven chart for different fee rates at 60% utilisation

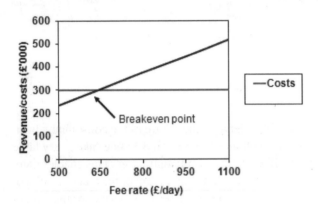

Tom should know from experience what fee rate is acceptable to most of his firm's current or prospective clients but, in practice, some may be willing to pay more, others less. So, he budgets for an average fee rate and this is assumed to be £750 per day. He calculates the profits as shown in Exhibit 12.5.

Exhibit 12.5 Profits achieved from budgeted utilisation

	£
Revenue: 156 days × £750/day × 3 people	351,000
Costs (from Exhibit 12.2)	300,000
Profit	51,000

If utilisation is only 50 per cent instead of 60 per cent, however, profit turns to a loss:

	£
Revenue: 130 days × £750/day × 3 people	292,500
Costs (from Exhibit 12.2)	300,000
Loss	7,500

Also shown in Exhibit 12.5 however is the effect of a lower than budget utilisation. So Tom needs to do a further analysis to show the effect of varying utilisation; and this is shown in Exhibit 12.6. Tom would then see that his breakeven utilisation is almost 52%.

Exhibit 12.6 Breakeven chart for different utilisation at a fee rate of £750 per day

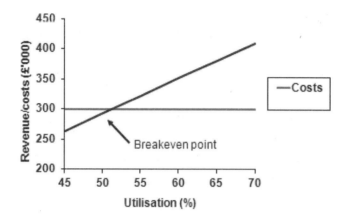

Utilisation, therefore, is a key factor to control in any consulting firm. Income depends on utilisation and fee rates. Whereas fee rates are set on an infrequent basis — maybe annually, or at the start of a project — utilisation has to be controlled on a daily basis. Once a day that could have been spent fee earning has passed in less profitable activity, it can never be recovered.

> *I have a friend, an architect, who works from home. He does not have a large income, although he claims he cannot take on more work. In fact, he is a great potterer; he will find odd tasks to do round the house, articles to read, games to play on his computer; he works probably no more than two or, at most, three hours each day. He could easily double his income by increasing the number of hours he works each day. But there is the man, there is his life-style and it is not something he would wish or needs to change.*

In commercial consulting practices such freedom is rarely possible. There is — or there should be — pressure on the consultant to maintain utilisation at what may seem high levels if a practice is to prosper.

TIME NOT AVAILABLE

But what of the time not earning fees? At this point, let us review the assumptions made in Exhibit 12.3 about time available.

Holidays and the working week

We have assumed that five weeks' annual holiday and statutory holidays (eight days) are all taken off from work.

Holidays away from work are of benefit to the business as well as the individual. After a break, the consultant comes back refreshed and recharged. It is tempting to postpone or forgo holidays; avoid the temptation if you can. Often, the benefit of a break is realised only in retrospect.

We have also assumed a five-day working week and that consultants are at work for an average working day. It is wrong to budget on the basis that individuals are to put in excessive effort. There is a certain machismo attached to long hours, working weekends, not taking holiday and so on. This is totally wrong; there is no intrinsic merit in spending excessive time at work — indeed, it can be counter-productive.

> *A friend, who works for a prestigious firm of management consultants, appeared one Sunday at lunch having spent the morning working at his office. I asked if this was a frequent occurrence, and did he get 'brownie points' for doing it? His comment was that it depended on your existing reputation. If it was good, you would be credited with having worked the extra hours; if it was poor, the comment would be, 'He has to come in on Sundays to keep up with the rest of the team'.*

Since then more attention has been given to work–life balance. Issues in this area can particularly arise when consultants are working away from home; long assignments can be debilitating and play havoc with personal and social lives. Consultant managers, therefore, should try to organise assignments so that consultants have a balance between those away from home and those where they can return home each evening. Various formulae are used by consultancy practices to cover those that are, of necessity, away; for example:

1. *The 7-7 formula:* a consultant should not need to leave home before 7.00am on Monday and should be home by 7.00pm on Friday. This may mean that the consultant does not appear on the client site un-

til lunchtime on Monday and leaves at Friday lunchtime, and the appropriate expectations will need to be set with the client.

2. *The 5-4-3 formula:* the consultant spends five days a week on client work, four of which will be on the client's site, entailing three nights spent away from home.

Obviously, there will be occasions where it is impossible or difficult to follow these formulae and, inevitably, there will be occasions when it is necessary to work extra hours. But these should be the exception rather than the rule, and be in response to unusual circumstances or a peak of workload.

Illness
Ideally — from the point of view of both the business and the individual — there should be no time lost through illness. In the example, an allowance has been made based on the average of past years. If it is less, that is good fortune; if more, bad luck.

Continuing professional development (CPD)
Continuing professional development embraces not only formal training courses, but also attendance at conferences, on-the-job development and so on. It can be very easy, given the pressures of day-to-day work, to allow other activities to take priority over CPD. And time away from work has an easily measurable opportunity cost for consultants, so training is very expensive. Consultancy, however, is a knowledge-based profession and it behoves consultants to maintain their knowledge assets. This can be achieved partly through their work experience, but time needs to be allocated to attend refresher and updating courses, and appropriate conferences.

Time might also be spent on sharing experience internally. One of the critical activities for any knowledge-based organisation is to capture individual experience and make it corporately available.

Moreover, professional institutes insist that time should be spent each year on CPD. The time allocated to training in Exhibit 12.3 should cover this.

It is important to recognise that consulting practices compete not only for clients but also for talent. In recent years, much attention has been paid to talent management. Consulting practices need to attract and retain good quality people if they are to survive and prosper. Part of the prospectus that is attractive to good candidates is the opportunity to develop their skills and capabilities – something offered through a good CPD programme (See Chapter 13 for more on this).

RULE 2: INVEST NON-FEE-EARNING TIME CAREFULLY

In the example in Exhibit 12.3, holidays, illness and CPD are budgeted at 48 days per person per year, leaving 212 days, of which 156 are budgeted for fee earning. How should the remaining 56 days be allocated?

As shown in Exhibit 12.1, time spent not on fees has to be allocated to:

- product development;
- marketing and selling;
- administration.

PRODUCT DEVELOPMENT

Consultancy 'products' are descriptions of the service or services that the individual or practice has on offer. Product development is covered in Chapter 11; at this point we need to consider the time demands implied.

Consultancy services do become outmoded and need refreshing and, as with all aspects of the business, require an investment of time. This investment needs to be focussed carefully; perhaps it is in this area that time can be most easily wasted.

Product development can be carried out as a specific activity but often combines theoretical development with operating experience. So, in practice, time spent on product development is spent packaging consultants' capabilities and experience and directing these to address client needs. It might consist of developing software for computers, a training course on a specific topic, or, as a lawyer or accountant, exploiting a change in legislation to the benefit of clients. And, at the end of a consultancy project, it might involve spending time assessing what was learned on the project and how it might be applied to new projects.

The rules for allocating time to product development are that the plan should fit the resources, and the resources the plan. In a commercial consulting firm, the amount of time given to product development will usually be among the lowest of the non-fee-earning activities.

MARKETING AND SELLING

Marketing

Marketing your firm's services is just as much a project as any of those carried out on behalf of clients. It, therefore, needs good project management: a set of objectives, plans for their attainment, resources allocated and controls for monitoring progress. The time budgeted for marketing will therefore depend on the marketing project plan.

In the case of TDH Ltd (and possibly larger firms too) this is worked out by a process of compromise and opportunism!

In practice, selling work and earning fees are likely to take priority over marketing, since they are closer to the realisation of cash revenue (see Exhibit 12.1). There is a risk, therefore, that insufficient time is given to marketing, but there must be a minimum level of activity to secure the future.

In preparing his budget, therefore, Tom should see how much time ought to be spent on selling before allocating time to marketing.

Selling
Selling takes time but it does not always result in sales. Time spent on selling, therefore, has to be jealously husbanded.

> *Some years ago, during a recession in consultancy, I noted a team of consultancy salespeople who seemed to be spending a lot of time around the office rather than out with clients. One of the salespeople explained to me, 'It's easy to be a busy fool. It would be easy to rush around the country — with the resultant costs — meeting people with whom there is no prospect of doing business. We are concentrating our efforts on identifying and selling only to good prospects and spending the rest of our time on longer-term marketing.'*

The amount of time to win a request for a proposal (RFP) or an invitation to tender (ITT) depends on the effectiveness of both marketing and selling. It is difficult to conclusively align success with a specific marketing initiative but it is sensible to analyse sales performance. The analysis may show a pattern amongst successful sales and suggest ways in which the sales level could be increased.

For the purpose of budgeting time, it is useful to have some idea of the 'score rate' of successful versus total proposals. As a rule, it is always easier to sell to existing clients; you have already established your credentials with them and they will therefore be more inclined to use your services. This may be reflected in your experience, which might show, for example:
- 90 per cent of proposals to existing clients are accepted. (These are called 'extension sales');
- 50 per cent of proposals to new clients are accepted.

These figures could be applied to the firm in the example, TDH Ltd. Tom's budget is shown in Exhibit 12.7, below. It shows that 97½ days should be allocated to selling.

Exhibit 12.7 TDH Ltd: sales budget

Average size of sale:	4 weeks' work (20 days)
Value of average size of sale: 20 days @ (£750/day)	£15,000

Assume that 90% of new sales lead to an extension sale. A new sale would then be worth, with its extension sale:

Value of new sale	= £15,000 + (90% × £15,000)
	= £28,500
The number of new sales required would be	Revenue required
	Value of new sale
	= £351,000 / £28,500
	= 13 (rounded up)

Assuming that proposals for new sales are only 50 per cent effective, the budget shows that 26 proposals for new sales and 13 extension proposals would be needed.

Time, therefore, needs to be allowed for 39 proposals. Assuming, say, 2½ days' selling time is required on average to secure the RFP, create and present the proposal, the total time for selling in the budget is 2½ × 39 = 97½ days

This is, of course, only for budgeting purposes; sales may be of different sizes and success rates vary. During a recession, more effort will be needed to secure sales — the market may diminish and there will be more competition for fewer opportunities.

ADMINISTRATION

Finally, time should be allowed for the administration of the business. (This does not include administrative work associated with specific projects, such as billing, writing letters or proof reading reports; these should be charged to the appropriate project.)

The business will need to spend time to plan and review its development; for example, if they are successful, TDH Ltd may want to add further consultants to the team and time has to be allowed for recruitment.

An allocation of half a day per month per person for administration has been made by Tom in his budget.

For Tom, Dick and Harriet, then, in their consulting practice, their annual budget could be as follows.

Exhibit 12.8 Annual budget for TDH Ltd

	Days per person per year
Net days available	212
Operating	156
Selling	32
Marketing	10
Product development	8
Administration	6
	212

MANAGING PERSONAL PERFORMANCE

The amount of time allocated to different activities can, of course, be tailored to the individual and their strengths. Most consultants, other than the most junior, will have a mix of responsibilities. The table below shows how you might distinguish the allocation of time for those in different roles:

There are some important features to note here:

- Even those whose role is primarily that of practice management spend time on selling and delivery.
- Other than the least experienced consultants, those who are involved in delivery will be expected to contribute to sales.

Exhibit 12.9 Personal time allocation

	Number of days p.a.		
	Selling	Delivering	Practice development
Consultant A — majors on delivery	25	187	0
Consultant B — strong sales person	160	30	22
Consultant C — practice leader	50	75	87
Consultant D — new consultant	0	212	0

This measure of time input needs to be complemented by what is meant to be produced from this investment. For delivery, it is simple – a total volume of fees earned. This might be determined by an equivalent day rate. For example, if this was £1,000 per day, then consultant A would be expected to bill £187,000 in the year.

Sales targets are more complex as they depend on the role of the consultant. A simple distinction often given in professional practices is 'finder' (main job is finding new business), 'minder' (looks after existing clients), and 'grinder' (main task is earning fees). The table below illustrates this (note that the figures are not related to the table above and assume that there are 200 days per year to be split between selling and delivery).

Exhibit 12.10 Personal targets for sales and fee earning

		New sales	Extension sales	Fee earning
Finder	Days allocated	120	40	40
	Days sold	600	400	40
	Conversion ratio	5	10	1
Minder	Days allocated	40	80	80
	Days sold	120	400	80
	Conversion ratio	3	5	1
Grinder	Days allocated	10	30	160
	Days sold	30	120	160
	Conversion ratio	3	4	1

Practice development is less susceptible to generic targets, which may, for example, relate to the development of an operating manual, sales collateral, the recruitment of a team, and a whole mix of other relevant activities.

RULE 3: CONTROL THE CASH

Consultancy firms have two principal features that militate against good cash control.

Firstly, expenses are mainly fixed and, because the largest portion relates to salaries, it is difficult to finance working capital by deferring payment of creditors. (There are ways of coping with this. One firm increased its cash by moving its salary payment date back a week. Another firm pays salary well in arrears, unlike most organisations that pay salaries in the current month. But both of these are one-off benefits.) TDH Ltd might make their expenses more variable by guaranteeing only a proportion of Tom, Dick and Harriet's remuneration; the balance being payable as a profit share at the end of the financial year. Nonetheless, there is a continual flow of cash out of the firm irrespective of the level of business.

Secondly, there is usually a considerable interval between making the sale and collecting payment for it, whilst the project is being carried out. For example:

May: project sold
June: project starts on fees
July: invoice sent for June's fees
September: invoice paid.

So salaries for June, July and August would need to have been paid before receiving income for this work.

The result is that high levels of work-in-progress can build up — work done for clients which has not yet been charged — unless there are special measures introduced to avoid this.

The monthly income and expenditure budget is:

- expenditure: £300,000/12 = £25,000;
- income: (156 days × 3)/12 × £750 = £29,250.

Note that income, above, is simply a measure of the increase in work-in-progress — not cash in. Cash will not arrive until after the client has been invoiced for the work and then paid the invoice. In some cases, a client might not be invoiced until the project has been completed — the worst case for cash flow. It could also leave an unhealthy balance of initiative with the client. For example, if TDH Ltd are owed £50,000 of fees by a single client, they would be vulnerable were that client to delay paying, default on paying, or dispute those fees. Indeed, in consultant mythology there have been several companies that purposely created disputes with their consultants so as to reduce the size of the outstanding bills.

Where possible, therefore, it is sensible to bill clients at regular stages during a project — say on a monthly basis. Even so, the working capital required is usually about three months' work-in-progress; TDH Ltd would, therefore, need about £75,000 working capital.

This would increase *pro rata* if they were to expand by taking on another consultant. Cash flow out would go up by more than £5,000 per month and a further £15,000 worth of working capital would be required. Note that this is a substantial proportion of their budgeted profits. This is typical of an expanding consultancy: previous years' surpluses can quickly be absorbed in financing increasing work-in-progress.

Some firms require stage payments at more frequent intervals than a month, but this, of course, represents an increase in administrative workload and is not suitable for projects that are thinly spread. An alternative is to bill at pre-determined work-in-progress levels, e.g. at £10,000 intervals for TDH Ltd.

A further possibility is payment partly in advance; this is ideal from the point of view of your cash flow, but the reverse for the client's and, therefore, less usual. Where there is some doubt about the client's ability or willingness to pay, however, the consultant may insist on, at least, some payment in advance. No provision has been made for bad debts in Tom's budget and he is relying on the quality of his credit control to see that they do not occur.

WHAT DO THE THREE RULES MEAN IN PRACTICE?

Experienced consultants will be familiar with the consequences of the three rules; those new to consultancy, particularly those who have not worked in a professional practice before, will become aware of them because of the administrative disciplines placed on them. Summarised below are some of the peculiar features of consulting practice which result from the rules.

Rule 1 Maintain utilisation — results in pressure on consultants to:
- keep a record of how they spend their time;
- maintain the proportion of time spent on feeable work;
- complete projects within the working time allocated;
- control their diaries ahead so that utilisation can be maintained.

Rule 2 Invest non-fee-earning time carefully — time has to be spent on activities other than earning fees but to be done well it requires that:
- the time invested is controlled as strictly, and the same disciplines applied, as in fee-earning work;
- it is given the correct priority with respect to other work; fee-earning work can always take higher priority than non-fee-earning work in the short term, but long-term neglect will be detrimental to the business.

Rule 3 Control the cash — cash control is a chore to consultants and it is better to have systems for invoicing and cash collection from clients which need little, if any, effort from consultants. Failing that, however, the requirements of this rule are to:

- agree payment terms with the client at the start of a project; if it is of any significant size or duration, insist on stage payments;
- ensure that this agreement is adhered to on your part — do not overlook invoicing in the flurry of other activities;
- monitor the value of work-in-progress on each project to ensure it does not become too large.

The major difficulties that specialist professionals have in making the transition to commercial consulting arise from the commercial context of the business. The rules set out must be observed to enable both the consulting firm to survive and prosper, and to enable professionals to practise their specialisms.

CHAPTER 13

THE PRACTICE ENVIRONMENT

How can you expect to govern a country that has 246 kinds of cheese?

Charles de Gaulle

Over the last 20–30 years, the pressure on organisations to cut costs has resulted in a reduced capacity to resource projects that are out of the ordinary routine of things. Increasingly this has meant that organisations have had to look externally to assemble the resources for major projects. This has contributed to the considerable growth in the number of consultants and organisations that offer consultancy seen over recent years.

This chapter is about working in a consultancy firm or practice. It should therefore be of interest both to those who might be contemplating a career in consultancy and to consultants who are reviewing their careers to help in making career decisions, as well as those involved in the management of a practice.

Before considering this, however, it is worth reflecting on why it is worthwhile for consultants to combine together in a practice. There are obvious benefits of companionship and economies of scale, but there are other practical reasons as illustrated in Exhibit 13.1.

Exhibit 13.1 The leverage of association

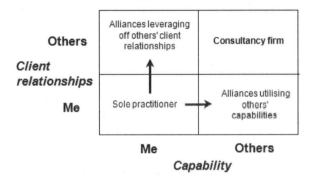

Me   Others
Capability

This shows that association provides leverage: consultants can introduce colleagues (who have different capabilities) to their contacts, whilst they might themselves be introduced on the same basis to colleagues' clients. Both processes increase the amount of business for the practice.

BECOMING A CONSULTANT

Sometimes an organisation will continue to use the services of a former employee on a consultancy basis so that they can continue to draw on their advice and experience. In this case, 'consultancy' simply refers to the contractual relationship between the two. It usually means that the individual has no benefits or guarantee of ongoing employment, which may be temporary and part time.

Plainly this describes the relationship between consultants and their clients, but (if you have been following this book thus far!) you will realise that there is much more to consultancy. The consultant may be involved in a project and have contracted not for input of time, but for output of deliverables. Consultancy skills are needed to do this; consultants need to bring a professional approach to their work. So in this chapter we will be considering consultancy as a profession, not simply as a contractual relationship.

THE BASIS OF REPUTATION
People can be successful as consultants only if their prospective clients accept them as such. This reputation can derive from the individual or from the organisation for which they work.

At one extreme is the guru. A guru is an individual who has achieved a substantial reputation for their expertise and is employed as a consultant because of this. A guru is sought in answer to the question, 'Who is the best person to help us on this problem?' and will have an individual reputation that is largely independent of the institution to which they belong. In many instances gurus are academics who market themselves by presenting papers at conferences, writing books and so on.

At the other end of the scale is the 'management mercenary': people who enter consultancy early in their careers, often with a lot of knowledge but little experience, fall into this category. They will probably join a firm of consultants and grow in skill under the supervision of more experienced professionals. (This is similar to the training given in other professions; for example solicitors or accountants serve out a period of articles.) Management mercenaries secure their work because they work in a firm of consultants rather than because of their own reputation, although this may change as they become more experienced. Internal consultants may well be in a similar position.

Independent consultants are a mix of the two. They will often work as associates or in small firms and will get their work by means of networking — personal contacts, previous clients and the like.

CAREER PROGRESSION IN CONSULTANCY

It is only in recent years that individuals have become consultants without previously working in a non-consultancy role. So now there are two points of entry to the profession.

Those who enter consultancy directly as their first job will probably work in an analyst role — reporting to more experienced consultants and assigned on work packages that are pretty well pre-defined. After some time they will move on to the role of consultant and this is the level at which those with previous work experience outside consultancy will join a consultancy practice.

For individuals new to consultancy, there appear to be at least three stages in their career development within the firm.

1. *To do operating work.* At the start of their fee-earning work, consultants will not be very choosy about the work they do — they will be happy to gain experience and learn their craft as a consultant.
2. *To do interesting operating work.* With increasing experience and growing confidence consultants will try to be more selective about the assignments they undertake.

3. *To develop into functions other than operating consultant.* Career progression in consultancy consists of developing in one or more of three areas:
   - Taking on commercial responsibilities — winning new business and managing relationships with clients;
   - Taking responsibility for projects of greater size, complexity and risk;
   - Having an area of specialist expertise that is of particular value to the firm and its clients.

These latter tasks may take up a considerable amount of the time of experienced consultants.

In developing in these areas, consultants become of greater value to their firm. Indeed, failure to develop in this way may mean that the firm may counsel an individual to leave! 'Up or out' is not an uncommon practice in consultancy firms — or any professional practice. It is not harsh — it is realistic: if increasing salary expectations are to be met, the consultant needs to command greater value.

Not all consultants have the ability or desire to move on to stage 3 and so long-term careers in consultancy firms are the exception rather than the rule. The reasons are that firstly, many people enter consultancy with the intention of leaving after three or four years, which they do. Secondly, for economic reasons there is considerable pressure for individuals to move on or move out. As people get older, their salary expectations become higher; a 42-year-old consultant expects to earn more than a 32-year-old one and if both have much the same value to the practice, there is the economic incentive to replace expensive people with cheaper equivalents. The alternative is for the longer-serving individual to increase their value, as a specialist, as a business developer or as a consultant manager, but this is not always possible.

Conversely, individuals may decide that they no longer want to be consultants, and move back into the non-consultancy world with the benefit of the experience they have gained. This can happen at various career stages in consultancy, including senior levels, when partners or directors of consulting firms move on to take the role of director of a public company, or a senior appointment in the public sector.

Another exit route which has become more common in recent years (and the one that I personally have followed) is to become a sole practitioner. This route is ideal for those who want to pursue a career in consultancy without being burdened with the managerial, administrative and political activities that ensue when taking a senior role in a large consultancy firm. Many sole practitioners and those who work for (and indeed have started up) small firms are 'graduates' of major consultancy firms.

New consultants entering a consultancy firm should therefore carefully consider what their next job might be and when the 'exit windows' occur as illustrated in Exhibit 13.2 below.

Exhibit 13.2 Exit windows

Exit window	Years after start	Comments
1	2–4	Will have learned basic craft of consultancy and reached point of diminishing returns in operating experience.
2	3–7	Should have taken on project management role, together with business development and internal management roles. Staying in consultancy beyond this point may make jobs outside consultancy more difficult to find.
3	7 +	Career options become fewer and may be limited to specialist or quasi-consultancy roles unless you are at the top of your practice.

The timing of the exit windows will vary according to your specialisation and market conditions. Lest all of this sounds very depressing, it is reassuring that many, if not most of the top people in consultancy firms entered with the expectation that they would spend only a short period in the profession.

Sole practitioners have the advantages of freedom of action and (potentially) making a lot more money than their employed counterparts. The advantages of entering a firm of consultants, however, are:

- working with other professionals: it can be very lonely being a sole practitioner;
- training: if you are new to consultancy it may be better to understand how the business works in an environment where there is existing consultancy expertise;
- avoidance of administration: as a sole practitioner you need to do all of your own administration;

- avoidance of feast or famine: sole practitioners have to secure contracts and then carry them out, this often leads to periods of alternating feast and famine; whilst operating, they are not selling and thus when the present contract comes to an end, there is no income until the next one is secured;
- scope for professional growth: the client is buying the reputation of a consulting firm as well as the individual consultant. As remarked above, this gives rather more scope for individuals to operate at the limits of their expertise or in new business sectors.

A MODEL OF THE CONSULTING BUSINESS

It is important to understand the consulting business. One way to think about a consultancy is as a process in which there are exchanges of value. Exhibit 13.3 illustrates that these take place between an individual consultant, the employing consultancy firm and the client.

Exhibit 13.3 Exchanges of value in the consulting business

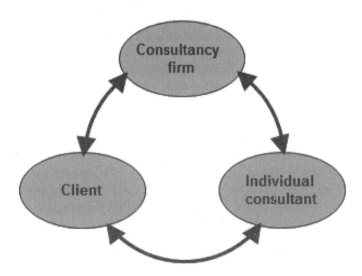

Exhibit 13.4 shows the transactions involved. Set out below are comments on each of these.

BETWEEN CLIENT AND CONSULTANCY FIRM

It does not automatically follow that an external firm of consultants needs to be used on every project to be carried out: the client could use their own staff or hire in the help required. The reasons why a client will turn to a firm of consultants are as follows.

- They bring a *capability* that means they can do the project better. 'Better' in this context need not mean only quality of output, but may also relate to timescale, risk, objectivity or a multitude of other factors.

Exhibit 13.4 Exchanges of value: transactions involved

To	From Consultancy firm	Client	Individual consultant
Consultancy firm		Fee income Corporate expertise and credibility Product development opportunities	Revenue Knowledge Business development
Client	Capability Problem orientation Technology transfer		Specialist knowledge Past experience Know-how
Individual consultant	Pay Development of: - consulting skills - technical competence - sectoral experience	Sectoral experience Practice of expertise Enlarging expertise Network	

- *Problem orientation.* A firm of consultants should have the breadth of resources to be able to provide sufficient consultants with the skills required to address the client's problem. The resources available within the client organisation are usually limited and there is the risk that the problem may be tailored to match the available solutions.

- The firm of consultants may have a proprietary approach which is suitable but available only to clients. Alternatively, the consultancy may have a distinguished reputation in a particular specialist area in which the client needs help. In both of these cases by working with the firm of consultants the client will have not only accomplished the project but also learned new approaches. The task of the consultancy firm in this respect is that of facilitating *technology transfer*. What a consultancy does is to take technology (i.e. knowledge or know-how of limited or no availability in the client's organisation) and apply it to the client's problem. The consultancy therefore needs to plan its technology acquisition, whether it is through people (by recruitment), knowledge (by training and contact with academia) or experience (from previous assignments).

What does the consultancy firm get from the client/consultant relationship?
- *Fee income* — payment for services.
- *Corporate expertise and credibility.* A consultancy firm accumulates corporate experience from the projects carried out in the past and in quoting these, underwrites its expertise. This expertise can be focussed on a particular market as well as on areas of specialisation.
- Consultancy should not be the mindless application of standard approaches; some innovation and flair are required on most assignments. Original approaches that are proven on a project may, however, be useful in applications elsewhere. For example, suppose a piece of computer software is developed on a project the same software might be applicable on other projects and, indeed, its availability could be a selling point. Undertaking work for clients therefore offers the consultancy firm scope for *developing new products and services*.

The exchanges between consultancy firm and client provide an insight into the personnel management and direction of consulting firms. The consultant is the medium whereby value is conveyed from consultancy to client; in prosaic terms, the consultant is the product. Products have a life cycle and so do particular consultant specialisations. The consultancy offerings of today, for example, have little in common with those of 30 years ago but 30 years could easily be the span of the career of a consultant. In that time they have to make sure they remain an attractive product to be marketed by their employer and bought by their clients. This means keeping up to date and maintaining special skills attractive to a market that has the funds to buy them. Consultancy is a profession where there can be individual obsolescence.

BETWEEN INDIVIDUAL CONSULTANT AND CONSULTANCY FIRM

All consultants or prospective consultants at some time or other consider whether they should work as a sole practitioner or join a firm of consultants. This decision can be illuminated by considering the exchange of values between the consultant and consultancy firm.

What the individual gets out of joining a consultancy is more than remuneration. Many become consultants to obtain a practical post-graduate qualification in business and thereby hope to enhance their value and attractiveness to future employers.

Whilst employed as a consultant, the individual gains by developing the following.

- *Consulting skills*: as should be obvious from the contents of this book, consulting is a process that demands particular skills and a period of work as a consultant develops these.
- *Technical competence*: larger consultancy practices may take individuals with little specialist knowledge or experience but with high potential, and develop them. In all firms the individual should aim to develop their specialist ability. A former colleague who had recently left consultancy remarked that he had forgotten how much administration was involved in line management. Consultancy allows specialist skills to be built up by concentrated experience. An advantage of working in a group of consultants is that it exposes the consultant to other specialisations. Because of this, in a firm of consultants it is possible to work on projects near the periphery of your expertise and thereby broaden it.
- *Sectoral experience*: a consultant will work with a variety of clients and will thus experience a far wider range of business environments and commercial sectors than if they were employed as an executive over the same period.

It is worth noting that the character of consultancy in recent years has changed in respect of the length of time a consultant may spend working with any single client. It is a deliberate strategy amongst large consultancy practices nowadays to sell projects that require work years of consultancy input. This means that a consultant can be confined to a particular project for months, if not years. This does not provide the variety of experience that may have attracted them into the profession. This phenomenon is not limited to large firms either; not long ago I came across a consultant working in a practice of 20 consultants, who had been engaged with the same client and project for more than 3 years.

More variety is available at senior levels but, even here, partners in large practices may find themselves wholly engaged with a single major client.

What the consultancy gets from the individual consultant is the following.

- The *revenue* from fee income they generate by working for clients.
- Their *knowledge*: this could be put to use among other consultants, through training and so on, thereby developing a greater in-house capability.
- Scope for *business development*: consultants with previous work experience will have their own network of contacts affording possible scope for promotion of the consultancy practice among them.

BETWEEN CLIENT AND INDIVIDUAL CONSULTANT

Although it may be the consultancy firm that wins a contract, it will be the individual consultant who carries it out. The client will form an opinion about the consultancy from the individual's performance of the project and it is the individual who is adding value to the client in exchange for the firm's fees. What the client will be looking for from the consultant is *specialist knowledge, past experience* and *know-how* relevant to the issues being addressed. The client will rely on the consultancy firm to provide a consultant (or consultant team) who has these in the right areas.

It follows that if you want to be a consultant, you have to have something worth selling. It can therefore be very difficult for generalists to enter the field of consultancy.

From the consultant's point of view, the value of being a consultant arises from doing projects for clients. This enables the consultant to practise and enlarge their expertise in various sectors.

Even in the best managed consulting organisations there are periods when a consultant (like an actor) is occasionally 'resting' between projects. This can be very trying for new consultants and illustrates the importance of the point made above: notwithstanding all the internal virtues of a consultancy firm, the greatest benefit to consultants is drawn from the work they do for clients.

THE RELEVANCE OF EXCHANGES OF VALUE TO A CONSULTANT'S CAREER

The idea of exchanges of value is thus very helpful in understanding consultancy and the role of the consultant in it. The key points relevant to a consultant's career are therefore as follows.

- If you want to become a consultant, you must have an expertise that prospective clients wish to buy. This may be focussed on technical expertise or knowledge of a commercial sector, and will be embodied in your knowledge, experience and know-how.
- If you plan to join, or are already part of, a consulting firm, consider your long-term future. If you do not foresee your role developing as a renowned expert, business developer or manager, does the firm offer you a long-term career? If not, what are the appropriate exit points for you?
- Decide what you want out of your consultancy experience that will add to your value on the job market. What does it imply in terms of operating and other tasks?
- What is the right environment to achieve these objectives? You need to decide whether you are willing and able to become a sole practitioner, or whether you should join a firm and, if so, whether it should be large or small.

WORKING IN A CONSULTING PRACTICE

Management consultancy firms suffer from many of the shortcomings of professional practices in general and have a few specialised problems of their own, too. This section is addressed to all who are undergoing the culture shock of entering a consultancy firm. The difficulties are more apparent in large firms so I will concentrate on them, but the same issues will apply to some extent to the small firm. They are explained in the assertions below.

CONSULTANTS ARE IMPOSSIBLE TO MANAGE

Or at least very difficult. This is because contrary behaviours are required from consultants:

- As consultants they are meant to be independent of their clients and make recommendations based on their own evaluations;
- By contrast, as members of a consulting firm, they need to follow the rules and guidelines established within the firm and to accept direction from the management.

The ideal therefore is a 'conforming individualist'. In practice what happens is that in a firm of 100 consultants there will always be 99 prepared to question the decisions of the hundredth and to tell them how things could be better.

A CONSULTANCY IS AN ARMY IN WHICH THE LOWEST RANK IS COLONEL

People entering consultancy often do so from distinguished careers to date; they will have been outstanding in their previous positions. A consultancy firm, however, is made up of people all of whom have similarly distinguished careers. Newcomers can have difficulty in adjusting to the fact that they are not the exceptional people they might have been in their previous employment. Furthermore, specialists whose advice has previously been unquestioned can be unsettled by the need to justify their conclusions or rewrite reports when subject to the quality assurance procedures in a consultancy firm.

A GOOD CONSULTANT IS NOT NECESSARILY A GOOD MANAGER

As noted in Chapter 12, the specialist tasks of a professional can easily crowd out the managerial ones. It is unusual, even at the most senior levels of any professional practice, to find individuals whose task is solely management; they will still have client relationships and perhaps delivery responsibilities. Those charged with management will therefore not be as preoccupied with it as their counterparts outside the professions.

Moreover, the qualities of a first-class consultant are not the same as those of a first-class manager. Promotions into managerial positions therefore have to be handled with care, as in all professions; in larger practices, it is sensible to have scope for career advance without the requirement of taking on managerial responsibilities — perhaps by providing parallel specialist and managerial grades.

THE IDEAL HAS TO BE TEMPERED BY COMMERCIAL NECESSITY

Consultants like to broaden their experience by enlarging the range of work they do and industries they work in. Conversely, clients are more attracted to individuals who already have experience of dealing with their problem in their industry.

Similarly, consultants like to select the assignments they take so as to achieve personal development goals. The incidence of sales rarely meets these needs, however, and there is a strong economic incentive for firms to keep consultants engaged in fee-earning work.

In both of these cases compromise is necessary, and for new consultants particularly it means that from time to time they have to perform assignments which are far from their ideal. Happily, most find that once they have more experience and seniority they are able to be more selective.

AND FINALLY...

Consultants sell their time for a price; the price is determined by the value of what they can achieve in that time. The rarer and more in demand your specialist knowledge, the higher the price it can command. Therefore, never forget what it is as a consultant you are selling to your clients or to your employer. It may be your skills as a technical specialist or your knowledge of a particular market or industrial sector, or within a consultancy practice, it may be a particular strength in research, product development, business development or management. Whatever it is, take care to husband and enhance your value by recognising where it lies and adding selectively to your knowledge and experience.

To end on a positive note: I have spent most of my working life as a management consultant, in large and medium-sized firms and — now — my own small practice. Each phase has had its good and bad points, but overall I have enjoyed it immensely. I hope that you and your clients, like me, will therefore get not only great value but also enormous fun from being part of the world of consultancy.

REFERENCES

Beckhard, R. and Harris, R.T., *Organisation Transitions: Managing Complex Change* (1987) Addison Wesley.

Blake, R.R. and Mouton, J.S., *Managing Intergroup Conflict in Industry* (1964) Gulf Publishing.

Cialdini, R.B., *Influence: Science and Practice* (2001) Allyn and Bacon.

Handy, C., *Understanding Organisations* (1981) Penguin Books.

Harrison, R., 'Understanding your organization's character' *Harvard Business Review* (May–June 1972).

Hersey, P., Blanchard, K.H. and Natemeyer,W.E., *Situational Leadership, Perception and the Impact of Power* (1978) Centre for Leadership Study.

Institute of Consulting, *Code of Professional Conduct* — www.iconsulting. org.uk.

Jay, A., 'Rate yourself as a client' *Harvard Business Review* (July–August 1977).

Kahneman D., *Thinking, Fast and Slow* (2011) Penguin Books

Maister, D., Green, C. and Galford, R., *The Trusted Advisor* (2002) The Free Press.

Schmidt, W. and Johnston, A., *'A Continuum of Consultancy Styles'* Occasional Paper of the University of Southern California Business Administration Department (1969).

PUBLISHING HISTORY

First edition (Practical Consulting) 1987
Second edition (Practical Management Consultancy) 1991
Third edition 1997
Fourth edition 2003
Fifth edition 2007
Sixth edition 2013
Seventh edition (The Art of Consultancy) 2019
ISBN 978-1-84140-970-2